Politics, Ethics and Performance

Anamnesis

Anamnesis means remembrance or reminiscence, the collection and re-collection of what has been lost, forgotten, or effaced. It is therefore a matter of the very old, of what has made us who we are. But *anamnesis* is also a work that transforms its subject, always producing something new. To recollect the old, to produce the new: that is the task of *Anamnesis*.

a re.press series

Politics, Ethics and Performance
Hélène Cixous and the Théâtre du Soleil

Hélène Cixous
edited by Lara Stevens

re.press Melbourne 2016

re.press
PO Box 40, Prahran, 3181, Melbourne, Australia
http://www.re-press.org

National Library of Australia Cataloguing-in-Publication entry

Creator: Cixous, Hélène, 1937- author.

Title: Politics, ethics and performance : Hélène Cixous and the
Théâtre du Soleil / Hélène Cixous ;
translated, edited and introduced by
Lara Stevens.

ISBN: 9780987268211 (paperback)

Series: Anamnesis

Subjects: Théâtre du Soleil.
Theater--Political aspects.
Political plays--History and criticism.
Art and morals.
Experimental theater--France--Paris.
Essays.

Other Creators/Contributors:
Stevens, Lara, translator, editor, writer of introduction.

Dewey Number: 792.015

Designed and Typeset by *A&R*

This book is produced sustainably using plantation timber, and printed in the destination market reducing wastage and excess transport.

Contents

Acknowledgements

First thanks are due to Hélène Cixous for writing these extraordinary essays and for giving me the opportunity to work with them in translation. Thanks to Denise Varney for introducing me to the work of Hélène Cixous and for being a constant supporter of my work and a dear friend. I am greatly appreciative for Bryan Cooke's insightful suggestions for the introduction, his willingness to spend hours discussing difficult philosophical concepts and, mostly, for his treasured friendship.

Thanks are also due to the French Trust Fund at the University of Melbourne and the French Research History Higher Degree Scholarship for their financial support that enabled the field trips to France which provided the backbone of this research and translation opportunity. I am very grateful to Helen Davies and all the donors of the French Trust Fund for their generosity.

I would like to thank my three (anonymous) referees for their extensive, incisive and generous comments on both the French and English versions of my Introduction. Their comments have led to many improvements and helped me to avoid several errors. I would also like to thank Natalya Hughes for permission to use her stunning work for the cover of this book.

I owe much to Justin Clemens for his infectious enthusiasm and encouragement for this book as well as his careful and considered editing of it. Thanks also to Paul Ashton for taking on the task of editing the book and for keeping independent presses alive. My deep gratitude also goes out to my friends Elisabeth and Philippe Guilleminot for giving up so much of their time to edit the French introduction. Also to my step-mother (and the most extraordinary linguist I know), Rosemary Benkemoun, who generously devoted days to nutting out the most difficult passages with me. Finally, to Franck Pendino at the Théâtre du Soleil for his extraordinary patience, responsiveness and helpfulness with this book throughout the entire process.

Thanks to my dear family for all their love and support, and mostly to Eddie Paterson who made this translation possible and makes all things in life an adventure and a joy.

Editor & Translator's Introduction

Politics, Ethics and Performance

This collection of essays by writer, philosopher and feminist Hélène Cixous spans twenty-nine years of her writing, thinking and working with the French theatre company the Théâtre du Soleil. The Théâtre du Soleil was founded by Ariane Mnouchkine in 1964 as a radical experimental theatre group. Cixous has been the company's scriptwriting collaborator and occasional dramaturg in devised work since the 1980s, and continues to work with the company today. The essays in this collection reflect on the development of the Théâtre du Soleil's unique performance aesthetics and the ethical and political concerns of a theatre company that has been committed to social justice from its inception.

The Théâtre du Soleil's artistic practice is motivated by a 1960s idealism that art can intervene socially and politically and provide a catalyst for real-world change. As the company describes in the program notes to the 1975 production of *l'Age d'Or* [*The Golden Age*]:

> We want to reinvent the rules of the game that unveil daily reality by showing it not as familiar and immutable, but as surprising and transformable. This will thus be a theatre directly taken from social reality, which is not mere observation, but rather encouragement to change the conditions in which we live. (in Neuschäfer 2004)[1]

Since the 1960s, the artists of the Théâtre du Soleil have devised performances that respond to national and international political issues using experimental aesthetics that draw upon a range of European and Asian theatrical traditions.

The members of the Théâtre du Soleil have always put their socialist ethos into practice by participating in or leading community activism. In 1973, the company created a short performance work for Michel Foucault's le Groupe d'Information sur les Prisons (GIP), which sought better prison conditions, and they signed a controversial petition for legalising abortion that was sponsored by Simone de Beauvoir (Miller 2007, 12). Mnouchkine

1. My translation.

also founded l'Association internationale de défense des artistes victimes de la répression dans le monde (AIDA), an organisation dedicated to freeing politically persecuted artists. AIDA has produced statements, sit-ins and public spectacles for artists who are suffering political discrimination or censorship. In 1991, Mnouchkine led a 30-day hunger strike to protest the French government's inaction in the face of the genocide occurring in Bosnia. In 1996 she gave the company's performance spaces – the Cartoucherie which is located in the Bois de Vincennes on the outskirts of Paris – over to 382 *sans papiers* who were expelled from their refuge at St. Bernard Church in Paris (Miller 2007, 12). The Théâtre du Soleil are also strongly committed to educating their large spectator publics about pertinent social issues as well as touring performances to factories and events organised by trade unions so as to make their theatre accessible to all classes of French society.

Not only do the essays in this collection respond to the dynamic and socially engaged work of the Théâtre du Soleil, but constitute an integral part of the company's objective to 'change the conditions in which we live'. They reinforce its broader desire to reveal to spectators the possibility of altering contemporary conditions of inequality and injustice. Prior to her work with the Théâtre du Soleil, Cixous had written several plays, most notably *Portrait de Dora* [*Portrait of Dora*] first performed as a radio play in 1972 and on stage in 1976. *Portrait of Dora* is a fictional re-imagining of Sigmund Freud's documented sessions using psychoanalysis on his young patient, 'Dora', and his misreading of her 'hysteria'. The play became a seminal text for feminist theatre. *Portrait of Dora* shows Cixous' interest in real historical events and people, gender politics as well as the problem of communication, truth and justice, all concerns that she continues to explore in this collection of essays.

Most of the essays here first appeared in print in French in the program notes to the performances, or as introductions to the published playtexts. This book is the first to bring them into dialogue with one another and make them available to an Anglophone readership. I have chosen to order the essays in this collection in reverse chronology so as to invite a retrospective view of Cixous' work. The most recent essay – 'The Irreparable' – was written in 2014 and the earliest – 'An Inextinguishable Spark' – was written in 1985. Each essay responds to one of the Théâtre du Soleil's major productions over the last quarter of a century including *Macbeth* (2014), *The Castaways of the* Fol Espoir *(Sunrises)* (2010), *The Mayflies* (2006), *The Last Caravanserai (Odysseys)* (2003), *Drums on the Dam – In the form of an ancient puppet play performed by actors* (1999), *And Suddenly Nights of Awakening* (1997), *The City of Perjury or the Awakening of the Erinyes* (1994), *The Atreides* (1990-1992), *The Indiad or the India of their Dreams* (1987), and *The Terrible and Still Unfinished Story of Norodom Sihanouk, King of Cambodia* (1985).

Cixous' essays respond to and take inspiration from the performances and the processes of collaborative research and experimentation that went

into creating them. Each essay is a commentary or provocation on the relationship between theatrical aesthetics, politics and ethics. Each essay addresses the political and ethical ambiguities of particular times, places and events and the experience of different groups that are 'othered', marginalised or treated with suspicion by the mainstream. The 'others' that Cixous engages with in these essays include racialised others, refugees, revolutionaries, those who resist colonial expansion, the lower classes, women, the ill or infected, victims of ideological fanaticism, avant-garde artists and writers, scientists whose discoveries revolutionised how we see and understand the world and ourselves, and peaceniks.

These essays comprise an integral part of Cixous' significant and extensive contribution to philosophy, poetry, fiction, feminist theory and theatre theory. More specifically, they directly consider the relationships between art/theatre/performance and transformative politics under neoliberalism—our contemporary situation, which is often described as a 'post-Marxist' historical moment that is dominated by capitalist ideology seemingly without alternative (Rancière 2011, 32–33). Cixous' essays raise pertinent ethical questions for the twenty-first century by exploring the contradictions between the promises of Western democratic freedoms and the limited access of the non-citizen to human rights protections; the role of theatre and performance in protesting injustice through storytelling; the difficulties and necessities of cross-cultural communication in art as in politics; and the treatment of women both historically and today.

Reading écriture féminine

Cixous' distinctive writing style presents a challenge to any reader. Her sentences are long and complex, often shifting between topics in a stream-of-consciousness manner that is reminiscent of James Joyce, the subject of Cixous' doctoral thesis and much of her literary analysis. Cixous' writing is dense with intertexual references, puns and wordplays, homonymy, homophony, assonance, alliteration and autobiographical details. Her sentences can be perplexing in their structure, length, their use of multiple intertexual references, neologisms and symbolism. She often breaks grammatical rules and generic conventions and revels in volatile and ambiguous language that invites readers to critically approach her essays and the performances to which they refer.

In an earlier essay 'Le rire de la Méduse' ['The Laugh of the Medusa'] (1975), Cixous justifies her development of a style of writing that she calls '*écriture féminine*'. Further developing the work of her friend and occasional collaborator, philosopher Jacques Derrida, *écriture féminine* aims to subvert and circumvent 'logocentrism' and 'phallogocentrism'. For Derrida, overturning logocentrism, is a radical disruption of the 'metaphysics of presence' in the

history of philosophy, which is to say immediate access to a fixed meaning of a word or text (1967, 11-12). Derrida reminds us that because the author of the written word is usually absent to the reader, writing always gestures towards what is absent. Writing can be taken out of context, misinterpreted or incorrectly copied and thus it always relies on deferred meaning. As such, much of Derrida's deconstructive mode of writing works to show that words or concepts are often haunted by what is not-present, by their past meanings and nuances (which are often contradictory to contemporary usage). He exposes what he describes as the 'spectres' of words by exploring their etymology in order to complicate their polysemy. Furthermore, he plays with the conjugation of verbs to create homophonic words that present conflicting meanings, thereby suggesting contradictions in language in its spoken form.

Phallogocentrism, a Derridian neologism, builds on the project of deconstructing language further by drawing in ideas and terms from psychoanalysis, specifically the theories of Jacques Lacan (Derrida 1992, 57-58). In particular it attends to Lacan's writings on the phallus as the desired object for both genders. For Lacan, the phallus is always lost or out of reach – the object of desire and the desire to fulfil the desire of the other that reveals the 'lack' or frustration of all desire. Derrida links logocentrism to the Lacanian phallus through their mutual allusion to what is absent. His deconstructive style of writing attempts to bring these non-presences into view with what is present, thereby demonstrating a complex relation between knowledge, understanding, writing and desire. Ultimately Derrida aims to show the implications of these often contradictory interconnections for contemporary ethical and political concepts such as 'hospitality' or 'democracy'.

Similarly, *écriture féminine* is a mode of writing that aims to expose and transform the privileging of the masculine presence that dominates the history of metaphysics and the history of the written word more generally. In 'The Laugh of the Medusa' Cixous writes: 'It is by writing, from and toward women, and by taking up the challenge of speech which has been governed by the phallus, that women will confirm women in a place other than that which is reserved in and by the symbolic, that is, in a place other than silence' (in Marks 1987, 251). Redressing women's historical exclusion from writing publically, Cixous insists that '[w]oman must write her self' in ways that 'confuse the biological and the cultural' (Cixous in Marks 1987: 245).

Cixous' understanding of 'woman' does not rely on a biologically determinist view of woman. Instead she posits the idea of woman as both presence and non-presence, of the experience of woman as 'a world all her own which she had been secretly haunting since early childhood'(in Marks 1987, 246). Cixous does not want women to deny the uniqueness of their biology, nor does she want women to be reduced to it. Cixous recognises that women are partially determined by the social but that the condition of women cannot be completely explained through a materialist mode analysis that only

attends to how women are 'constructed' throughout history. In developing a mode of writing that attends to sexual difference, Cixous furthers the feminist deconstructive project by marshaling a range of strategies in her use of language. These include homophonic wordplay to evoke multiple simultaneous meanings, or by changing the gender of a definite article and/or the ending of a noun. (This latter strategy for subverting the rules of grammar is untranslatable into English, given that English nouns are not gendered.)

Cixous' multi-vocal mode of writing is deconstructive in the ways that it playfully draws attention to the contradictions of language and reveals the impossibility of an intrinsic or stable meaning of words and signs. Cixous develops a number of new terms that seek to overturn the embedded hierarchies in the relation between words and the things to which they refer. In the essay 'Theatre surprised by puppets', for example, Cixous creates the neologism '*architectent*' that turns the noun '*l'architecture*' into a verb that creates a rhythm and assonance with the word '*textes*' that precedes it in the sentence. With the neologism '*architectent*', Cixous seeks to indicate the residue left over by dreams upon waking. Cixous explains that her dreams imprint monumental edifices on the mind that are made up of both text and image, yet are neither text nor image.

Écriture feminine also defies the traditional temporal logics of writing, received syntactical and grammatical rules, and clearly demarcated voices. Cixousian sentences are prone to changing tense mid-way through, as well as making abrupt movements between first, second and third person pronouns. Cixous often shifts from diegesis to dialogue without warning, and from descriptions of the everyday and the familiar to the abstractly philosophical, expecting the reader to keep pace. She shows the impossibility of anchoring meaning in language. Instead, she wants to open words and sentences up to multiple possible and layered interpretations. Elsewhere she has stated her desire to create a text that 'runs far ahead of the reader and ahead of the author … and requires the reader to run' (in Calle-Gruber and Cixous 1997, 7). A reader who is 'running' with the text is a more active and possibly more critical reader, one who is always questioning meaning and sense, and one who can accept the un-tameability of words and their meanings.

These strategies have a particular function for her writing on theatre that William McEvoy identifies as her attempts to demonstrate that theatre is and should be untheorisable due to its embodied nature and textual poetics (2009: 20). As McEvoy writes:

> Cixous's texts are concerned both to explain theatre theoretically and to textually perform theoretical concepts in a way that suggests limits to modes of theory based on explanation and analysis … Theory stabilises and actualises knowledge whereas theatre requires it to be suspended and recovered through an experiential process. (2009: 21-22)

This intertwining of performance and theory leads to the creation of what McEvoy calls 'critico-creative texts' (2009: 28) that take inspiration from Artaud's attempts to capture the energies of live performance and break free from the limitations of text. It might also be described as 'performative writing', writing that moves beyond the metadiscursive function in order to act as well as reflect.

Cixous' texts are littered with quotation, paraphrasing, allusions and parodies. Ian Blyth and Susan Sellers have elsewhere called these citations 'acts of textual ventriloquism' (Blyth and Sellers 2004, 5). The question of citation is central to Cixous' interrogation of the art of writing and the art of performance. The essays in this collection are interlaced with what Cixous has elsewhere described as *citationsecrets*, secretcitations, her double language and uncited intertexual references embedded within the text (Cixous 2009, 76). Cixous' citations draw attention to the unoriginality and recycled nature of all writing, including her own. This express citationality weaves the rich fabric of her exchanges with the historical and contemporary authors that she most admires, such as Joyce, William Shakespeare, Marcel Proust, Derrida, or the Brazilian writer Clarice Lispector. The voices of these authors haunt the pages of the essays in this collection according to Cixous' own theories of 'haunting'; which is to say, these other voices inform the settings, characters and events depicted in her plays and critical essays.

Cixous rarely cites her intertextual allusions. Instead, she hints at their past lives in ways that invite the reader to seek out their sources. In the essays gathered here, Cixous plays with citation by switching between the traditional French novelistic convention of demarcating characters' voices using hyphens and separate lines and the English use of quotation marks. Whereas English novels generally demarcate characters' speech using quotation marks, European writers adopted the hyphen form to differentiate between dialogue that is not citational and quotation marks for direct citation only. The hyphen form allows writers to retain the sense of an uninterrupted stream-of-consciousness.

Cixous uses both hyphens and quotation marks in these performative essays to blur the boundaries between direct and indirect speech, thoughts and narration. For example, in the essay 'The Communion of Misfortunes' she shifts between quoting from Euripides' Iphigenia *in Aulis*, her 'dialogue' with the Ancient Greek playtext and a distanced commentary on the experience of the Chorus:

> The Chorus is the Hero of Foreboding. It is in a state
> of Tragic Rage:
> 'I feel this is going to end badly, this is going to end badly, this is going to end badly'
> Finally, the worst, is that it ends badly
> The Chorus suffers the pain of Job: all its fears are realised.

My translation has retained Cixous' use of these conventions in order to preserve her marked distinction between these two different modes of representing speech—a distinction that seeks to undermine the stability of 'representation' itself.

Cixous also plays with citation by making her own voice as author and/or narrator and the voices of her characters bleed into one another. In the essay 'Striking Sticks', for example, the authorial voice becomes conflated with the voice of the captain of a sea voyage and with the spectators of the performance. She writes:

> My body is in the body of someone else. Or perhaps it is my head. Who plays the Seigneur? asked a spectator. It's Madame Li who plays the Seigneur, I say. And yet. What if it was the nephew Hun who played him. But no. It is the Seigneur who plays Hun so that Hun can play him.

The precarity of the author as she dissolves into the other voices in the essay's narrative de-stabilises the reliability of the text and its truth claims, blurring any clear demarcation between fiction and non-fiction. Theatre scholar and writer Mireille Calle-Gruber describes this narrative mode as turning the sentence back on itself and recycling it in order to show the process of writing in flux (1997, 5).

The use of a plurality of voices in Cixous' essays mimics the changeability of the actor who moves between characters, often within the same play in a Théâtre du Soleil production. The actors commonly employ the Brechtian techniques of showing themselves performing the role to highlight the tensions between their performance of character and their performance of self in the everyday. Moreover, the Théâtre du Soleil often find ways to signal the writing process as part of the performance. For example, the play *The Last Caravanserai* begins with a film that shows a hand writing a letter in Farsi. A voice-over that switches between French and Farsi reveals the content of the correspondence between Mnouchkine and an anonymous refugee woman. In addition, Cixous' program notes to the same production were originally published in her handwriting, marking her unique imprint on the text. The materiality of Cixous' writing, which includes crossed-out words and other markings on the page, show the ordinarily hidden aspects of her writing, thinking and editing processes. As such, *écriture féminine* is a highly self-reflexive mode of writing and a metatheatrical subject of some Théâtre du Soleil productions, adding more layers of complexity to the essays brought together here.

Écriture féminine is sometimes compared to poetry because of its explicit evasion of fixed meaning and its lyrical and rhythmic qualities. The rhythms and flows of *écriture féminine* are vital to its composition. Cixous is interested in the materiality of the word and what this materiality evokes, for example, as sound, rather than in its literal meaning. The musicality of

her language is evident in lines such as: 'music plays itself and goes from self or from silk, seeping, listening, escaping' ('Theatre surprised by puppets'). Here the alliteration and assonance of 'silk, seeping, listening, escaping' creates a *legato* that propels the reader forwards through its smooth and sonically pleasing rhythms. Cixous' sensitivity to music leads her to reflect on the music in Théâtre du Soleil productions, created by Jean-Jacques Lemêtre. For Cixous, music operates at the same emotional level as thought. As she writes in 'Acknowledging Debts': 'thought only speaks musically. It doesn't know, it feels'. *Écriture feminine* is writing that synchronises with the rhythms of thought and thus its effects on the reader aim to be affective rather than didactic.

While formal and linguistic experiments are today familiar to readers of postmodern fiction, Cixous' style is particularly unusual in the context of the writing in this collection. Here *écriture féminine* is employed for literary or performance analysis, political commentary or to interrogate philosophical problems. Art or literary criticism, politics and philosophy often aim to impose interpretative meaning on a text or event and Cixous' work is a deliberate and radical rejection of this undertaking. As she notes, *écriture féminine* is 'not a way of repressing or obliterating theory but of giving it a place which is not an end in itself' (Cixous in Blyth and Sellers 2004, 114). These essays offer commentaries on politics, ethics and performance that are not ends in themselves; rather, they are starting points that invite readers and scholars to engage with their open-ended provocations.

The use of *écriture féminine* to comment on contemporary political and ethical questions is its own intervention into and counter-response to the neoliberal rhetoric that has saturated the media and political rhetoric in the West since the 1980s. The technocratic language of neoliberalism is full of concealed contradictions, particularly in its frequent references to 'free markets' and 'free' flows of labour, goods and capital. The language of freedom often conceals the very limitations that economic liberalism and its austerity measures have imposed upon the vast majority of labouring subjects who are forced to live with the precarity of labour casualisation, job insecurity and reduced social welfare. In this collection, Cixous uses *écriture féminine* to bring to light some of these contradictions and explore the relationship between theatrical performance and contemporary politics.

Cixous has noted elsewhere that poetry is the most truthful form of writing because it is always alluding to the absent and so it is always in process (1997, 4). She uses a mode of poetic prose that gestures towards the absent, silenced and invisible to evoke what is unspeakable, unheard, imperceptible or concealed in the public political sphere such as the treatment of refugees by Western governments, the plight of women, the corruption of governments and the political influence of large corporations over judicial and governmental decisions. She also interrogates the right and function of art/

theatre to interrogate these difficult ethical problems through her discussions on the aestheticisation of violence in art and the role of art in activist politics. Cixous' performative mode of writing uses the language and concepts of theatrical performance to invite readers and spectators to rethink these urgent and difficult ethical, political and artistic questions outside the familiar rhetorical modes used by Western political leaders and the mainstream media.

Navigating the text

All translations and footnotes in this collection are mine. The translation and editorial choices that I have made attempt to retain the integrity of Cixous' original sentences in order to allow the Anglophone reader some insight into the richness and complexity of her writing. Where it is possible to do so, I have attempted to keep intact the length and word order of Cixous' sentences to give the reader an impression of the drawn-out, stream-of-consciousness, rhythmic flows of her language and the double or multiple entendres. In keeping the structural integrity of Cixous' sentences, I aim to help the reader navigate the text. To capture the word play of these sentences without interrupting their fluidity, I sometimes use the convention of putting possible meanings, interpretations of a word, or homophones in the same line and dividing them with a '/'. I hope this aids the reader to view the sentence as a whole, rather than breaking concentration to look elsewhere on the page for a fuller explanation.

For more detailed and complex explanations of word play I have provided some footnotes. These footnotes seek to offer a limited guide to navigating some of the complexity of Cixous' writing by pointing out some of her uncited references, wordplay and use of different languages. The footnotes are, however, far from exhaustive; they offer merely one possible reading among several. They aim to give the reader a taste of the breadth of Cixous' thought, its layers of intertexuality and the musicality of her writing.

Given the complexity of *écriture feminine*, Cixous' writing largely resists translation. Indeed, Cixous states in an interview that her texts are almost 'untranslatable' (2000, 339). She recognises that any translator of her work has to 'be faithful by being unfaithful' and that it is necessary for the 'translator to take the risk and the responsibility, to give up something here and, on the contrary, invent something there' (2004a, 8). Yet Cixous also celebrates the idea of error and failure in writing as both a reflexive sign of the writing process and a means of showing the text as always-in-process. This collection, has many moments of unfaithful faithfulness, but also provides readers with both the English translation and the original French. I encourage readers with some knowledge of French to refer to the original text in order to more deeply consider the sentences that are particularly enigmatic.

The personal as political

It is frequently noted that Cixous' biographical details shape her personal politics and unique mode of writing. Of particular relevance to this collection, Cixous' interest in what it means to be 'other' is closely bound to her personal history. Cixous was born in 1937 to a Jewish family and grew up in Clos Salembier, a non-French part of Algiers, in pre-independence Algeria. Here she and her family were treated as outsiders and foreigners by both the French colonial residents and the native Algerians. Her family's position as non-religious Jews meant they were excluded from both the Jewish community and the local Muslim population (Calle-Gruber and Cixous 1997, 197). Anti-Semitism was also rife during her childhood, shadowed as it was with the Nazi invasion of France and Marshal Philippe Petain's collaboration with the fascists in France from 1940-1944.

When Cixous migrated to France in the 1950s, she describes feeling like an outsider not only because of her accent and her ancestry but, predominantly, because of her gender (1997, 204). Her social position as female, bisexual, Algerian Jew with Spanish, Hungarian, German and French grandparents made her multiply 'other'. The essays in this collection frequently touch on the problems of imperialism, the residues of colonisation and the socio-cultural place of the foreigner. The essays explore the displacement of old empires through the French language – formerly one of the great imperial and diplomatic languages of modernity. In the essay 'Our Show', Cixous shows the difficulties of using the language of the coloniser, even for artistic purposes. She draws attention to the problems encountered when art tries to redress some of the wrongdoings inflicted on colonised subjects by the colonisers when she asks: 'How do we not replace your foreign language with our French language?'. Cixous shows how the language of the coloniser retains its history of authority, power and hierarchy, as well as its history of usurping the voices and agency of colonised subjects. As such, she problematises the role of socially committed theatre in its attempt to speak for the other, even if that communication begins as a mutually respectful cross-cultural dialogue.

In tracing the decline of French imperialism, the essays are also interested in framing new empires and their discontents. Essays such as 'If you allow me, I'm going to speak to you about love…' and 'An Inextinguishable Spark' are responses to the aftermath of colonial rule in the former British India and French Cambodia, and the atrocities and upheavals that accompanied these nations' difficult transitions to independence. Yet they are also commentaries on the extraordinary and inspiring political figures that emerged in these periods. 'If you allow me, I'm going to speak to you about love…' reflects on the legacy of Mohandas Karamchand Gandhi who became a preeminent model of non-violent activism and influenced civil rights movements

all over the world for generations to follow. 'An Inextinguishable Spark' considers the achievements of the Cambodian King, Norodom Sihanouk, who, despite his own personal loss, showed his enemies compassion and forgiveness in order to rebuild his fractured nation after the retreat of the Khmer Rouge into exile.

Cixous' ancestry has not only influenced her political beliefs but has equally impacted on the development of *écriture féminine.* As a result of her hybrid ancestry, she speaks and reads a number of languages fluently including German, French, English, Hebrew, Latin and ancient Greek. It is frequently noted that Cixous' multilingual skills have contributed to her irreverent attitude to language and the possibility of fixed meaning since the nuance of meaning shifts in each different language (Blyth and Sellers 2004, 6). Not only do her texts move between languages, but language also becomes a game to be scrutinised, pulled apart and re-constructed in neologisms and portmanteau words that more effectively express multiple and often contrary meanings.

It is not only Cixous' dense style that makes these essays challenging to read. All the essays refer to performances that readers may not have viewed. Sometimes Cixous reflects on a single theatrical work over several different essays. The commentaries on particular performance aesthetics – many of which are unique to the Théâtre du Soleil – are invariably more meaningful to those people who have seen the performances live or on DVD. In an effort to help readers better comprehend and navigate the essays, I have divided the collection into ten sections and have grouped together the essays that respond to a particular theatrical performance. Each section begins with a brief synopsis of the relevant Théâtre du Soleil play and an outline of the context of its performance. Each essay retains Cixous' original notes printed at its conclusion to mark the traces of its first publication date and performance context.

Cixous and the theatre

Cixous' oeuvre is famously expansive. It includes works of fiction, plays, literary theory, feminist theory and philosophy, screenwriting, librettos, reviews, biographies, cultural commentary and poetry. Though her work offers such wide-ranging contributions, her impact on theatre and performance has been critical. Cixous' significance to twentieth century theatre extends far beyond her early plays written in the 1970s, and even beyond her work with the Théâtre du Soleil. Her theoretical writings on the theatre and the place of women in the theatre, particularly the essay 'Aller à la mer' ['Going to the Sea/Mother'] (1977) have shaped twentieth century feminist thinking about future directions for the theatre and the place of women within it. 'Going to the Sea/Mother' is an exasperated

critique of theatre in the 1970s, which she criticises for the way in which it reproduces patriarchal family structures and constantly places women in the role of victims (Cixous 1984, 546). It is also a call to women to come together to reclaim the live qualities of theatre and its potential to represent women experiencing their identities as multiple by playing roles that move beyond those that they are consigned to in patriarchal societies (Cixous 1984, 547).

In the essays collected here, Cixous' earlier feminist project is expanded through the notion of 'hospitality'. Cixous applies the idea of hospitality to thinking through contemporary socio-political problems and the unique qualities of theatre and performance as compared to other artforms. For Cixous, the theatre requires actors, authors, directors, musicians and spectators to strip themselves of their egos and open themselves up to the other. That other might be an other of a different gender, but might equally be someone of a different race, generation, or even species. While governments often fail to extend hospitality towards the foreign other, Cixous notes that theatre is a place of 'hosting the other' *par excellence.* It is the place where we share our stories and the stories of others, even if we do so incompletely or inadequately. In Cixous' terms, the theatre is the place that reminds us that 'we are singular plural beings, coinhabited coinhabitants cohaunting cohaunteds' ('Striking Sticks').

Cixous links her critique of imperialism in her essays from the 1980s to the lack of hospitality shown towards to refugees at the turn of the twenty-first century. In the essays 'Striking Sticks' and 'Theatre surprised by puppets', Cixous expands upon the idea of hospitality by claiming that actors host the other when they play different character roles. These essays explore the aesthetic of the play *Drums on the Dam* in which the actors pretended to be Bunraku puppets controlled by puppet masters, played by other actors. This performance aesthetic required the actors to give up the agency of both their bodies and their voices. They moved on stage seemingly according to the dictates of the puppet master and their lines were spoken by other actors situated off-stage. In submitting to these others, the actors performed an act of self-othering that invited others in, and which provided a visual and auditory performance of the body as multiple.

Cixous further notes that it was not only the actors who were overcome by their characters but also the author whose body was taken over during the writing process. In writing *Drums on the Dam,* Cixous describes how she hosted an imaginary Chinese poet 'Hxshi-Xhou' whose name is homophonous with 'Cixous'. Hxshi-Xhou, she claims, wrote the fable for her as Cixous 'ventriloquised' Hxshi-Xhou's story. This might be read as yet another act of citation and the author's self-othering or an act of speaking for the other in the language of the dominant culture which recalls many of the problems of colonial writing.

In the essays in this collection, Cixous argues that the greatest value of theatre today is its role as a place that can reveal to us as spectators, writers and artists that we are deaf and blind. For Cixous, theatre is a 'large ocular globe, this open Eye, that humans pass through with their eyes blindfolded' and has the responsibilities of a watchman ('Acknowledging Debts'). It is the very artifice of theatre that makes it the ideal medium for unveiling the lies of the everyday – whether in the media or in the politeness of our quotidian social interactions. For Cixous, theatre continues to be the place where habit is broken, a place that thrives on displacement, estrangement and contingency. It is also a place of solidarity and shared experience where communities of artists and the general public come together. She explains that theatre has always been a house of judgment where the spectator public is called upon to act as witness. Theatre is, for Cixous, the place where we see, fleetingly, that things could be different to the way they currently are, when an alternative decision or action could be taken. Cixous argues that theatre reminds us that these moments of contingency and the possibility of change also occur in our everyday lives, and that we must be vigilant if we are to recognise them as such when they arise.

Locating the self-other

My desire to make Cixous' essays available to an Anglophone readership is in part motivated by my personal history. I was fortunate enough to have first read Cixous' plays and theoretical writings in Melbourne, Australia, as an undergraduate student and enthusiast of feminist theatre. Yet my desire to translate these essays was motivated by more than just my position as a Western feminist and theatre scholar. I came of age in Australia during the Prime Ministership of John Howard and his Immigration Minister Philip Ruddock, of the right-wing Liberal Party. I saw the attitudes towards and treatment of refugee men, women and children change substantially in the eleven years that Howard was in power. I followed the media stories of off-shore detention centres. I visited some of the centres located in remote regions of Australia and witnessed the appalling treatment of the detained asylum seekers.

Both my parents were migrants to Australia. My mother's family emigrated from Sri Lanka in 1957 and my father migrated as an adult from England in 1980. When my maternal grandparents emigrated in the mid-1950s, Australian immigration was still regulated by the White Australia Policy. My Dutch Burgher grandparents had to prove that they and their children had sufficiently 'white' ancestry to be allowed to settle in Australia. This racist immigration policy was only made unlawful when the Whitlam Government passed the Racial Discrimination Act in 1975. Its legacy, however, has been revived in the last two decades in asylum seeker policy under

a number of different Australian governments, from both sides of the political spectrum. As Cixous writes in 'What is a refugee? Are you a refugee?': 'History repeats itself, barely disguised'.

The essays in this collection that respond to the play *The Last Caravanserai (Odysseys)* reflect on the human effects of contemporary immigration policy in France and Australia in particular. Cixous knows from personal experience that one cannot rely on the nation state for hospitality. The paradox of the democratic state is that it can only ever offer 'conditional hospitality' to those outside the state. In the essay 'What is a refugee? Are you a refugee?' Cixous notes that the word 'refugee' comes into French from the Latin after the French King Louis XIV revoked the Edict of Nantes and turned the Calvinist Protestants living in Catholic France into fugitives. She tries to understand how this revocation altered French attitudes towards foreigners in the long term.

At the time of writing this in 2015, Europe is experiencing what has been labelled the 'European migrant crisis'. Refugees from the Middle East and North Africa are fleeing the escalating conditions of war, civil war, violence, instability and religious fanaticism. The flow of migrants into the European Union is expected to reach 1.5 million people this year alone. Meanwhile, deadly terrorist attacks on Paris, Beirut, Ankara, and Bamako in November 2015, claimed by different radicalised Islamic groups, further highlight the spread of violence across borders. As the European Union negotiates with Turkish President Recep Tayyip Erdogan (despite his dubious human rights record) to broker a deal that will ensure Turkey acts as a buffer to migrants wanting to gain access to Europe from the Middle East, this is a moment in history in which a politics of hospitality is acutely relevant.

Cixous has written that language has an 'infinite hospitality' (Cixous 2005, 207). Accordingly, the essays collected here give temporary shelter to visions of a more ethical and humane future. In this time in history in which the other is vilified, demonised and feared in the West – whether it is the Muslim other, old women or the refugee child – the essays gathered here draw on the ambiguities and contradictions of theatrical and political representation in ways that invite readers to locate the self in the other and the other in the self, in order to complicate our contemporary ethical obligations. The essays show the unavoidable difficulties of any political or artistic action in the face of injustice but are also constant reminders of Cixous' ethical imperative: 'How can we never play any role?'

Lara Stevens
December 2015
Melbourne, Australia

WORKS CITED

Blyth, Ian, and Susan Sellers. 2004. *Hélène Cixous: Live Theory*. New York; London: Bloomsbury.

Calle-Gruber, Mireille, and Hélène Cixous. 1997. *Hélène Cixous, Rootprints: Memory and Life Writing*. London; New York: Routledge.

Cixous, Hélène. 1984. "Aller À La Mer." Translated by Barbara Kerslake. *Modern Drama* 27 (4): 546–48.

Cixous, Hélène. 2000. "An Interview with Hélène Cixous." *Paragraph* 23 (3): 338–43.

Cixous, Hélène. 2005. *Stigmata: Escaping Texts*. London; New York. Routledge.

Cixous, Hélène. 2009. *Hyperdream*. Cambridge, UK; Malden, MA: Polity.

Derrida, Jacques. 1967. *De La Grammatologie*. Paris: Editions de Minuit.

Derrida, Jacques. 1992. *Acts of Literature*. Psychology Press.

Marks, Elaine (ed). 1987. *New French Feminisms*. New York: Pantheon.

McEvoy, William. 2009, '"Leaving a space for the non-theorisable": Self and Other in *Hélène* Cixous's Writing for Theatre', *The European Legacy*, 14 (1): 19–30.

Miller, Judith Graves. 2007. *Ariane Mnouchkine*. London: Routledge.

Neuschäfer, Anne. 2004. "1970-1975: Ecrire Une Comédie de Notre Temps - La Filiation Avec Jacques Copeau." Mai. http://www.theatre-du-soleil.fr/thsol/a-propos-du-theatre-du-soleil/l-historique,163/1970-1975-ecrire-une-comedie-de.

Rancière, Jacques. 2011. *The Emancipated Spectator*. London: Verso.

Politique, éthique et spectacle

Ce recueil d'essais de l'écrivain, philosophe et féministe Hélène Cixous couvre 29 années de son écriture, de sa pensée et de son travail avec la troupe du Théâtre du Soleil, ce collectif artistique expérimental et radical fondé par Ariane Mnouchkine en 1964. Cixous a pris part aux créations collectives du Théâtre du Soleil en tant qu'écrivain ou dramaturge depuis les années 1980 et elle continue aujourd'hui encore à travailler avec la troupe. Ce recueil d'essais reflète le développement de l'esthétique unique du Théâtre du Soleil et les préoccupations éthiques et politiques d'un collectif qui se préoccupe de justice sociale depuis sa création.

La pratique des artistes du Théâtre du Soleil se nourrit de l'idéal des années 1960 qui considère que l'art peut intervenir socialement et politiquement pour catalyser des changements dans la société. On peut ainsi lire dans le programme de *L'Âge d'Or* (1975):

> Nous voulons réinventer des règles du jeu qui dévoilent la réalité quotidienne en la montrant non pas familière et immuable, mais étonnante et transformable. Ce sera donc un théâtre en prise directe sur la réalité sociale qui ne soit pas un simple constat, mais un encouragement à changer les conditions dans lesquelles nous vivons. (Neuschäfer 2004)

Depuis les années 1960, les membres du Théâtre du Soleil montent des spectacles qui reflètent leurs combats politiques nationaux ou internationaux et puisent leur esthétique dans les traditions théâtrales asiatiques et européennes.

Les artistes du Théâtre du Soleil ont toujours mis en pratique leur conviction socialiste en s'engageant dans l'activisme communautaire. Ainsi en 1972, la troupe crée un court spectacle pour le Groupe d'Information sur les Prisons (GIP) dirigé par Michel Foucault, qui cherche à améliorer les conditions de détention. Certaines des artistes sont signataires du « Manifeste des 343 », la pétition controversée, parrainée par Simone de Beauvoir, en faveur de la légalisation de l'avortement (Miller 2007, 12). Mnouchkine est également l'un des membres fondateurs de l'Association Internationale de

Défense des Artistes victimes de la répression dans le monde (AIDA) destinée à défendre les artistes persécutés par les gouvernements de leur pays grâce à des déclarations, des sit-ins et des spectacles en faveur de ceux qui sont victimes de discrimination politique ou de la censure. En 1995, Mnouchkine fait une grève de la faim de 30 jours pour protester contre l'inaction française envers le génocide en Bosnie. En 1996, elle héberge dans son théâtre de la Cartoucherie—situé dans le Bois de Vincennes, à la périphérie de Paris —382 sans-papiers qui avaient été expulsés de l'église Saint-Bernard à Paris (Miller 2007, 12). Le Théâtre du Soleil poursuit également une mission sociale d'éducation de ses nombreux spectateurs et veille à ce que ses spectacles soient accessibles à toutes les classes de la société française.

Les essais contenus dans ce recueil ne reflètent pas seulement le travail socialement engagé du Théâtre du Soleil, mais ils visent à créer, en accord avec les principes de la compagnie, des pièces capables de « changer les conditions dans lesquelles nous vivons ». Ils renforcent le projet de révéler aux spectateurs la possibilité de modifier les conditions actuelles d'inégalité et d'injustice. Avant de travailler avec le Théâtre du Soleil, Cixous avait écrit plusieurs pièces, notamment le *Portrait de Dora,* d'abord diffusé à la radio en 1972 puis monté à la scène en 1976. Le *Portrait de Dora* est une reconstitution des séances d'analyse de la jeune « Dora » racontées par Sigmund Freud , et de son diagnostic problématique d'« hystérie ». La pièce compte maintenant parmi les textes fondateurs du théâtre féministe. Le *Portrait de Dora* montre l'intérêt de Cixous pour les événements réels et les personnages historiques, pour la politique des sexes ainsi que les problèmes de communication, de vérité, de justice, toutes ces préoccupations demeurant au cœur des essais de cette collection.

La plupart de ces essais figuraient dans les programmes des spectacles, ou en introduction des pièces éditées. Ce recueil est le premier à les faire dialoguer et à les rendre accessibles à un lectorat anglophone. J'ai choisi d'organiser ces essais en une chronologie inverse qui donne une vue rétrospective de l'œuvre de Cixous. L'essai le plus récent – « L'irréparable » – a été écrit en 2014 – et le plus ancien, « Une étincelle inextinguible » – en 1985. Chaque essai correspond à l'un des spectacles majeurs du Théâtre du Soleil donné au cours du dernier quart du vingtième siècle, parmi lesquels figurent *Macbeth* (2014), *Les Naufragés du Fol Espoir (Aurores)* (2010), *Les Ephémères* (2006), *Le Dernier Caravansérail (Odyssées)* (2003), *Tambours sur la Digue - Sous forme de pièce ancienne pour marionnettes jouée par des acteurs* (1999), *Et soudain des nuits d'éveil* (1997), *La Ville parjure ou le Réveil des Érinyes* (1994), *Les Atrides* (1990-1992), *L'Indiade ou l'Inde de leurs rêves* (1987), et *L'Histoire terrible mais inachevée de Norodom Sihanouk, roi du Cambodge* (1985).

Les essais de Cixous répondent à ces spectacles et s'en inspirent à la fois, évoquant les recherches collaboratives et les expérimentations qui ont mené à leur réalisation. Chaque essai est un commentaire ou une invitation

à relier esthétique théâtrale, politique et éthique. En outre, chaque essai est une réponse à un moment spécifique, à un lieu ou un événement historique précis et raconte l'expérience de groupes « autres », marginalisés ou abordés avec méfiance par le grand public. Ces « autres » auxquels Cixous s'intéresse dans ces essais comprennent les personnes distinguées par leur race, les réfugiés, les révolutionnaires, ceux qui résistent à l'expansion coloniale, les classes inférieures, les femmes, les malades ou infectées, les victimes du fanatisme idéologique, les artistes et écrivains avant-gardistes, les scientifiques qui ont fait des découvertes qui ont changé notre façon de voir le monde et nous-mêmes, et les pacifistes.

Ces essais illustrent la contribution importante de Cixous aux domaines de la philosophie, la poésie, la fiction, la théorie féministe et la théorie du théâtre. Plus précisément, ils montrent les relations existant entre entre art, théâtre et spectacle et dénoncent la politique de transformation sous l'actuel néolibéralisme – souvent décrit comme un moment historique « post-marxiste », dominé par une idéologie capitaliste apparemment sans alternative (Rancière 2011, 32-33). Ces essais soulèvent des questions éthiques importantes pour les XXe et XXIe siècles, telles que les contradictions entre les promesses de libertés démocratiques de l'occident et le refus des droits de l'homme pour les non-citoyens, le rôle du théâtre et du spectacle comme moyen de combattre l'injustice, les difficultés et nécessités de communication interculturelle dans l'art comme dans le monde politique, et la condition féminine dans l'histoire et aujourd'hui.

Écriture féminine

Le style d'écriture particulier de Cixous représente un défi pour tous les lecteurs. Ses phrases sont longues et complexes ; souvent elles évoluent entre les sujets en un « flux de conscience » qui rappelle le procédé utilisé par James Joyce, sujet de la thèse doctorale de Cixous et de nombre de ses analyses littéraires. L'écriture de Cixous est remplie de références, calembours, jeux de mots, jeux de sonorités (homonymie, homophonie, assonance, allitération) et allusions autobiographiques. Ses phrases peuvent dérouter le lecteur en raison de leur structure, de leur longueur, de l'utilisation de plusieurs citations, néologismes et symbolisme. Elle bouscule souvent les règles grammaticales ou les conventions génériques et se complaît dans des phrases fragiles et ambiguës qui invitent les lecteurs à aborder de manière critique ses essais et les spectacles auxquels elles se rapportent.

Dans son essai « Le rire de la Méduse » (1975) Cixous revendique un style qu'elle nomme « écriture féminine ». Approfondissant les travaux de son ami et collaborateur occasionnel, le philosophe Jacques Derrida, Cixous voit dans l' « écriture féminine » un moyen de subvertir et contourner le « logocentrisme » et le « phallogocentrisme ». Pour Derrida, contourner le «

logocentrisme » signifie en finir avec la « métaphysique de la présence » dans l'histoire de la philosophie, qui vise à donner un accès immédiat au sens fixe d'un mot ou un texte (1967, 11-12). Derrida nous rappelle que, puisque l'auteur d'un texte est la plupart du temps absent pour le lecteur, l'écriture désigne toujours une absence. Un texte peut être enlevé de son contexte, mal traduit ou mal copié et repose donc toujours sur un sens différé. En tant que telle, la déconstruction de Derrida montre que les mots ou les concepts sont souvent hantés par ce qui n'est pas présent, par leur signification antérieure et leurs nuances (en contradiction souvent avec l'usage contemporain). Derrida révèle ce qu'il appelle les « spectres » des mots en s'appuyant sur leur étymologie afin de compliquer leur polysémie. De plus, il joue sur la conjugaison des verbes pour créer des homophones aux sens contradictoires, mettant ainsi en évidence les contradictions au sein du langage sous sa forme orale.

Le « phallogocentrisme », ce néologisme derridien, poursuit le projet de déconstruire la langue en empruntant idées et termes à la psychanalyse, et notamment aux théories de Jacques Lacan (Derrida 1992, 57-58). Derrida fait tout particulièrement référence aux écrits de Lacan sur le « phallus » comme objet de désir des deux sexes. Pour Lacan le « phallus » est toujours manqué ou hors de portée – l'objet du désir et le désir de remplir le désir de l'autre qui révèle le manque ou la frustration de tout désir. Derrida fait un lien entre le « logocentrisme » et le « phallus » Lacanien en raison de leur évocation commune de ce qui est absent. Cette écriture déconstruite essaye de confronter ce qui est présent et non-présent, pour montrer la relation complexe qui existe entre le savoir, la compréhension, l'écriture et le désir. Enfin Derrida montre les implications de ces interrelations, souvent contradictoires, en ce qui concerne des concepts éthiques et politiques contemporains, comme « l'hospitalité » ou « la démocratie ».

De la même façon, l'écriture féminine est un mode d'écriture qui vise à dénoncer et transformer la prédominance masculine dans l'histoire de la métaphysique et l'histoire de l'écrit en général. Dans son essai « Le rire de la Méduse » Cixous écrit: « C'est en écrivant, depuis et vers la femme, et en relevant le défi du discours gouverné par le phallus, que la femme affirmera la femme autrement qu'à la place à elle réservée dans et par le symbole c'est-à-dire le silence » (1975, 43). Tâchant de revenir sur la difficulté historique pour les femmes d'écrire pour un large public, Cixous insiste : « Il faut que la femme s'écrive » afin de « confondre le biologique et le culturel » (1975, 39).

La définition de la femme chez Cixous ne renvoie toutefois pas à un déterminisme biologique. Au contraire, Cixous avance l'idée d'une femme à la fois comme présence et non-présence, d'une expérience de femme comme celle « d'un monde sien qu'elle hantait secrètement depuis sa petite enfance » (1975, 39). Cixous ne veut pas que les femmes renient leur spécificité biologique, ni qu'elles soient réduites à cette biologie. Cixous reconnait que

les femmes sont déterminées en partie par la vie sociale, mais que la condition des femmes ne peut pas s'expliquer complètement par une analyse matérialiste qui ne s'intéresse qu'à la question de savoir comment les femmes sont « construites » historiquement. En créant un mode d'écriture attentif à la différence sexuelle, Cixous continue le projet féministe de déconstruction en déployant toute une gamme de stratégies dans son usage de la langue. Ces stratégies comprennent des jeux de mots homophoniques pour évoquer plusieurs significations simultanées, ou des changements de genre ou de terminaison d'un nom. (Ce bouleversement des règles grammaticales ne peut pas être rendu en anglais, étant donné que les noms en anglais n'ont pas de genre.)

L'écriture multivocale de Cixous est un exemple de déconstruction dans la mesure où elle attire l'attention sur les contradictions de la langue et révèle l'impossibilité de la signification intrinsèque des mots et des signes. Cixous crée un certain nombre de mots nouveaux qui visent à renverser les hiérarchies existant entre les mots et les choses auxquelles ils renvoient. Dans son essai « Théâtre surpris par des marionnettes », par exemple, Cixous crée le néologisme « architectent », faisant du substantif « architecte » un verbe rythmant et assonant avec le mot « textes » qui le précède. Grâce à l'emploi du néologisme « architectent », Cixous désigne ce qui reste des rêves au moment du réveil. Cixous explique que ses rêves impriment sur son esprit des édifices monumentaux constitués de textes et d'images, mais qui ne sont cependant ni texte, ni image.

L'écriture féminine défie également la logique temporelle traditionnelle de l'écriture, les règles syntaxiques et grammaticales, et les délimitations nettes des voix des personnages dans le théâtre. Les phrases de Cixous changent souvent de temps à mi-chemin, ou bien alternent soudainement les pronoms de première, deuxième ou troisième personne. Cixous passe souvent sans avertir du récit au dialogue, et des descriptions du quotidien aux abstractions philosophiques, attendant du lecteur qu'il suive. Elle montre l'impossibilité de l'ancrage du sens dans le langage. Au contraire, elle cherche à ouvrir les mots et les phrases à une multitde d'interprétations possibles. Par ailleurs, elle a exprimé sa volonté de créer un texte qui « court loin devant le lecteur et en avance de l'auteur, ou lorsque le texte court simplement, il nécessite que le lecteur doive courir aussi » (in Calle-Gruber et Cixous 1997, 7).[1] Un lecteur qui « court » avec un texte est un lecteur plus actif et peut-être plus critique, toujours prêt à s'interroger sur le sens d'un mot ou d'une phrase, et qui peut accepter le fait que les mots et leurs significations ne puissent pas être apprivoisés.

Ces stratégies ont aussi une fonction particulière dans ses écrits sur le théâtre ; William McEvoy y voit la tentative de Cixous de démontrer que le

1. Ma traduction.

théâtre n'est pas et ne devrait pas être théorisable en raison de sa corporalité et de sa dimension poétique (2009: 20). Selon McEvoy :

> Dans ses textes, Cixous cherche à la fois à expliquer le théâtre théoriquement et à mettre en texte des concepts théoriques d'une manière qui suggère qu'il y a des limites à la théorie basée sur l'explication et l'analyse … La théorie stabilise et actualise la connaissance alors que le théâtre exige qu'elle soit suspendue et récupérée grâce à un processus empirique. (2009: 21-22)2

Cette imbrication du spectacle et de la théorie chez Cixous mène à la création de ce que McEvoy appelle des « textes critico-créatifs » (2009: 28) qui s'inspirent des tentatives d'Artaud pour capturer les énergies du spectacle vivant et se libérer des limitations du texte. Elle pourrait également être définie comme une « écriture performative », c'est-à-dire une écriture qui va au-delà de la fonction métadiscursive pour agir autant que réfléchir.

Les textes de Cixous sont parsemés de citations, paraphrases, allusions et parodies. Ian Blyth et Susan Sellers ont ailleurs qualifié ces citations comme « acts of textual ventriloquism » (« ventriloquisme textuel ») (Blyth and Sellers 2004, 5). La question de la citation est au cœur de la recherche de Cixous sur l'art de l'écriture et l'art du spectacle. Les essais de ce recueil sont parcourus de ce que Cixous a ailleurs décrit comme des « citationsecrets », ces double sens et références intertextuelles incorporés dans le texte sans citation (2009, 76). Les citations de Cixous attirent l'attention sur le manque d'originalité et le caractère répétitif de toute écriture, y compris la sienne. Ces citations explicites forment un tissu riche d'emprunts aux auteurs passés ou contemporains qu'elle admire le plus comme Joyce, William Shakespeare, Marcel Proust, Derrida, ou l'écrivain brésilienne Clarice Lispector. Les voix de ces auteurs hantent les pages des essais qui suivent, suivant la théorie de « l'hantologie » définie par Cixous elle-même ; en d'autres termes, ces voix informent les lieux, les personnages et les événements de ses pièces et essais critiques.

Cixous explicite rarement ses allusions intertextuelles. Elle donne plutôt un indice de leurs vies passées de manière à inviter le lecteur à chercher leurs sources. Dans les essais réunis ici, Cixous joue sur les conventions pour introduire les voix de ses personnages : elle utilise des traits d'union et retours à la ligne, selon la tradition des romans français, ou bien des guillemets, suivant la tradition des romans anglais. Alors que les romans anglais recourent aux guillemets pour les dialogues des personnages, les écrivains européens ont adopté le trait d'union pour différencier le dialogue qui n'est pas une citation, de la citation directe. Le trait d'union permet aux écrivains de conserver l'allure d'un flux de conscience ininterrompu.

Cixous utilise à la fois des traits d'union et des guillemets dans ces essais performatifs pour brouiller les frontières entre discours direct et indirect,

2. Ma traduction

pensées et narration. Par exemple, dans l'essai « La Communion des Douleurs », elle alterne les citations d'*Iphigénie à Aulis* d'Euripide, son propre « dialogue » avec la pièce de la Grèce antique et un commentaire distancié sur l'expérience du Chœur:

> Le Chœur est le Héros du Pressentiment. Il est dans l'état
> de Rage Tragique:
> 'Je sens que cela va mal finir, cela va mal finir, cela va mal finir'
> – finalement, le pire, c'est que ça finit mal.
> Le Chœur souffre du mal de Job: toutes ses craintes sont exaucées.

Ma traduction tâche de respecter les usages de Cixous, et de préserver la distinction marquée entre ces deux modes de discours rapporté – une distinction qui cherche à ébranler la stabilité de ce que veut dire « rapporter » les discours.

Cixous joue aussi avec la citation en rendant sa propre voix d'auteur/ narrateur indifférenciable de celle de ses personnages. Dans l'essai « Coups de baguettes », par exemple, la voix de l'auteur se confond avec la voix du capitaine d'un voyage en mer tout comme avec les pensées des spectateurs de la pièce. Elle écrit :

> Mon corps est dans le corps de quelqu'un d'autre. Ou bien c'est ma tête. Qui joue le Seigneur? demandait un spectateur. C'est Mme Li qui joue le Seigneur, dis-je. Et pourtant. Si c'était le neveu Hun qui le jouait? Mais non. C'est le Seigneur qui joue Hun pour que Hun le joue.

La précarité de l'auteur, qui se fond dans les autres voix du récit, déstabilise la fiabilité du texte et ses prétentions à la vérité, brouillant toute démarcation nette entre fiction et non-fiction. La spécialiste du théâtre Mireille Calle-Gruber décrit ce mode de récit comme celui qui tourne la phrase sur elle-même en la recyclant, afin de montrer le processus de l'écriture en flux (1997, 5).

La pluralité des voix dans les essais de Cixous imite les changements du comédien qui va d'un personnage à un autre, souvent dans la même pièce dans le cas d'un spectacle du Théâtre du Soleil. Les comédiens se montrent souvent en train de jouer leur rôle – une technique brechtienne destinée à mettre en évidence les tensions entre le personnage de théâtre et l'acteur dans son quotidien. En outre, le Théâtre du Soleil trouve souvent le moyen de signaler le processus d'écriture dans le cadre du spectacle. Par exemple, la pièce *Le Dernier Caravansérail* commence par un film qui montre une main en train d'écrire une lettre en farsi. Une voix-off qui alterne entre le français et le farsi révèle le contenu de la correspondance entre Mnouchkine et une femme réfugiée anonyme. De plus, le programme de ce spectacle est imprimé dans l'écriture manuscrite de Cixous elle-même, qui marque ainsi le texte de son empreinte unique. La matérialité de l'écriture de Cixous, avec des mots raturés et des taches sur la page, dévoile certains aspects de

son écriture, de sa pensée et des processus de rédaction. En tant que telle, l'écriture féminine est un mode d'écriture fortement introspectif et un sujet méta-théâtral rencontré dans certaines pièces créées par le Théâtre du Soleil, ce qui ajoute encore à la complexité des essais réunis ici.

L'écriture féminine est parfois comparée à la poésie en raison de ses évasions du sens fixe et de ses qualités lyriques et rythmiques. Les rythmes et le flux de l'écriture féminine sont essentiels à la composition des mots dans les phrases. Cixous s'intéresse à la matérialité du mot et à ce que cela évoque, par exemple, la façon dont la sonorité d'un mot ou sa place dans une phrase peut créer un autre sens qui est complètement différent. La musicalité de son langage est évidente dans les passages tels que: « la musique aussi joue d'elle-même et va de soi ou de soie, s'écoulant s'écoutant s'échapper » (« Théâtre surpris par des marionnettes »). Ici les allitérations et assonances « de soi ou de soie, s'écoulant s'écoutant s'échapper » créent un legato qui propulse le lecteur à travers ses rythmes phoniques souples et agréables. Cixous offre aussi quelques réflexions concernant la musique des spectacles du Théâtre du Soleil, composée par Jean-Jacques Lemêtre. Pour Cixous, la musique fonctionne au même niveau émotionnel que la pensée. Comme elle l'écrit dans l'essai « Reconnaissance de dettes », « la pensée ne parle que musicalement. Elle ne sait pas, elle sent ». L'écriture féminine se synchronise avec les rythmes de la pensée et donc ses effets sur le lecteur ont tendance à être plus affectifs que didactiques.

Bien que les expérimentations sur le langage soient aujourd'hui assez familières aux lecteurs de romans postmodernes, le style de Cixous détone tout particulièrement dans le cadre de ce recueil, où il est mis en œuvre pour analyser les textes littéraires, les gestes des comédiens, la musique, la mise en scène, pour faire un commentaire politique ou pour se livrer à des questions philosophiques. Alors que la critique d'art ou littéraire, la politique ou la philosophie visent souvent à imposer un sens à un texte ou à un événement, l'écriture de Cixous rejette radicalement ce processus. Ces essais offrent des commentaires sur la politique, l'éthique et le spectacle qui ne sont pas des fins en soi ; au contraire, ce sont des points de départ qui invitent les lecteurs et les chercheurs à participer à ces provocations ouvertes.

Le choix de l'écriture féminine pour réagir aux questions politiques et éthiques contemporaines s'inscrit en réaction contre la rhétorique néolibérale qui domine les médias et le discours politique des pays développés depuis les années 1980. Le langage technocrate du néolibéralisme regorge de contradictions dissimulées, en particulier dans ses fréquentes références aux « marchés libres » et aux mouvements « libres » du travail, des produits, et du capital. Le langage de la « liberté » dissimule souvent les contraintes que le libéralisme économique et ses mesures d'austérité ont imposées à la grande majorité des travailleurs dans le monde, obligés de vivre dans la précarité et l'insécurité de l'emploi, avec de moins en moins de protections

sociales. Dans les essais qui suivent, Cixous recourt à l'écriture féminine pour examiner la relation entre le spectacle de théâtre et la politique contemporaine à la lumière de ces contradictions.

Cixous a noté par ailleurs que la poésie est la forme la plus sincère de l'écriture, car elle fait toujours allusion à ce qui est absent, et donc est toujours en mouvement (1997, 4). Cixous utilise une prose poétique tendue vers ce qui est absent, réduit au silence ou rendu invisible, de façon à évoquer ce qui dans la sphère politique est indicible, inouï, imperceptible ou tu, des sujets tels que le traitement des réfugiés par les gouvernements occidentaux, la condition féminine, la corruption des gouvernements, ou encore l'influence des grandes entreprises sur les décisions judiciaires et gouvernementales. A travers ses discussions sur l'esthétisation de la violence dans les œuvres d'art et sur le rôle de l'art dans l'activisme politique par exemple, elle met également en question la légitimité et le rôle du théâtre et de l'art en général en matière de questionnement éthique. L'écriture performative de Cixous utilise le langage et les concepts de la représentation théâtrale pour inviter les lecteurs et les spectateurs à réfléchir aux questions éthiques, politiques et artistiques, qui sont urgentes et toujours difficiles à résoudre, en dehors des modes rhétoriques familiers utilisés par les dirigeants politiques occidentaux et les médias.

A travers les essais

Toutes les traductions et les notes de bas de page dans ce recueil sont miennes. La traduction et mes choix éditoriaux tentent de préserver l'intégrité des phrases originales de Cixous afin de donner au lecteur anglophone un aperçu de la richesse et de la complexité de son écriture. Chaque fois qu'il a été possible de le faire, j'ai gardé intacts la longueur et l'ordre des mots dans les phrases de Cixous pour donner au lecteur une idée du courant de conscience ininterrompu, des flux rythmiques de son écriture et de la polysémie. En préservant la syntaxe de Cixous, j'espère aider le lecteur à se frayer un chemin dans le texte. Pour rendre les jeux de mots dans ces phrases, sans en interrompre la fluidité, je recours parfois au trait oblique pour signaler les diverses significations possibles d'un mot, ou ses homonymes. J'espère que cela aidera le lecteur a appréhender la phrase dans son ensemble, sans le déconcentrer en l'invitant à regarder ailleurs pour une explication plus complète.

Pour des explications plus détaillées et complexes, j'ai ajouté quelques notes de bas de page. Ces notes visent à guider le lecteur pour qu'il puisse pénétrer un aspect de la complexité de l'écriture de Cixous en soulignant certaines allusions, ses jeux de mots et son utilisation de différentes langues. Cependant ces notes ne sont pas exhaustives et se bornent à offrir une interprétation possible parmi d'autres. Elles visent à donner au lecteur un aperçu

de l'ampleur de la pensée de Cixous, de la richesse de l'intertextualité et de la musicalité de son écriture.

Compte tenu de la complexité de l'écriture féminine, l'écriture de Cixous résiste à la traduction. Dans un entretien, Cixous déclare que ses textes sont presque « intraduisibles » (2000, 339). Elle reconnaît que tout traducteur de son œuvre doit être « fidèle tout en étant infidèle »3 (in Blyth and Sellers 2004, 8). Pourtant, Cixous voit aussi dans l'erreur et l'échec de l'écriture à la fois de réfléchir au processus de l'écriture et de présenter le texte comme étant toujours en cours d'élaboration. Ce recueil offre de nombreux exemples d'infidélité fidèle, mais offre aussi au lecteur le texte original en français accompagné de sa traduction en anglais. J'invite les lecteurs qui ont quelque connaissance du français à consulter le texte original pour saisir au mieux le sens des phrases qui sont particulièrement ardues.

Le privé et le politique

Il a été souvent noté que la biographie de Cixous a fortement influencé ses convictions politiques et son écriture unique. Dans les essais qui suivent, par exemple, le rapport à sa vie personnelle et à l'histoire de sa famille a fortement nourri sa réflexion sur ce que veut dire être « autre ». Née en 1937 dans une famille juive, Cixous a grandi au Clos Salembier, un quartier non-français d'Alger avant l'indépendance. Au Clos Salembier, elle et sa famille étaient traitées comme des étrangers par les colons français comme par les indigènes algériens. En tant que juifs non-religieux, les membres de sa famille étaient exclus à la fois de la communauté juive et de la population musulmane locale (Calle-Gruber et Cixous 1997, 197). S'ajoutait à celui un profond sentiment d'antisémitisme à la suite de l'invasion nazie en France et de la collaboration du maréchal Philippe Pétain avec les fascistes entre 1940 et 1944.

Cixous raconte comment, à son arrivée en France dans les années 1950, elle a été traitée comme une étrangère, non seulement à cause de son accent et de son ascendance, mais, principalement, à cause de son appartenance sexuelle (Calle-Gruber et Cixous 1997, 204). Sa situation sociale de femme, bisexuelle, juive algérienne, avec des grands-parents originaires d'Espagne, de Hongrie, d'Allemagne et de France l'ont rendue « autre » à plusieurs niveaux. Les essais qui suivent abordent les problèmes de l'impérialisme, les effets de la colonisation et la place socio-culturelle de l'étranger. Ils examinent la survie des anciens empires à travers la langue française – autrefois l'une des grandes langues impériales et diplomatiques de la modernité. Dans l'essai « Notre spectacle », Cixous montre les difficultés que pose l'usage de la langue du colonisateur, même à des fins artistiques. Elle dénonce entre autres l'impossibilité pour l'art de réparer certains méfaits des puissances

3. Ma traduction

colonisatrices à travers la question: « Comment ne pas remplacer ta langue étrangère par notre langue française? ». Cixous montre comment la langue du colonisateur conserve la trace de l'autorité, du pouvoir et de la hiérarchie, ainsi que les traces d'usurpation des voix dues colonisés. Elle s'interroge ainsi sur le théâtre engagé socialement et sur sa tentative de prendre la parole à la place de l'autre, même si la communication commence avec un dialogue interculturel respectueux des différences.

S'ils reetracent la chute de l'impérialisme français, les essais s'intéressent également aux nouveaux empires et à l'insatisfaction qu'ils génèrent. Des essais tels que « Si vous permettez, je vais vous parler d'amour ... » et « Une étincelle inextinguible » décrivent les conséquences de la colonisation de l'Inde par les Anglais et du Cambodge par les Français, et tout particulièrement les atrocités et les bouleversements qui ont accompagné la difficile transition de ces nations vers l'indépendance. On y trouve aussi des commentaires sur ces hommes politiques, extraordinaires sources d'inspiration, qui ont lutté pour leur pays dans ces périodes de transition. « Si vous permettez, je vais vous parler d'amour ... » s'intéresse à Mohandas Karamchand Gandhi, apôtre de la non-violence, dont l'influence sur les mouvements des droits civiques s'est fait sentir partout dans le monde. « Une étincelle inextinguible » évoque le roi du Cambodge, Norodom Sihanouk, qui, malgré son infortune personnelle, a su faire preuve de compassion et pardonner à ses ennemis pour parvenir à reconstruire son pays après le retrait des Khmers rouges.

Les origines familiales de Cixous n'ont pas seulement influencé ses convictions politiques, mais elle ont eu aussi des répercussions sur le développement de son écriture féminine. Cixous parle de nombreuses langues comme l'allemand, le français, l'anglais et l'hébreu, le latin et le grec ancien. Il a été souvent noté que le multilinguisme de Cixous a contribué à son attitude irrévérencieuse envers la langue et la fixité du sens, du fait que les sens varient d'une langue à une autre (Blyth and Sellers 2004, 6). Non seulement ses textes évoluent entre différentes langues, mais la langue elle-même demande à être examinée, malmenée et reconstruite à l'aide de néologismes et de mots-valises qui expriment de façon plus efficace des significations multiples et souvent contraires.

Ce n'est pas seulement le style dense de Cixous qui rend ces essais difficiles à lire. En effet ces textes évoquent tous des spectacles que les lecteurs n'ont pas obligatoirement vus. Parfois, Cixous poursuit l'analyse d'une pièce sur plusieurs essais différents. Ses commentaires sur certaines formes d'esthétique théâtrale – dont plusieurs sont spécifiques au Théâtre du Soleil – sont toujours plus significatifs pour ceux qui ont vu les spectacles en direct ou sur DVD. Pour aider les lecteurs à s'y retrouver dans ces essais, j'ai divisé le recueil en dix chapitres et regroupé les essais qui correspondent à une performance théâtrale donnée. Chaque partie commence par un bref résumé de la pièce du Théâtre du Soleil concernée et un aperçu du contexte du

spectacle. De plus, les notes originales de Cixous figurent à la fin de chaque essai , préservant ainsi les traces de leur première publication ainsi que du contexte du spectacle.

Cixous et le théâtre

L'œuvre de Cixous est vaste, c'est bien connu. Elle comprend des romans, des pièces de théâtre, de la théorie littéraire, de la théorie féministe, de la philosophie, des scénarios, des livrets, des critiques, des biographies, des commentaires culturels et de la poésie. Bien que ces contributions s'attachent à de nombreux domaines différents, leur impact sur le théâtre et l'art du spectacle a été marquant. L'importance de Cixous dans le domaine du théâtre du XXe siècle s'étend bien au-delà de ses premières pièces écrites dans les années 1970, et même au-delà de son travail avec le Théâtre du Soleil. Ses écrits théoriques sur le théâtre et sur la place des femmes au théâtre, en particulier l'essai « Aller à la mer » (1977), ont influencé la pensée féministe du XXe siècle pour ce qui est de l'avenir du théâtre et du rôle des femmes dans le théâtre. « Aller à la mer » est une critique exaspérée du théâtre des années 1970, auquel Cixous reproche de reproduire les structures familiales patriarcales et de cantonner les femmes dans le rôle de victimes (1984, 546). C'est aussi un appel aux femmes à manifester pour revendiquer les qualités vivantes du théâtre et sa capacité à représenter les femmes prenant conscience de leur riche diversité et jouant des rôles bien éloignés de ceux auxquels elles sont réduites dans les sociétés patriarcales (1984, 547).

Dans les essais rassemblés ici, le premier projet féministe de Cixous s'enrichit de la notion d' «hospitalité ». Cixous utilise le concept d'hospitalité pour réfléchir à des problèmes socio-politiques contemporains et à la capacité unique au théâtre et au spectacle à accueillir « les autres ». Pour Cixous, le théâtre exige que les comédiens, auteurs, musiciens et spectateurs se dépouillent de leur ego pour s'ouvrir aux autres. L'autre pourrait être d'un sexe différent, mais aussi quelqu'un d'une autre race, d'une autre génération, ou même d'une autre espèce. Alors que les gouvernements échouent souvent à accueillir l'autre étranger, Cixous constate que le théâtre est un lieu d'accueil par excellence. C'est le lieu où l'on partage les histoires des autres, même si c'est d'une façon incomplète ou insuffisante. Selon les termes de Cixous, le théâtre est le lieu qui peut nous rappeler « que nous sommes des êtres singuliers pluriels cohabités cohabitants cohantés cohantants » (« Coups de baguettes »).

Dans ses essais des années 1980, Cixous fait un lien entre sa critique de l'impérialisme et l'absence d'hospitalité à l'égard de l'autre racialisé et des réfugiés au tournant du XXIe siècle. Dans les essais « Coups de baguettes » et « Le Théâtre surpris par les marionnettes », Cixous recourt à l'idée d'hospitalité en montrant que les comédiens « accueillent » les autres

en jouant des personnages différents. Ces essais analysent l'esthétique du spectacle *Tambours sur la digue* dans lequel les comédiens jouaient le rôle de marionnettes de Bunraku manipulées par des marionnettistes, eux-mêmes joués par d'autres comédiens. L'esthétique de ce spectacle nécessitait que les comédiens renoncent à la fois à leur corps et à leur voix. Ils devaient donner l'impression de se mouvoir en fonction des ordres du marionnettiste, tandis que leurs répliques étaient prononcées par d'autres comédiens situés hors scène. En se soumettant à ces autres, les comédiens effectuaient un acte d'auto-altérité, invitant les autres en eux, et donnant de ce corps multiple une image visuelle et auditive.

De plus Cixous note que les comédiens n'étaient pas les seuls à être agis par leurs personnages : l'auteur voyait également son corps agi au cours du processus d'écriture de *Tambours sur la digue.* Dans « Coups de baguettes » Cixous raconte qu'elle a accueilli en elle un poète chinois imaginaire, Hxshi-Xhou/Xi-Xou, dont le nom rime avec le sien. Cixous prétend que Xi-Xou a écrit la fable de *Tambours sur la digue* alors qu'elle se contentait de « ventriloquer » pour raconter l'histoire de Xi-Xou. On pourrait y voir un effet de l'intertextualité et de l'auto-altérité de l'auteur, ou bien le fait de parler pour l'autre dans la langue de la culture dominante qui rappelle nombre de problèmes soulevés par l'écriture coloniale.

Dans les essais qui suivent, Cixous affirme que la plus grande richesse du théâtre aujourd'hui est de révéler aux spectateurs, écrivains et artistes que nous sommes tous sourds et aveugles. Pour Cixous, le théâtre est un « grand globe oculaire, cet Œil ouvert, dans lequel passent ces humains aux yeux bandés » et qui assume les responsabilités d'un gardien (« Reconnaissance de dettes »). C'est l'artifice même du théâtre qui est le moyen idéal pour dévoiler les mensonges quotidiens – ceux des médias ou ceux qui résultent de nos interactions sociales de tous les jours. Pour Cixous, le théâtre continue d'être le lieu où les habitudes sont bousculées, un lieu qui joue sur le déplacement, la distance et l'inattendu. C'est aussi un lieu de solidarité et de partage, où les communautés d'artistes et le grand public peuvent se retrouver. Selon elle, le théâtre a toujours été un tribunal où le spectateur est appelé comme témoin. Le théâtre est le lieu où nous pouvons voir de façon fugace que les choses pourraient être autrement, si une décision différente était prise ou si l'on agissait autrement. Selon Cixous, le théâtre nous rappelle que ces moments d'urgence et ces possibilités de changement se produisent également dans la vie de tous les jours, et que nous devons être vigilants si nous voulons les reconnaître quand ils se présentent.

Trouver l'auto-altérité

Mon désir de rendre les essais de Cixous accessibles à un public anglophone est en partie motivé par mon histoire personnelle. J'ai eu la

chance de découvrir les pièces de théâtre et les écrits théoriques de Cixous à Melbourne en Australie, en tant qu'étudiante passionnée par le théâtre féministe. Pourtant, mon envie de traduire ces essais n'est pas seulement née de mon travail en tant que chercheuse dans le domaine du théâtre féministe et politique. J'étais au lycée puis à l'université en Australie pendant le mandat du premier ministre John Howard et de son ministre de l'immigration Philip Ruddock, appartenant à l'aile droite du Parti Libéral. J'ai été témoin du changement d'attitude envers les réfugiés pendant les onze années qu'Howard était au pouvoir. J'ai suivi dans les médias les histoires relatives au traitement de ces hommes, femmes et enfants dans les centres de détention offshore. J'ai visité quelques centres de détention situés dans des régions éloignées d'Australie et ai été témoin de la façon épouvantable dont ces demandeurs d'asile étaient traités.

Mes deux parents ont émigré en Australie. La famille de ma mère a quitté le Sri Lanka en 1957 et mon père est venu d'Angleterre à l'âge adulte au début des années 1980. Quand mes grands-parents maternels ont émigré au milieu des années 1950, la politique migratoire australienne privilégiait encore le 'White Australia'. A cause de cela, mes grands-parents d'origine burgher hollandaise ont dû prouver qu'eux et leurs enfants avaient suffisamment d'ascendance « blanche » pour être autorisés à s'installer en Australie. Cette politique migratoire raciste n'est devenue illégale que lorsque le gouvernement de Gough Whitlam a adopté la loi contre la discrimination raciale en 1975. Cette politique, cependant, a été relancée par les partis de droite comme de gauche durant les deux dernières décennies en matière de politique envers les demandeurs d'asile. Comme Cixous l'écrit dans « Qu'est-ce qu'un réfugié? Vous êtes un réfugié? » : « L'histoire se répète, à peine déguisée ».

Les essais qui correspondent à la pièce *Le Dernier Caravansérail (Odyssées)* font référence aux conséquences humaines de la politique migratoire contemporaine en France et en Australie notamment. Cixous sait par expérience personnelle que l'on ne peut pas compter sur les chefs d'état pour accueillir les réfugiés. Paradoxalement les pays démocratiques ne peuvent offrir qu'une « hospitalité conditionnelle » à ceux qui ne sont pas leurs citoyens. Dans l'essai « Qu'est-ce qu'un réfugié? Êtes-vous un réfugié? » Cixous remarque que le mot « réfugié », originaire du latin, est entré dans la langue après la révocation de l'édit de Nantes par Louis XIV qui poussa les calvinistes à fuir la France catholique. Elle essaie de comprendre comment cette révocation a modifié de façon définitive l'attitude envers les étrangers.

A l'heure où ces lignes s'écrivent, l'Europe tente de négocier la « crise des réfugiés ». Venus du Moyen-Orient et d'Afrique du Nord, les réfugiés fuient des conditions épouvantable crées par la guerre civile, la violence, l'instabilité et le fanatisme religieux. On prévoit que le flux des migrants dans l'Union européenne atteindra 1,5 millions de personnes cette année. De plus

les attaques terroristes meurtrières sur Paris, Beyrouth, Ankara, et Bamako en novembre 2015, revendiquées par différents groupes islamistes radicalisés, montrent que la violence se propage au-delà des frontières. Alors que l'Union européenne est en train de négocier avec le président turc, Recep Tayyip Erdogan (pourtant soupçonné d'atteintes aux droits de l'homme) en vue d'un accord historique qui ferait de la Turquie une zone tampon entre l'Europe et le Moyen-Orient, une politique de l'hospitalité serait particulièrement bienvenue.

Cixous a pu écrire que les langues offrent une « hospitalité infinie » (Cixous 2005, 207). De la même façon, les essais rassemblés ici accueillent la vision fugitive d'un avenir plus éthique et plus humain. En cette période de l'histoire où « l'autre » est vilipendé, diabolisé et redouté dans le monde occidental – qu'il s'agisse d'un musulman, d'une femme âgée ou d'un enfant réfugié – ces essais jouent sur les ambiguïtés et les contradictions de la représentation théâtrale et politique pour nous inviter nous lecteurs à trouver notre moi en l'autre et l'autre en nous, et rendre plus complexes nos obligations éthiques contemporaines. Certes ces essais dénoncent les difficultés inhérentes à toute action politique ou artistique face à l'injustice, mais ils sont autant de rappels du mot d'ordre éthique de Cixous : « Comment ne jouer aucun rôle? »

Lara Stevens
Décembre 2015
Melbourne, Australie

RÉFÉRENCES BIBLIOGRAPHIQUES

Blyth, Ian, and Susan Sellers. 2004. *Hélène Cixous: Live Theory.* New York; London: Bloomsbury.

Calle-Gruber, Mireille, and Hélène Cixous. 1997. *Hélène Cixous, Rootprints: Memory and Life Writing.* London; New York: Routledge.

Cixous, Hélène. 1975. 'Le rire de la Méduse.' *l'arc,* pp. 39-54.

Cixous, Hélène, and Barbara Kerslake. 1984. 'Aller À La Mer.' *Modern Drama* 27 (4): 546–48.

Cixous, Hélène. 2000. 'An Interview with Hélène Cixous.' *Paragraph* 23 (3): 338–43.

Cixous, Hélène. 2005. *Stigmata: Escaping Texts.* London; New York: Routledge.

Cixous, Hélène. 2009. *Hyperdream.* Cambridge, UK; Malden, MA: Polity.

Derrida, Jacques. 1967. *De La Grammatologie.* Paris: Editions de Minuit.

Derrida, Jacques. 1992. *Acts of Literature.* Psychology Press.

McEvoy, William. 2009, '»Leaving a space for the non-theorisable»: Self and Other in *Hélène* Cixous's Writing for Theatre', *The European Legacy,* 14 (1): 19–30.

Miller, Judith Graves. 2007. *Ariane Mnouchkine*. London: Routledge.
Neuschäfer, Anne. 2004. '1970-1975: Ecrire Une Comédie de Notre Temps - La Filiation Avec Jacques Copeau.' Mai. http://www.theatre-du-soleil.fr/thsol/a-propos-du-theatre-du-soleil/l-historique,163/1970-1975-ecrire-une-comedie-de.
Rancière, Jacques. 2011. *The Emancipated Spectator*. London: Verso.

Translations

Macbeth

The play: *Macbeth*
Author: William Shakespeare
Translation: Ariane Mnouchkine
Creators: The Théâtre du Soleil
First performed: 30 April 2014 at the Cartoucherie of Vincennes, Paris
Director: Ariane Mnouchkine
Music: Jean-Jacques Lemêtre
Dramaturg: Hélène Cixous

Synopsis: *Macbeth* or *The Tragedy of Macbeth* by William Shakespeare, believed to have been written between 1599 and 1606, dramatises the destructive psychological and political effects of those who are ambitious to attain power by violent means. The play tells the story of a revered Scottish general, Macbeth, who receives a prophecy that he will become King of Scotland. Hungry for power, Macbeth takes action to bring about the prophecy by murdering King Duncan. He then embarks upon an increasingly violent campaign and tyrannical rule to conceal his act of regicide. He is haunted by guilt and paranoia which feeds his growing madness and eventually leads to his death and his wife's suicide. For the fiftieth anniversary of the creation of the Théâtre du Soleil troupe (1964-2014), Ariane Mnouchkine returned to staging a Shakespeare play after having staged the Shakespeare plays *Richard II* in 1981, *Twelfth Night, Or What You Will* in 1982 and *Henry IV* in 1984 as a series. These productions preceded the arrival of Hélène Cixous into the troupe's collective creation in 1985 which marked a new dramaturgical direction for the company.

Résumé de la pièce: *Macbeth* est une tragédie de William Shakespeare, écrite entre 1599 et 1606 qui brosse le portrait d'un homme dévoré par l'ambition. La pièce raconte l'histoire d'un général écossais vénéré, Macbeth, qui reçoit une prophétie: il deviendra roi d'Écosse. Assoiffés de pouvoir, et motivé par sa femme, Macbeth prend toutes les mesures pour réaliser cette prophétie en assassinant tout d'abord le roi Duncan, puis tous ceux qui tenteront d'entraver son assension. Il s'embarque alors dans une fuite en avant de plus en plus violente. Hanté par la culpabilité et la paranoia, la folie meurtrière croissante des Macbeth les conduiront au suicide pour l'une et à la mort pour l'autre. À l'occasion du cinquantième anniversaire de la création de la troupe du Théâtre du Soleil (1964-2014), Ariane Mnouchkine retrouve Shakespeare après l'avoir monté sous la forme d'un cycle (*Richard II* en 1981, *La nuit des rois* en 1982 et *Henri IV* en 1984), avant que ne débute en 1985 une autre direction dramaturgique avec la naissance du compagnonnage avec Hélène Cixous.

The Irreparable[1]

But what happened to the great Macbeth, this victorious General with a brilliant career? A beautiful man, loved by his family, respected, admired, showered with deserved honours, saluted by the King. He had everything to be happy. A loving wife, distinguished like a noble Roman. A magnificent castle. And what beautiful countryside! Everything was smiling on him.

And thus from one day to the next, a gloom (a curtain of darkness)—falls—It was the Monday that followed the triumph. Even so, that cannot be (the fault of) these old prophetic witches? It is as if the future had been thrown on him and had devoured his brain with its poisoned teeth. As if a telegram from the devil had arrived. One word: Kill! A horrible idea comes to knock at the door of his thought. Thought? Not even. It is as if the plague had knocked at the door of his castle. A second of hesitation. A second? Not even. It is as if he had already opened the door before opening. As if someone had preceded his movement. His wife?

To the second there has been this terrible need to do what we don't have do, and, suddenly, what we cannot do, we do it. Done. And already everything is ruined and decomposed: reason, heart, feeling, food, sleep. One can no longer sleep, nor get up. Time no longer has a past nor a present. It is without rest and without return. The first second had been fatal for him, we can only go forward in blood, in blood, going down in blood.

[The great Derangement invaded the world. What lives is not living. What is dead is not dead. Dreams chased from their region wander on the outside in hallucinations. Everything is lost, friendship, confidence, wife, illusions, taste. Even fear leaves him.]

And the people, in this story?

The people? Ah! Yes! It's true. Usually, in the plays of Shakespeare, when there is a country, there is also a people. The people, the Macbeths had never thought of them! All their strength, busyness, concentrated on

1. The French title of this essay, '*L'irréparable*', references a poem of the same name by Charles Beaudelaire that appears within his well-known collection 'Fleurs du Mal', originally published in 1857. Beaudelaire's '*L'irréparable*' is a poem about the relentless suffering that comes with the emotion of remorse.

L'irréparable

Mais qu'est-ce qui est arrivé au grand Macbeth, ce général victorieux à la carrière brillante? Un bel homme, aimé des siens, respecté, admiré, comblé d'honneurs mérités, salué par le roi. Il avait tout pour être heureux. Une femme aimante, distinguée comme une noble romaine. Un château magnifique. Et quel beau paysage! Tout lui souriait.

Et voilà que du jour au lendemain, une ténèbre (un rideau de ténèbres)—tombe—C'était le lundi qui suivait le triomphe. Ça ne peut quand même pas être (la faute des) ces vieilles sorcières prophétiques? C'est comme si l'avenir s'était jeté sur lui et lui avait mordu le cerveau avec ses dents empoisonnées. Comme si un télégramme du diable était arrivé. Un mot: Tue! Une idée horrible vient frapper à la porte de sa pensée. Pensée? Même pas. C'est comme si la peste avait frappé à la porte de son château. Une seconde d'hésitation. Une seconde? Même pas. C'est comme s'il avait déjà ouvert la porte avant d'ouvrir. Comme si quelqu'un avait précédé son mouvement. Sa femme?

À la seconde il y a eu ce besoin foudroyant de faire ce qu'on ne doit pas faire, et, subitement, ce qu'on ne peut pas faire, on le fait. Fait. Et déjà tout est ruiné et décomposé: la raison, le cœur, le sentiment, la nourriture, le sommeil. On ne peut plus ni dormir, ni se réveiller. Le temps n'a plus de passé ni de présent. Il est sans repos et sans retour. La première seconde lui a été fatale, on ne peut plus qu'aller de l'avant dans le sang, dans le sang, descendant dans le sang.

[Le grand Dérangement a envahi le monde. Ce qui vit n'est pas vivant. Ce qui est mort n'est pas mort. Les rêves chassés de leur région errent à l'extérieur en hallucinations. Tout est perdu, l'amitié, la confiance, l'épouse, les illusions, le goût. Même la peur le quitte.]

Et le peuple, dans cette histoire?

Le peuple? Ah! Oui! C'est vrai. D'habitude, comme dans les pièces de Shakespeare, quand il y a un pays, il y a aussi un peuple. Le peuple, les Macbeth n'y avaient jamais pensé! Toutes leurs forces, affairées, tendues vers ce petit objet maléfique: la couronne. Tout l'espace du cœur est occupé par le terrible désiré. Jamais on n'avait vu une telle pureté dans le mal, une telle passion dans la tentation, nous semble-t-il.

this little evil object: the crown. All the space in the heart is occupied by the terrible desired. Never have we seen such purity in evil, such a passion in temptation, it seems to us.

Us? Us, the forgotten ones, the rejected ones, we are seized by fright and incomprehension. How do we get there, which is to say beyond all pleasure, all satisfaction, there where the end is continuous and language vomits itself up?

Evil is just behind the door. You hear it screaming. He (Macbeth) would have never had to think about opening the door. Too late knocks like lighting.

Careful! We would not (do not) ever have to leave the Macbeths to open the door, we think. Evil is ready. It only waits for this moment. Careful! Evil is continuous. You've been warned?

1 February 2014

Nous? Nous, les oubliés, les rejetés, nous sommes saisis d'effroi et d'incompréhension. Comment en arrive-t-on là, c'est-à-dire au-delà de tout plaisir, de toute satisfaction, là où la fin est sans arrêt et la langue se vomit elle-même?

Le mal est juste derrière la porte. Vous l'entendez hurler. Il (Macbeth) n'aurait jamais du penser à ouvrir la porte. Trop tard frappe comme la foudre.

Attention! Nous ne devrions (devons) jamais laisser les Macbeth ouvrir la porte, pensons-nous. Le mal est prêt. Il n'attend que cet instant. Attention! Le mal est sans arrêt. Vous êtes prévenus?

1er février 2014

The Castaways of the Fol Espoir (Sunrises)

The play: *The Castaways of the* Fol Espoir *(Sunrises)*
Creators: The Théâtre du Soleil
First performed: 3 February 2010 at the Cartoucherie of Vincennes, Paris
Director: Ariane Mnouchkine
Collective creation: partly written by Hélène Cixous, freely adapted from the unfinished and posthumously published Jules Verne novel *The Survivors of the 'Jonathan'* (1909), adapted by his son, Michel Verne
Music: Jean-Jacques Lemêtre
Costumes: Nathalie Thomas, Marie-Hélène Bouvet, and Annie Tran

Synopsis: The play is constructed as a mise-en-abyme between two different worlds. The first setting takes place in 1914 and recounts the story of a team of socialist filmmakers living in La Marne, a commune on the West coast of France. The filmmakers are shooting a silent film in the three days prior to the beginning of the First World War. The second narrative in the play takes place between 1889 and 1895 and follows the lives of the characters within the silent film. This narrative tells the story of a shipwreck on the coast of Cape Horn on Hornos Island, the southernmost headland of the Tierra del Fuego archipelago of Chile. The castaways of the wreck—who are migrants, socialists, criminals and gentry—are faced with the possibility of creating a new kind of society, an opportunity to realise their utopian dreams. The play explores the idealism and promise of the late 19th and early 20th century as the characters stand, unknowing, on the precipice of a century of extreme violence and inhumanity.

Résumé de la pièce: Pendant l'été 1914, l'imminence de la Première Guerre mondiale précipite le tournage d'un film dont l'histoire se passe entre 1889 et 1895. Ces deux périodes de la toute fin du XIXe siècle et du tout début du XXe siècle alternent, comme alternent aussi le « parlé » (la vie de cette troupe improvisée de cinéastes socialistes décidés à faire du cinéma d'éducation et de recréation populaire en 1914) et le « muet » (le spectateur assiste au tournage de certains épisodes de leur film). La structure du spectacle est donc une mise en abîme: les comédiens du Théâtre du Soleil incarnent des passionnés de cinéma qui tournent un film dont ils interprètent eux-mêmes les personnages. L'histoire de ce film est le naufrage d'un navire sur une île, à la pointe de la Magellanie. Les passagers du navire vont tenter de créer une société nouvelle, un modèle pour l'humanité future, à une époque charnière ou toutes les utopies du siècle naissant semblaient possibles.

Caught in the Headlights

'A margin of immeasurable importance' this is what Proust feels in the clarity of a wasp's small buzzing in the Summer sky of 1913, and it wasn't a gnat, nor a bird, but 'an airplane filled with men, and watching over us'.

This celestial gnat-airplane-horse, this miniscule resonating vessel that gives us all the height of the friendly and breathtaking Summer sky, this is our performance. It is comparable to miniscule Japanese paper flowers, little pieces of indistinguishable life which, barely have they dived into a bowl of theatre filled with water, than they stretch out, contort, make color, become houses, fellows, trees, navigators, statesmen, opera singers, convicts, characters finally! and all Europe and its surrounds, the oceans and the Americas.

This index of immeasurable importance, we will also have experienced it in opening a short novel by Jules Verne one day in the year 2008, which had survived 100 years after its author, and can be found a little lost on the shelf of a secondhand bookseller in a Parisian market. Hardly have we dipped our eyes into his infusion of words than we see a monumental swarming climbing towards the sky on the ruined paper.

So here we are in the Summer of the year 1895, it is perhaps immediately after 1904. What happiness these days bring! We are at the marvelous beginnings of the most enthusiastic of centuries, the twentieth, this electrical time, which arrives accelerating with all speed.

Think about it! We had never seen, since the Galilean revolution, such a concentration of discoveries. In the sciences, the revolution is total, absolute: here we have formal logic, here set theory. Here *Science and Hypothesis*—this revolutionary text by Poincaré, and so in 1905 Planck's law and the theory of quantum mechanics ensues. We are soon going to stop being heavier than the air, if this continues. The new century spreads its wings. Each young year shines with a new fire. We are at the *crossroads*. It is as if there was an alchemical reaction between the different revolutions that reach fruition at the same time. And from this, the illuminating flight of intimate continents, the momentum of psychoanalysis. This year, Freud finds the keys to the unconscious. It is this sensation of being caught in the headlights that inspires the fabulous explorations of Jules Verne, tales for children of all ages that

Une sensation de Phare

« Un coefficient d'incalculable grandeur » voilà ce que sent Proust dans la netteté du petit bourdonnement de guêpe dans le ciel de l'été 1913, et ce n'était ni un moucheron, ni un oiseau, mais « *un aéroplane monté par des hommes, et veillant sur nous* ».

Ce moucheron-aéroplane-cheval céleste, cette infime monture sonore qui nous donne toute la hauteur du ciel d'été amical et vertigineux c'est notre spectacle. Il est comparable à ces minuscules fleurs de papier japonais, petits morceaux de vie indistincts qui, à peine sont-ils plongés dans un bol de théâtre rempli d'eau, s'étirent, se contournent, se colorent, deviennent des maisons, des bonshommes, des arbres, des navigateurs, des hommes d'état, des cantatrices, des bagnards, des personnages enfin quoi! et toute l'Europe et ses environs, les océans et les Amériques.

Cet indice de grandeur incalculable on l'aura eu aussi en ouvrant un jour de l'an 2008 un petit roman de Jules Verne, qui avait survécu cent ans à son auteur et se retrouvait un peu perdu à l'étal d'un bouquiniste dans un marché de Paris. À peine avait-on trempé un regard dans son infusion de mots que sur la ruine de papier on voit monter vers le ciel un fourmillement monumental.

Nous voilà en été de l'an 1895, c'est peut-être tout de suite après en 1904. Quels bonheurs ces jours-ci! Nous sommes aux commencements merveilleux du plus enthousiasmant des siècles, le vingtième, ce temps électrique, qui arrive en accélérant de toutes ses vitesses.

Pensez! On n'a jamais vu, depuis la révolution galiléenne, une telle concentration de découvertes. En sciences, la révolution est totale, absolue: ici nous avons la logique formelle, ici la théorie des ensembles. Ici « La Science et l'Hypothèse » ce texte révolutionnaire de Poincaré, et voici en 1905 la loi de Planck et il s'ensuit la théorie de la mécanique quantique. Nous allons bientôt cesser d'être plus lourds que l'air, si ça continue. Le nouveau siècle déploie ses ailes. Chaque jeune année brille d'un feu nouveau. Nous sommes *au carrefour.* C'est comme s'il y avait une réaction alchimique entre les différentes révolutions qui arrivent à leur terme en même temps.Et par ici, l'essor éclaireur des continents intimes, l'élan de la psychanalyse. Cette

we are, little happy and intrepid visionaries from this Time which no longer takes 'no' for an answer.

In these few years, let's say between 1890 and 1914, everything changed. There is not one nook of physics, mathematics, chemistry, biology that is not blown apart. You remember, the breath of happiness! From the smallest to the largest things, everything is uncovered and transported as if on another continent. It is as if we were moving from Paris or Berlin to Patagonia in the beat of a wing. Hold on, do you see this young man lying in a meadow in Normandy, his head in the future? It is Marcel Proust. The weather is nice. He listens: he hears the buzzing of insects in the blue of the sky: and it is the revolution of all the senses/in all senses of the word. What? A shining insect? An airplane: superhuman emotion. We don't see it; and then we 'see' it: men, no, angels, celestial knights are above us, and time and space are metamorphosed! Two kilometres by train is but two thousand metres in the vertical infinity. Human perspectives undergo lighting-transformations.

And thus literature and airplanes tie the knot, in Kafka as in Proust, as in Shambala: we take flight! We make the imagination soar in other ways. Distances and extreme extremities are the door of our new dreams. Think! One day Ader flies three centimetres from the sun and ten years later we are at the stars. From now on we desire and conquer with electrical motors. Thanks to us—the automobile! The telephone! And: Radio! We will go further, to the edge, to the poles. Careful! Over there is the unknown. Shackleton approaches the South Pole with his *Endurance.*

We have never seen an age as fiery and as eager for challenges and new energy.

Nietzsche has just told us: 'man is a promising animal'. Oh yes, that is promising! Man is an inventive animal. And receptive: it is as if there were, in those years, a propagation phenomenon by a proximity of spirits, a contagion of life forces. Electricity, this defining event, will have lit more than a lamp: from now on, the history of humanity also takes place during the night. The fact that we can live, work, and create during the night is a technical miracle. And as we are still at the *absolute-beginning*, habit, the monster that snuffs out everything, has not yet tarnished the sparkle of all that is wonderful.

It is in these intoxicating years that our characters *embark*. We rush forth. It is natural in these auspicious times that we had the idea and the desire to change the world, and also to paint it, in its new movements, its adventures, its child's play.

And naturally the vast political sphere is also seized by convulsions. It cracks at the seams. Classes, borders, regimes, thrones, powers, social models, everything is agitated, shaken up by the Spirit of liberty, because everything is bound up together: the automobile and the workers' movements,

année Freud trouve les clés de l'inconscient. C'est cette sensation de *Phare* qui inspire les fabuleuses explorations de Jules Verne, récits pour les enfants de tous les âges que nous sommes, petits voyants et intrépides heureux de ce Temps qui ne connaît plus le non.

En ces quelques années, disons de 1890 à 1914, tout a changé. Il n'y a pas un recoin de physique, de mathématique, chimie, biologie, qui ne soit bouleversé. Vous vous souvenez, le souffle du bonheur! Des plus petites aux plus grandes choses tout est soulevé et transporté comme sur un autre continent. C'est comme si on passait de Paris ou Berlin d'un coup d'aile en Patagonie! Tenez, vous voyez ce jeune homme allongé dans un pré de Normandie, la tête au futur? C'est Marcel Proust. Il fait beau. Il écoute: il entend un bourdonnement d'insecte dans le bleu du ciel: et c'est la révolution de tous les sens. Quoi? Cet insecte qui brille? Un aéroplane: l'émotion surhumaine. On ne le voit pas; et puis on le « voit »: les hommes, non, des anges, des chevaliers célestes sont là-haut, et le temps et l'espace sont métamorphosés! Deux kilomètres en train ce n'est pas deux mille mètres dans l'infini vertical. Les points de vue humains subissent des transformations-éclair.

Et voilà comment la littérature et les aéroplanes font la noce, chez Kafka comme chez Proust, comme au Shambala: on décolle! On fait voler l'imagination autrement. Distances et extrêmes extrémités sont à la portée de nos nouveaux rêves. Pensez! Un jour Ader vole à trois centimètres du sol et dix ans plus tard on est aux étoiles. Dorénavant nous désirons et conquérons avec moteur électrique. À nous l'automobile! Le téléphone! Et: la Radio! Nous irons plus loin, jusqu'au bout, jusqu'aux pôles. Attention! par là-bas c'est l'inconnu. Shackleton approche du Pôle Sud avec son *Endurance.*

On n'a jamais vu une époque aussi fougueuse et aussi avide d'extension et de nouvelles forces.

Nietzsche vient de nous dire: « l'homme est un animal prometteur ». Oh oui, ça promet! L'homme est un animal inventeur. Et récepteur: c'est comme s'il y avait, en ces années, un phénomène de propagation par contiguïté des esprits, une contagion des forces de vie. L'électricité, cet événement absolu, aura allumé plus qu'une lampe: désormais l'histoire de l'humanité a lieu aussi la nuit. Le fait qu'on puisse vivre, travailler, créer la nuit, est un miracle technique. Et comme nous sommes encore aux *tout-commencements*, l'Habitude, le monstre qui éteint tout, n'a pas encore terni l'éclat du merveilleux.

C'est dans ces ans enivrants que nos personnages *entreprennent.* On s'élance. Il est naturel, en ces temps propices, que l'on ait l'idée et l'envie de changer le monde, et de le peindre aussi, dans ses mouvements nouveaux, ses aventures, ses enfances de l'art.

Et naturellement la vaste sphère politique est elle aussi saisie de convulsions. Ça craque aux coutures. Classes, frontières, régimes, trônes,

psychoanalysis, linguistics and minority rights. Subtly, politically, morally, we advance in the sciences and in alliances: in the same season when the first issue of the journal that dares to call itself *Humanity*, appears in France, Einstein's article entitled 'On the Electrodynamics of Moving Bodies' appears in Germany. *Relativity, Humanity*, move forwards together. What do Jaurès and Einstein have in common? At least one trait: their reasoned and careful love of peace.

If it is *Peace* of which we speak and think about so much, it is because all this technical and political 'progress' doesn't move forward without a paradoxical progress: war also matures, fed by jealousies, rivalries and inordinate appetites. As the world grows it also grows in voraciousness. This fabulous epoch is also the time of bitter imperialist greed, of nationalist conflagrations. Europe wants to eat the other continents. Little England has a stomach fat enough for two continents, France spreads over Africa and up to Asia, Germany doesn't calm its temper. The dragons whip the air with their murderous tails.

Don't think about it. Never had art been so luxurious. Opera intoxicates us: are we too sick to go, we can subscribe to 'theatre phone'[1] and listen to Wagner, Debussy or Strauss from our bed. That's what Proust does. The faraway is in the room, in the attic. And here we have it, cinematography! Naturally the first thing it does, in this age when the *Voyage* has become the most widespread thing in the world, is to go to the moon.

And if we went there? If we looked for the moon on the earth? What would it look like? It would be white, shining and virginal. It would be an island. Imagine it. We could trace the model of the future of humanity from there. We would draw the ideal democracy three thousand years after Aeschylus.

Jaurès said in his first editorial from 18 April 1904 that: 'Humanity does not yet exist, or at least it hardly exists…'. He wanted to speak about the humanity of humankind, naturally, the humanist humanity, the humanity-equality, justice, sharing. *Humanity*! 'Humanity doesn't exist yet' *but it will come*. It is coming. Oh! Yes, it is *the century of humanity* that is coming, we say to ourselves. And it announces itself as modern, dynamic. The air is mythological. Human beings are overgrown, enlarged, stretched out, carried beyond their perimeters. They aspire.

And Jaurès said: or it '*hardly*' exists. And so, if this 'hardly' was, it was us. We would make the effort to make it just come to life, a little, modestly, ideally, scene by scene.

We begin to accomplish the prophesies of Rimbaud. We take on humanity. We find a new language with which to paint the unknown quantity in images. And women too! They *will be in front*.

1. A telephonic distribution system that allowed people to listen to live opera and theatre over the phone.

pouvoirs, modèles sociaux, tout est agité, secoué par l'Esprit de liberté, car tout est lié: l'automobile et les mouvements ouvriers, la psychanalyse, la linguistique et les droits des minorités. Subtilement, politiquement, moralement, on avance en sciences et en solidarités: dans la même saison où paraît en France le premier numéro du journal qui ose s'appeler *l'Humanité*, paraît en Allemagne l'article d'Einstein intitulé « De l'électrodynamique et des corps en mouvement ». *Relativité*, *Humanité* s'avancent ensemble. Qu'ont-ils en commun Jaurès et Einstein? Au moins un trait: l'amour prudent et raisonné de la paix.

Si *La Paix*, on en parle, on y pense tellement, c'est que tous ces « progrès » techniques et politiques, ne vont pas sans un progrès paradoxal: la guerre aussi mûrit, nourrie de jalousies, de rivalités, d'appétits démesurés. Le monde en s'agrandissant fait croître les voracités. Cette époque fabuleuse c'est aussi le temps amer des avidités impérialistes, des inflammations nationalistes. L'Europe veut manger les autres continents. La petite Angleterre a un estomac gros comme deux continents, la France s'étale sur l'Afrique et jusqu'en Asie, l'Allemagne ne décolère pas. Les dragons fouettent l'air de leurs queues meurtrières.

N'y pensons pas. Jamais l'art n'a été aussi fastueux. L'opéra nous enivre: sommes-nous trop malades pour y aller, nous pouvons nous abonner au théâtrophone et écouter Wagner, Debussy ou Strauss de notre lit. Ce que fait Proust. Le lointain est dans la chambre, dans le grenier. Et voilà le cinématographe! Naturellement la première chose qu'il fait, à cette époque où *le Voyage* est devenu la chose du monde la mieux partagée, c'est d'aller dans la Lune.

Et si nous y allions? Si nous cherchions la lune sur la terre? De quoi aurait-elle l'air? Elle serait blanche, brillante et vierge. Ce serait une île. Imaginons. On pourrait y tracer le modèle de l'humanité future. On dessinerait la démocratie idéale trois mille ans après Eschyle.

Jaurès a bien dit dans son premier éditorial du 18 avril 1904 que « l'Humanité n'existe pas encore, ou bien elle existe à peine... » Il voulait parler de l'Humanité humaine, naturellement, l'humanité humaniste, l'humanité-égalité, justice, partage. *L'Humanité*! « L'Humanité n'existe pas encore » *mais elle viendra*. Elle vient. Oh! Oui c'est *le siècle de l'Humanité* qui vient, se dit-on. Et elle s'annonce moderne, dynamique. L'air est mythologique. Les êtres humains sont prolongés, agrandis, étendus, portés au-delà de leurs périmètres. Ils aspirent.

Et Jaurès a dit: ou elle existe « *à peine* ». Eh bien, si cet « à peine », c'était nous. On prendrait la peine de la faire naître à peine, un peu, modestement, idéalement, scène par scène.

Nous commençons à accomplir les prophéties de Rimbaud. Nous nous chargeons d'humanité. Nous trouvons une nouvelle langue pour peindre en images la quantité d'inconnu. Et les femmes, aussi! Elles *seront en avant*.

How far will we go? Further than India, further than Chile and Argentina! Today, it is 29 June 1914.

What could stop us?

16 October 2009

Jusqu'où irons-nous?! Plus loin que l'Inde, plus loin que le Chili et l'Argentine! Aujourd'hui, nous sommes le 29 Juin 1914.

Qu'est-ce qui pourrait nous arrêter?

16 octobre 2009

Les Éphémères

The play: *The Mayflies*
Creators: The Théâtre du Soleil
First performed: 27 December 2006 at the Cartoucherie of Vincennes, Paris
Director: Ariane Mnouchkine
Music: Jean-Jacques Lemêtre
Dramaturg: Hélène Cixous
Scenography: Everest Canto de Montserrat
Costumes: Nathalie Thomas and Marie-Hélène Bouvet

Synopsis: *The Mayflies* is an intimate epic, divided into two parts, that explores the lives of ordinary middle-class people in France at the beginning of the twenty-first century. For the first time, Ariane Mnouchkine stages her memories and those of the actors in the troupe. Performed on moving trolleys that are pushed by other actors with choreographic elegance, the play unfolds through an episodic structure that mimics the flux of life, driven by the rhythms of the music played by Jean-Jacques Lemêtre. The play reveals ordinary men and women experiencing joy, sadness, suffering and death. The telephone plays an important role in the show as the object that transmits good and bad news to the characters. *The Mayflies* is thus a sort of collective evocation of the intimate weaving of our present moment.

Résumé de la pièce: *Les* Éphémères est une épopée intime, divisée en deux parties, qui explore la vie de petites gens en France à l'aube du XXIème siècle. Pour la première fois, Ariane Mnouchkine met en scène des souvenirs qui l'ont marquée, entremelés de ceux des comédiens de la troupe. Installés sur des structures mobiles, poussées par des partenaires, avec une élégance chorégraphique, la pièce se déroule en épisodes continus, tel le flux de la vie, rythmés par la musique incessante de Jean-Jacques Lemêtre. Des hommes et des femmes ordinaires sont traversés par la joie, la douleur, la souffrance et la mort. Le téléphone joue un rôle important dans le spectacle comme objet qui transmet les bonnes et les mauvaises nouvelles aux personnages. *Les* Éphémères est ainsi une sorte de rituel d'évocation collective de ce qui a intimement tramé le present de chacun.

The Mayflies

Mayfly.
Like little dragonflies, these archiptères,1 that live a day, once, an hour, a life more incandescent than brief...

- *Where does our passing-furtive show take place?*
- *In France. Not far, in the depths of just opposite.*
- *When?*
- *Just now and another time again today.*
  From yesterday's point of view and today, when out of the shadow flickering the past reignites the present. Once more.
- *Who?*
- *The actors, researchers, divers into the absolute, who discover in the recesses of the heart our interior images, marvellous watchmen, watchwomen, watchmen of trembling watchwomen. The musician who returns our lost music to us. Us, in short, and suddenly pulled from daily sloth, by the noise of a reminiscence. Us taken back from life. Only just.*
- *A text?*
- *That happens before the text, faster, behind thought, on the tip of the tongue, at the point of the flame. How 'to speak' the state of illumination? This free-flowing light, intimate.*
- *A word?*
- *Apocalypse, clearly. Behold, the hidden is unhidden.*[2]
- *One minute! We have just enough time to see, but not to know. Vision dazzles*

1. Ancient common name for several orders of insects.

2. Cixous creates a neologism with the word '*décaché*' translated as the negation of '*caché*' meaning 'hidden', thus '*décaché*' as 'unhidden'.

Les Ephémères

Ephémère.
Comme ces petites libellules, ces archiptères, qui vivent un jour, une fois, une heure, vie d'autant plus incandescente que brève…

- *Où se passe notre spectacle passant-furtif?*

- *En France. Pas loin, dans les profondeurs du juste à côté.*

- *Quand?*

- *À l'instant et encore une fois aujourd'hui même.*
  À l'angle d'hier et aujourd'hui, quand sortant de l'ombre en vacillant le passé se rallume au présent. Encore une fois.

- *Qui?*

- *Les comédiens, chercheurs, plongeurs d'absolu, qui découvrent dans les recoins du coeur nos images intérieures, merveilleux veilleurs, veilleuses, veilleurs des veilleuses tremblantes. Le musicien qui nous rend nos musiques perdues. Nous, en somme, et subitement tirés de la paresse quotidienne, par le bruit d'une réminiscence. Nous, repris de vie. De justesse.*

- *Un texte?*
  Cela se passe avant le texte, plus vite, derrière la pensée, au bout de la langue, à la pointe de la flamme. Comment 'parler' l'état d'illumination? Cette lumière filante, intime.

- *Un mot?*

- *Apocalypse, évidemment. Voilà que le caché est décaché.*
  Une minute! On a juste le temps de voir, mais pas de savoir. La vision nous éblouit et nous coupe le souffle. La révélation est éphémère. On ne peut qu'essayer de la peindre, au-delà de la parole, par non-dits, à tâtons, hésitations, caresses, délicatement. Par 'Ephémères', comme une prière rejetée, la joie d'une peine retrouvée. Comme l'expérience inattendue de l'immortalité des sentiments, immortalité brève, intermittente mais oui, immortelle, oui.

us and cuts off the breath. The revelation is ephemeral.[3] *One can only try to paint it, beyond speech, by the not-saids, by fumblings, by hesitations, caresses, delicately. By 'Mayflies', like a rejected prayer, the joy of a rediscovered pain. Like the unexpected experience of the immortality of feelings, brief immortality, intermittent but yes, immortal, yes.*

Les Ephémères
A show by the Théâtre du Soleil, at the suggestion of Ariane Mnouchkine, music by Jean-Jacques Lemêtre.

3. The word for 'mayflies' in the French is '*les ephémères*' and Cixous plays on its double meaning with 'ephemeral'.

Les Ephémères

Un spectacle du Théâtre du Soleil, sur une proposition d'Ariane Mnouchkine, musique de Jean-Jacques Lemêtre.

The Last Caravanserai (Odysseys)

The play: *The Last Caravanserai (Odysseys)*
Creators: The Théâtre du Soleil
First performed: 2 April (The Cruel River) and 22 November 2003 (Origins and Destinies) at the Cartoucherie of Vincennes, Paris
Director: Ariane Mnouchkine
Dramaturg: Hélène Cixous
Music: Jean-Jacques Lemêtre
Set: Guy-Claude François
Paintings and dyeing: Didier Martin and Ysabel de Maisonneuve
Costumes: Nathalie Thomas and Marie-Hélène Bouvet

Synopsis: *The Last Caravanserai (Odysseys)* is a theatrical response to Western governments' treatment of asylum seekers fleeing persecution and conflict. The six-hour play in two parts was performed as episodic scenes that depict refugee experiences in French and Australian camps and detention centres, flashbacks to daily life in their home countries and the events that caused the refugees to flee or be sent into exile. The refugee narratives depicted in the play were developed out of recorded interviews with refugees told from the camps or detention centres of Sangatte (near Calais, France), Mataram (on the island of Lombok, Indonesia), Villawood (NSW, Australia) and Auckland (New Zealand). Some of the recorded refugee testimonials feature in the performance as voice-overs.

Résumé de la pièce: *Le Dernier Caravansérail (Odyssées)* est une réponse théâtrale au traitement des gouvernements occidentaux envers les réfugiés qui fuient la persécution et la guerre. À partir des témoignages de réfugiés venus de tous les horizons, Ariane Mnouchkine et le Théâtre du Soleil ont tissé une vaste épopée sur les exilés de notre monde moderne. Cette pièce de six heures, divisée en deux parties, est organisée en épisodes qui se déroulent sur divers points de la planète à travers une multitude de décors, en faisant entendre de nombreuses langues. Du Kurdistan à Sangatte, de l'Iran à l'Angleterre, de l'Indonésie à l'Australie, chaque fragment saisit quelques instants de destins singuliers et donne ainsi la parole aux réfugiés, aux exilés, aux sans-papiers que nous avons d'ordinaire bien du mal à entendre. Les histoires des réfugiés sont extraites d'entretiens realisés avec les réfugiés issus des camps ou centres de détention à Sangatte (près de Calais, France), Mataram (île de Lombok, Indonesie), Villawood (NSW, Australie) et Auckland (Nouvelle-Zélande).

At the Beginning of Our Memories

At the beginning of our memories there was the War. The Iliad was a story. After the War: the Odyssey.

Those who didn't come home to their countries, neither living nor dead, roaming for a long time across the entire earth.

Today, the new Wars throw hundreds of thousands, millions, of new fugitives onto our planet, fragments of dislocated worlds, the trembling scraps of ravaged countries for which the names no longer signify a sheltered home but, instead, debris or prisons: Afghanistan, Iran, Iraq, Kurdistan ... the list of poisoned countries grows each year.

But how to tell the story of these innumerable odysseys?

How many new little theatres would we need to invent in order to give each terror-stricken fate its ephemeral shelter?

But how can our theatre transport these theatrical shells and these wisps of human beings on its ocean of wood and stars? It is a whole people of disparate and threatened foreigners that form these atoms fleeing from the political gusts, in our centuries sewn together by barbed-wire threads.

'What will become of us?' say those who have left their name, their family, their roots, very far behind them, that we call 'refugees', 'clandestines', '*sans papiers*', 'migrants'. And who, between themselves, nobly call one another 'voyagers'. They are brutally travelled, 'the contents' of cargo carriers and trucks, inching their way across borders, and they don't know where or when this dangerous voyage will end that pushes them from coastal port to door after door to confront the meagerness of contemporary hospitality.

They travel without hope and without end but buoyed by belief. In place of religion, a naïve faith in the existence of a country where the democratic deities that we spoke to them about live: liberty, respect.

So where is this country? Where will they arrive? When will they arrive? Will they ever/never arrive?

And us, sitting in our relatively moderate country, who are we? Their fellow creatures? Their witnesses? Their enemies? Their friends? Former travellers who have forgotten?

Or the people that the voyage waits for at the turning point?

Program Extract

Au commencement de nos mémoires…

Au commencement de nos mémoires il y eut la Guerre. L'Iliade en fit un récit. Après la Guerre: l'Odyssée.

Ceux qui ne sont pas rentrés au pays, ni vivants ni morts, errent longtemps par toute la terre.

Aujourd'hui, de nouvelles Guerres jettent sur notre planète des centaines de milliers, des millions de nouveaux fugitifs, fragments de mondes disloqués, bribes tremblantes des pays ravagés dont les noms ne signifient plus abri natal mais décombres ou prisons: Afghanistan, Iran, Irak, Kurdistan…, la liste des pays empoisonnés augmente chaque année.

Mais comment raconter ces odyssées innombrables?

Combien de nouveaux petits théâtres faudrait-il inventer pour donner à chaque destin affolé son éphémère hébergement?

Mais comment notre théâtre peut-il transporter ces coquilles de théâtres et ces brins d'êtres humains sur son océan de bois et de toiles? C'est tout un peuple occasionnel d'étrangers disparates et menacés que forment ces atomes fuyant sous les rafales politiques, dans nos siècles cousus de fils barbelés.

'Qu'allons-nous devenir?' disent ceux qui ont laissé leur nom, leur famille, leurs racines très loin derrière eux, que l'on appelle 'réfugiés', 'clandestins', 'sans papiers', 'migrants'. Et qui s'appellent entre eux, noblement les 'voyageurs'. Ils sont brutalement voyagés 'contenus' dans des cales et des camions, faufilés aux frontières, et ils ne savent pas où et quand finira ce voyage dangereux qui les pousse de port en côte et de porte en porte à mesurer la maigreur de l'hospitalité contemporaine.

Ils voyagent, sans espoir et sans fin, mais animés par la croyance. Au lieu de religion une foi naïve en l'existence d'un pays où vivent les déités démocratiques dont on leur a parlé: la liberté, le respect.

Où donc est ce pays? Où arriveront-ils? Quand arriveront-ils? Arriveront-ils jamais?

Et nous, assis dans nos pays relativement modérés, qui sommes-nous? leurs semblables? leurs témoins? leurs ennemis? leurs amis? D'anciens voyageurs qui ont oublié?

Ou des gens que le voyage attend au tournant?

Extrait du programme du spectacle

Our Show

How to not…

How do we not replace the speech from your mouth with my well intentioned speech?

How do we not replace your foreign language with our French language?

How do we keep your foreign language without being remiss in our politeness and hospitality towards the spectator public, our guest in the theatre?

How, without understanding in words, can we still understand in our heart?

How do we not exploit the anguish of others in making theatre?

How do we not sin through the illusion of comprehension and fear of incomprehension?

How can we put ourselves as near as possible to the place of the other without taking her over?

How can we not translate? Which is to say: how not to translate? We must translate/translate well.

How do we not let ourselves be seduced by the throng of good feelings?

How can we not embellish? Neither on one side nor the other.

How can we slide between good and bad conscience, these Siamese twins?

How can we say everything without a word?

How can we become human, by which we mean, never enough nor too much?

How can we never give up to the absolute what we will never attain?

How do we act out a character without taking mastery over it?

How can we leave aside being a refuge for the foreigner?

How can we never play any role?

And if we don't arrive/are not successful? This is the refugee's question on their journey.

Program extract

Notre spectacle

Comment ne pas...

Comment ne pas remplacer la parole de ta bouche par ma parole même de bonne volonté?

Comment ne pas remplacer ta langue étrangère par notre langue française?

Comment garder ta langue étrangère sans manquer de politesse et d'hospitalité à l'égard du public, notre hôte dans le théâtre?

Comment, sans se comprendre en mots, se comprendre quand même en cœur?

Comment ne pas s'approprier l'angoisse des autres en faisant du théâtre?

Comment ne pas pécher par illusion de compréhension et par crainte d'incompréhension?

Comment se mettre aussi près que possible de la place de l'autre sans la prendre?

Comment ne pas traduire? C'est-à-dire: comment ne pas traduire? Il faut bien traduire.

Comment ne pas se laisser séduire par la meute des bons sentiments?

Comment ne pas en rajouter? Ni d'un côté ni de l'autre.

Comment se glisser entre la bonne conscience et la mauvaise conscience, les siamoises?

Comment tout dire sans un mot?

Comment devenir humain c'est-à-dire jamais assez ni trop?

Comment ne jamais renoncer à l'absolu que l'on n'atteindra jamais?

Comment être l'acteur d'un personnage et non son maître?

Comment se laisser être un refuge pour l'étranger?

Comment ne jouer aucun rôle?

Et si on n'y arrive pas? C'est la question du réfugié en son voyage.

Extrait du programme du spectacle

What is a Refugee?
Are You a Refugee?

Refugee

1685: the word (it's a Latin word) enters into the French language (at the same time as it does into English) under the violent blow caused by the Revocation of the Edict of Nantes.[1] Louis XIV, the great king weakened and bigoted, turned the Protestants (what the English call the 'Huguenots') into fugitives, stripped of their rights and their freedoms. Thus, it is France and her monarch that introduces the wretched word into Europe: the word but not the fact. Between three and five hundred thousand Protestants are on the road. They make the journey that becomes the model of all flights in our world up until today: secret crossings of borders, underground resistance, threats of the galleys and of death.

All at once, these refugees—Voltaire says that their number and dissemination in the universe is even more significant than the Jews—don't call upon the laws of hospitality in vain: England, Switzerland, Holland and Brandenburg freely welcome this human manna that assures them an ethical and economic profit. And, further away, America and even Africa accept colonies of Calvinists.

Louis XIV strikes a blow of autoimmunity to the kingdom: under the pretext of defending the Catholic religion, he rips from himself bodies and goods, commerce, industry, finance, arts, sciences and the rest.

A primitive stage for France, emblematic of many other expulsions—executions right up until these days. The most tragic of last century being that of the Jews under Petain. History repeats itself, barely disguised.

Elsewhere, like here, it's the same model: each time, a State in a trance of hatred takes something into its own body that it no longer recognises as its own and tears it to pieces with its own teeth.

1. The Edict of Nantes of 1598, created by Henry IV of France, was a decree that allowed Calvinist Protestants to practice their religion without persecution in Catholic France.

Qu'est-ce qu'un réfugié? Êtes-vous un réfugié?

Réfugié

1685: le mot (c'est un mot latin) entre dans la langue française (en même temps que dans l'anglaise) sous le coup violent de la Révocation de l'Edit de Nantes. Louis XIV, le grand roi ramolli et embigoté, transforme les protestants (les huguenots, disent les Anglais) en fugitifs dépouillés de leurs droits et de leurs libertés. Ainsi, c'est la France et son monarque qui inaugurent l'infortuné mot en Europe; le mot mais pas le fait. Entre trois cent et cinq cent mille protestants sont sur la route. Ils font le périple qui devient le modèle de toutes les fuites de notre monde jusqu'à aujourd'hui: passage furtif de frontières, clandestinité, menaces de galère et de mort.

Toutefois, ces réfugiés, dont Voltaire dit que leur nombre et leur dissémination dans l'univers sont plus importants encore que ceux des juifs, n'invoquent pas en vain les lois de l'hospitalité: l'Angleterre, la Suisse, la Hollande, le Brandebourg accueillent volontiers cette manne humaine qui leur assure un profit éthique et économique. Et, plus loin, l'Amérique et même l'Afrique reçoivent des colonies calvinistes.

Louis XIV porte au Royaume un coup auto-immunitaire: sous prétexte de défendre la religion, il s'arrache à lui-même corps et biens, commerce, industrie, finance, arts, sciences et le reste.

Scène primitive pour la France, emblématique de bien d'autres expulsions—exécutions jusqu'à nos jours. La plus tragique du siècle dernier étant celle des juifs sous Pétain. L'histoire se répète, à peine déguisée.

Ailleurs, comme ici, c'est le même modèle: chaque fois, un Etat en transe haineuse s'en prend à son propre corps qu'il ne reconnaît plus comme sien et le déchiquète de ses propres dents.

Mais tout avait commencé aux temps prophétiques comme le raconte la Bible: l'idée de Ville et l'idée de Ville-de-refuge sont jumelles depuis que Iahvé a ordonné à Moïse (Nombres XV) la fondation de six villes—qui serviront de villes de refuge aux fils d'Israël, à l'hôte et au résident au milieu

But everything had begun in Prophetic times, as the Bible tells us: the idea of the 'City' and the idea of the 'City of refuge' are contemporaneous since Yahweh[2] commanded Moses (Number XV) to lay the foundations of six cities—that will serve as cities of refuge for the children of Israel, to the guest and the resident among them, so that refuge can be found there for whoever struck a person by accident—as soon as he passed over Jordan, towards the land of Canaan.

Thus was Rome also made, founded as a City and Refuge by Romulus.

Each society, each State, each nation, establishes itself in inter or intra-communitarian tension, deflecting in advance the spectre of persecution, and in this gesture, inscribing in its foundation the program of expulsion.

The flight of a people seems to take diverse forms: since the flight from Egypt, prepared in haste and driven through the passage of the Red Sea, time spent in the wilderness, to the frantic flight of Iraqi Kurds bombarded by their half-brother enemies and leaving cities and villages, empty handed, feet badly shod while running and dying from climbing the mountain that separates them from the Promised Land (in the case of Iran), the examples mount up: the flight of Spanish Republicans or the flight of Kosovars.

But it's always the same beginning, the same mourning, and for the fantasy driver, the same ghost of a Promised Land, constituted by haste instead of a suitcase and a roof, it's always the same mirage because there must be one. We flee, it is Easter, we do not know towards what we go, but we paint this idealised country in gold and we repeat its proper name and we wait for it to grant the age-old right of asylum.

– *Goodbye dear father, the Taliban are going to kill me, I leave for London*, writes the young Afghani. And the anxious father: *London? To do what?—We said you must look for refuge in England.*

Yes, the imaginary solution holds in a proper name to which we cling, putting faith and destiny into the laws of a place that today take the place of protective gods or kings who are respectful towards the foreigner, those known by all Greeks and Romans. Instead of Apollo, those who pray today invoke the Rights of Man and Democracy of which they have heard spoken. Rumour is the same character that it was at the beginning, before radio and the telephone.

The model of seeking refuge has not changed. In the end, the refugee catches a glimpse of the Promised Land. He sees it with his eyes, either he stands on Mount Nebo[3] like Moses in order to see the country where he will not put his feet, or, alternately, having fled Nazism, then Vichy, he arrives at the foot of the Pyrenees that promise him Spain: but, exhausted, Walter Benjamin surrenders to death. Standing on the plateau at Calais, the

2. A Hebrew term for God.

3. A mountain range in Jordan where Moses is said to have stood.

d'eux, pour que s'y réfugie quiconque a frappé une personne par mégarde—dès qu'il aura passé le Jourdain, vers le pays de Canaan.

Ainsi en fut-il aussi de Rome fondée comme Ville et Refuge par Romulus.

Chaque société, chaque Etat, chaque nation s'instaure dans la tension inter ou intracommunautaire, parant d'avance au spectre de la persécution et inscrivant par ce geste dans sa fondation même le programme de l'expulsion.

La fuite d'un peuple semble prendre des figures diverses: depuis la fuite d'Egypte, préparée à la hâte et conduite du passage de la Mer Rouge en traversée du désert, jusqu'à la fuite éperdue des Kurdes irakiens bombardés par leurs demi-frères ennemis et quittant villes et villages, mains vides, pieds mal chaussés en courant et mourant pour escalader la montagne qui les sépare de la Terre Promise (en l'occurrence l'Iran), les exemples se pressent: fuite des républicains espagnols ou fuite des Kosovars.

Mais c'est toujours le même départ, le même deuil, et pour fantasme conducteur le même fantôme d'une Terre Promise, constitué à la hâte à la place de la valise et du toit, c'est toujours le même mirage car il en faut un. On fuit, c'est Pâques, on ne sait pas vers quoi l'on va mais on peint en or ce pays idéalisé dont on répète le nom propre et dont on attend qu'il accorde le droit d'asile immémorial.

Adieu père chéri, les talibans vont me tuer, je pars pour Londres, s'écrie le jeune Afghan. Et le père angoissé: *Londres? Pour quoi faire?—On dit qu'il faut chercher refuge en Angleterre.*

Oui, le salut imaginaire tient dans un nom propre auquel on s'accroche, mettant sa foi et son destin entre les lois d'un lieu qui prend aujourd'hui la place des dieux protecteurs ou des rois respectueux de l'étranger, que tous les Grecs et les Romains connaissaient. Au lieu d'Apollon, les suppliants d'aujourd'hui invoquent les Droits de l'Homme et la Démocratie dont ils ont entendu parler. La Rumeur est le même personnage qu'elle fut à l'origine, avant la radio et le téléphone.

Le modèle du réfugiement n'a pas changé. À la fin, le réfugié arrive en vue de la Terre Promise. Il la voit de ses yeux, soit qu'il se tienne sur le mont Nébo comme Moïse pour apercevoir le pays où il ne mettra pas les pieds, soit qu'ayant fui le nazisme, puis Vichy, il arrive au col des Pyrénées qui lui promet l'Espagne; mais, épuisé, Walter Benjamin se rend à la mort. Debout sur le plateau calaisien, le réfugié de cette année voit briller la blancheur des falaises anglaises. Ah! Si l'on pouvait être la mouette et d'un coup d'aile…

L'avenir, la liberté, l'identité, le toit, le moi, l'adresse d'un homme abrité, il voit tout ce qu'il n'a pas.

Il n'y a qu'un pas. Celui de: *Tu n'entreras pas.*

Certes, 60.000 fugitifs brièvement hébergés à Sangatte, un jour, un mois, deux mois, ont réussi à 'gagner' (est-ce le mot juste) le pays rêvé. Mais à quel prix? 10.000 dollars? jusqu'au dernier dollar. Ce n'est rien. Parfois c'est

refugee of that year sees the shining whiteness of the English cliffs. Ah! To be a seagull and with the flap of a wing…

The future, liberty, identity, the roof/you, me,[4] the address of a protected man, he sees all that he doesn't have.

There is only a 'no'/one step. That of: *You will not enter.*

Certainly, 60,000 fugitives temporarily housed at Sangatte, one day, one month, two months, succeed in 'winning' (is this the right word) the country of their dreams. But at what cost? 10,000 dollars? To the last dollar. It is nothing. Sometimes it's the husband or wife that the journey has raised, overturned, led astray, killed, raped. Lost, separated. We arrive, if we arrive, only by half, half dead, or barely alive. Before the entrance, before the law.[5]

Thus arises the question that plagues and terrifies:

What is a refugee? Are you a refugee? Can you prove that you are, point by point, that being defined by international law as 'refugee'?

The refugee is the person who has to have proof that he has all the qualities of a 'refugee'. Which is to say, that he really has nothing. That he conforms to the criteria that constitute a man as 'refugee'. That he is in danger of dying for the good. That he is not a fake. A pretender. A liar. An imposter. A thief of rights. That he is an orphan, as one must be. That he is without ground, without fatherland, without resources, without help. Before the tribunal that examines him—there he is under suspicion, accused, warned, and if by bad luck he presents himself pleading before Australia, he is called an aggressor and locked up in Penal Colonies, without due process, without lawyer, without a fixed term assigned to his plea, expelled from place and time. We are in flight from the henchmen of Saddam Hussein for twenty years, wandering hidden, from Kuwait to the borders of Iran, we are citizens of nowhere and owners of nothing, and, to top it all off, we arrive in Australia!

There, even children find neither grace nor pity.

In Australia, we rediscover the hardships of past centuries, we separate families, we push to madness and suicide the Afghanis who are stupefied to find themselves behind barbed wire again, the Iranians who had dreamed. So Prime Minister Howard delights: these people who rely on the only tree in the camp, those there who sew their lips and those who cut themselves on barbed wire, we can clearly see from this that they are violent, brutes who don't have any right to civilised Australia. They revolt and attempt suicide!

---

4. Cixous creates homophony between 'the roof' and 'me', in French: '*le toit*' and '*le moi*'. '*Le toit*' also homophonous with '*le toi*' meaning 'you'.

5. 'Before the law' refers to a parable written by German novelist Franz Kafka, 'Vor dem Gesetz' in German. 'Before the law' also refers to Jacques Derrida's essay of the same name that responds to Kafka's parable by reflecting on its metafictional layers which leads Derrida to confront the problem of how and which kinds of writing get classified as 'literary'.

l'époux ou l'épouse que la route a enlevé, enlevée, égarée, tué, violée. Perdus, séparés. On n'arrive, si on arrive, qu'à moitié; à moitié mort, ou un peu vivant. Devant l'entrée, devant la loi.

C'est alors que se pose la question qui harcèle et affole:

Qu'est ce qu'un réfugié? Etes-vous un réfugié? Pouvez-vous prouver que vous êtes, point par point, l'être défini par les lois internationales comme 'réfugié'?

Le réfugié est celui qui doit avoir les preuves qu'il a tout du 'réfugié'. C'est-à-dire, qu'il a bien rien. Qu'il obéit aux critères qui font d'un homme un 'réfugié'. Qu'il est en danger de mort pour de bon. Qu'il n'est pas un faux. Un simulateur. Un menteur. Un imposteur. Un voleur de droits. Qu'il est orphelin comme il faut. Qu'il est sans sol, sans patrie, sans ressource, sans secours. Devant le tribunal qui l'examine, le voilà soupçonné, accusé, prévenu et, si par malheur il s'est présenté en suppliant devant l'Australie, le voilà appelé agresseur et enfermé au Bagne, sans forme de procès, sans avocat, sans terme assigné au supplice, expulsé et du lieu et du temps. On est en fuite devant les sbires de Saddam Hussein depuis vingt ans, errant caché, du Koweït aux lisières des pays d'Iran, on est citoyen de nulle part et propriétaire de rien, et, pour couronner le tout, on arrive en Australie!

Là, même les enfants ne trouvent pas grâce ni pitié.

En Australie, on retrouve la dureté des siècles dépassés, on sépare les familles, on pousse à la folie et au suicide les Afghans stupéfaits de se retrouver en barbarie, les Iraniens qui avaient rêvé. Alors, le Premier ministre Howard se réjouit : ces gens qui se pendent au seul arbre du camp, ceux-là qui se cousent les lèvres et ceux qui se déchirent sur les barbelés, on voit bien par là que ce sont des violents, des brutes qui n'ont aucun droit à la civilisation australienne. Ils attentent à leurs jours et se révoltent!

Voilà la preuve qu'ils sont eux-mêmes les terroristes dont ils osent prétendre avoir été victimes.

Coupables! s'écrie l'Australie géante convulsée par la crainte que lui causent quelques milliers de malheureux.

Quant à ceux qui, ayant échappé au naufrage, ont été vendus aux autochtones ruinés de l'île de Nauru, où ils sont enfermés à vie, à jamais privés de terre, d'espace, de liberté, dans cette cage sans exemple, cernée de grillages, sur ce rocher sans végétation et sans eau potable, dépendant des approvisionnements en conserves et en liquide qui viennent par bateau, sans doute meurent-ils d'effroi et de nostalgie. Mieux eût valu mourir de la main des talibans mais sur leur propre terre natale, se disent-ils.

Il y a aujourd'hui des cas de déportation de réfugiés qui dissimulent leur nom.

Depuis Moïse et Josué, depuis les Héraclides, le droit d'asile s'est vu restreindre et chagriner de siècle en siècle par les royaumes et les états-nations. L'être-réfugié devient de moins en moins sacré, de plus en plus criminalisé.

Here is the proof that they are terrorists themselves, though they dare to pretend to have been victims of terrorism.

Guilty! Cries the giant Australia, convulsing with a fear that creates several thousand wretched people.

According to those who, having escaped from the shipwreck, have been sold to the ruined natives of the Island of Nauru, where they are locked up for life, forever deprived of land, space, freedom, in that cage without parallel, surrounded by bars, on this rock without vegetation and without drinkable water, dependent on the provisions of pickles and liquid that come by boat, without doubt, they will die of fright and nostalgia. Better had they died at the hands of the Taliban, but on their own native soil, they say.

Today there are cases of deportation of refugees who conceal their name.

Since Moses and Joshua, since the Herclids, the right of asylum has seen a constricting and saddening from century to century by royal kingdoms and nation-states. The refugee figure becomes less and less sacred, more and more criminalised.

And so the XX century produces *the event*: the mass deportation of people who become stateless in Europe between the two wars.

According to Hannah Arendt, the worst begins here: the Jews, and not only, but also entire populations, are on roads that lead nowhere, except to camps.

For her, it's after the Russian Revolution, with totalitarianisms, a change in the structure of the Nation-state, in the experience of the border, in its relationship to citizenship, an original and terrible moment of which the cruel results are evident today.

Certainly, there have been analogous events in non-European cultures that we don't speak about enough: China, India, Africa, and often, in these cultures, our Europe has played its malevolent role.

The Europe that invented *the Refugee* has debts to pay back to the refugee.

To Biblical people, the word 'exodus' goes hand in hand with the word 'asylum'. What are they doing with that today?

And exile? Two words: the exiled is not necessarily he who asks for asylum. It can even be he who *asks for exile*, as was the renowned case of Victor Hugo refusing the amnesty offered by the little Emperor and camping on his island. There is, in the aura of exile, the memory of poets since Ovid through to Dante and Mandelstam, shape-shifters of pain into sublime oeuvres. Exile remains individual. A refugee can feel exiled: that he is already a worker of mourning on a poetic path. An exiled person, from the separation from his native soil, develops a strength that brings him closer to himself.

The refugee dreams of relief, of new beginnings. To be reborn perhaps?

Program Extract

Et voici qu'au XXe siècle se produit *l'événement :* la déportation massive de gens qui deviennent apatrides dans l'Europe entre les deux guerres.

Selon Hannah Arendt, le pire commence là : les juifs, et pas seulement, mais aussi des populations entières, sont sur les routes qui ne mènent nulle part sauf aux camps.

Pour elle, c'est, après la révolution russe, avec les totalitarismes, un changement de structure dans l'Etat-nation, dans l'expérience de la frontière, dans le rapport à la citoyenneté, un moment original et terrible dont les suites cruelles sont manifestées aujourd'hui.

Certes, il y a eu des événements analogues dans des cultures non européennes dont on ne parle pas assez, Chine, Inde, Afrique, et souvent, dans ces cultures, l'Europe que nous sommes a fait son travail maléfique.

L'Europe qui a inventé *le Réfugié* a des comptes à lui rendre.

Aux peuples bibliques revient le mot exode comme le mot asile. Qu'en font-ils aujourd'hui?

Et l'exil? Deux mots: l'exilé n'est pas nécessairement *demandeur d'asile.* Il peut même être *demandeur d'exil,* comme ce fut l'illustre cas de Victor Hugo refusant l'amnistie offerte par le petit Empereur et campant sur son île. Il y a, dans l'aura de l'exil, le souvenir des poètes depuis Ovide jusqu'à Dante et Mandelstam, transfigurateurs de la peine en Œuvre sublime. L'exil reste individuel. Un réfugié peut se sentir exilé: c'est qu'il est déjà un travailleur du deuil, en chemin poétique. Un exilé fait de l'éloignement du sol natal une force qui le rapproche de lui-même.

Le réfugié rêve d'apaisement, de recommencement. Renaître peut-être?

Extrait du programme du spectacle

Hospitality?

Jacques Derrida nicknamed and renamed it *hostipitalité* in 1996, in order to remind us of the forgotten secrets of the word and of the paradoxical and bitter folds of the concept that the language conceals.

The Latin word brings together at the same time, not *hostis,* in the sense of the foreigner as guest, which is to say: the invited guest (but *hôte* in French is, at the same time, the welcoming *hôte,* and the welcomed *hôte,* and that brings into play the difference and the disagreement[1]) and *hostis*—the public enemy foreigner, the enemy of the nation. Yes, he is thus the foreigner signified in the French language as: the enemy. *Ost,* in old French, is the army of the enemies. Thus our hostile host, our invited guest, supposedly welcome, becomes suspect and out of place/unwelcome.

To *hostis* is added, mixed in and substituted with *hospes,* he who receives and he who is received. From the outset, the foreigner as guest/host, as enemy, has a lot of trouble distinguishing one from the other.

For Kant, hospitality must be universal, all men, humans, have the right to this hospitality. Thus all human foreigners too.

But the non-human, the animal for example, is excluded. So be it. So no cat[2] at my place then?

And the gods?

The question poses itself through religion; today, the question of the right of asylum and of the refugee or immigrant becomes weighed down by the welcome of god. In effect, the foreigner arrives with his language, his family perhaps, and his god almost always. As we know, that doesn't leave the self. That even reanimates communalisms and fundamentalisms.

So it is thus that the Kantian universal human hospitality leads to thinking about the political and ethnic difficulties of concrete hospitality, lived experiences in this day and age.

---

1. The disagreement, or '*différend*' in the original text, is a legal term that, according to Jean-Francois Lyotard in *Le Différend* (1983), describes a conflict that cannot be determined because a single rule of judgment is not applicable to both (or all) arguments.

2. '*Pas de chat*' also means 'the step of a cat' and is a common sequence of movements in classical ballet.

L'Hospitalité?

Jacques Derrida l'a surnommée et renommée l'*hostipitalité* en 1996, afin de nous rappeler aux secrets oubliés du mot et aux replis paradoxaux et amers du concept tels que la langue les recèle.

C'est que le mot latin rassemble à la fois, pas *hostis*, le sens d'étranger en tant qu'hôte, disons: *l'invité* (mais *hôte* en français est à la fois *hôte* l'accueillant, et *hôte* l'accueilli, et cela fait entrer toute la différence et le différend) et *hostis* l'étranger-ennemi public, l'ennemi du pays. Oui, il en est ainsi l'étranger signifie dans la langue: l'ennemi. *Ost*, en vieux français, est l'armée des ennemis. Voilà notre hôte hostilisé, notre invité, supposé bienvenu, suspect et malvenu.

A *hostis* s'ajoute, se mêle, se substitue *hospes*, celui qui reçoit et celui qui est reçu. D'emblée l'étranger, l'hôte, l'ennemi ont bien du mal à se distinguer.

Pour Kant, l'hospitalité doit être universelle, tout ce qui est homme, humain, a droit à cette hospitalité. Donc tout étranger humain.

Mais le non-humain, l'animal par exemple, est exclu. Soit. Pas de chat chez moi alors?

Et les dieux?

La question se pose à travers la religion; aujourd'hui, la question du droit d'asile et de l'accueil du réfugié ou immigré s'alourdit de l'accueil du dieu. En effet, l'étranger arrive avec sa langue, sa famille peut-être, et son dieu presque toujours. Comme on le sait, cela ne va pas de soi. Cela ranime même les communautarismes et les intégrismes.

C'est ainsi que l'hospitalité universelle humaine kantienne amène à penser les difficultés politiques et ethniques de l'hospitalité concrète, actuelle.

L'hospitalité inconditionnelle voudrait accueillir sans limites, sans condition aucune ni dans le temps, ni dans le nombre, ni dans la définition. C'est le rêve. En réalité elle n'existe ni plus ni moins que la justice brillant, idéale et absolue, au-dessus du droit. *L'hospitalité* en réalité, et tous nous le vivons ainsi, est toujours et immédiatement *conditionnelle*.

Mais, comme Jacques Derrida y insistait en dépistant *l'hostipitalité*, on a besoin des deux hospitalités, l'inconditionnelle et la conditionnelle. Elles sont indissociables, elles s'inspirent et se retiennent l'une l'autre. A l'hospitalité

Unconditional hospitality would like to welcome without limitations, without any condition neither in time nor in number nor in definition. It is the dream. In reality, it exists no more or less than shining justice, ideal and absolute, above the law. *Hospitality* in reality, and every way we live it, is always and immediately *conditional.*

But as Jacques Derrida insisted in detecting *hostipitalité*, we need hospitalities, the unconditional and the conditional. They are inseparable; they inspire and retain the one in the other. From conditional hospitality, unconditional hospitality asks to always offer more generosity. Conditional hospitality, it handles carefully and it is not an evil: if we don't set limits, if we don't formulate rights, ideal love would one day topple over in hating exasperation and reject it.

Hospitality must, we would ideally want it, to offer to carry itself beyond, *a little* beyond the reasonable, the tempered. We would like it to shine without searing intensity and without calculation. That would be a form of holiness that is unaware of itself, one would offer a roof, yourself, without appetite, with serenity, without wanting to boast about one's self and feed on one's own generosity, without satisfying one's own request for friendship or recognition. That would happen 'naturally' by situating itself, from the outset, beyond self-interest.

As an example. To be hospitable to a human being, just as we are to the cat, we don't wait for it to repay us with goodness or to say thank you. In a neutral purity.

There are people who are capable of this.

The States, by definition, no. Today in Europe, hospitality, the foreigner, the right of asylum, immigration are under question. Everything having changed, lines of solidarity just as much as the causes of hatred.

In this today, Theatre, like Philosophy, searches in order to understand what has happened to the hospitality that came from the Bible or from the Greeks, what is happening to it, what will happen to it, what we can want to elaborate on in new ethical attitudes and by new juridical and political devices.

But we don't ask ourselves to be hospitable to the death. Only to not want to remake the host/guest in his image, but rather to remake the foreigner as each one of us was one day or another, in order not to forget that each person has the right to be an other.

Program Extract

conditionnelle, l'hospitalité inconditionnelle demande de tendre à toujours plus de générosité. L'hospitalité conditionnelle, elle, ménage et ce n'est pas un mal: si l'on ne donnait pas des limites, si l'on ne formulait pas les droits, l'amour idéal basculerait un jour dans l'exaspération haineuse et le rejet.

L'hospitalité doit, on le voudrait idéalement, tendre à se porter au-delà, *un peu* au-delà du raisonnable, du tempéré. On voudrait qu'elle brille sans fulgurance et sans calcul. Ce serait une forme de sainteté qui s'ignore, on offrirait le toit, le toi, sans appétit, avec sérénité, sans vouloir s'enorgueillir et se nourrir de sa propre bonté, sans satisfaire sa propre demande d'amitié ou de reconnaissance. Cela se ferait 'naturellement', en se situant d'emblée au-delà des intérêts du moi.

Comme une évidence. Etre hospitalier à l'être humain, comme on l'est au chat dont on n'attend pas qu'il rende le bien ou dise merci. Dans une pureté neutre.

Il y a des gens qui en sont capables.

Les Etats, par définition, non. Aujourd'hui en Europe, hospitalité, étranger, droit d'asile, immigration sont en question. Tout ayant changé, les liens de solidarité comme les causes de la haine.

Dans cet aujourd'hui, le Théâtre, comme la Philosophie, cherche à comprendre ce qui est arrivé à l'hospitalité qui venait de la Bible ou des Grecs, ce qui lui arrive, ce qui va lui arriver, ce qu'on peut vouloir élaborer dans de nouvelles attitudes éthiques et par de nouveaux dispositifs juridiques et politiques.

Mais on ne nous demande pas d'être hospitalier jusqu'à la mort. Seulement de ne pas vouloir refaire l'hôte à son image, mais plutôt de se refaire étranger comme chacun l'a été un jour ou un autre, afin de ne pas oublier que chacun a le droit d'être un autre.

Extrait du programme du spectacle

Our Hosts[1]

Who are these refugees that our actors welcome into their soul and their body? Who stay for a fleeting moment in one caravanserai or another? Who are they that welcome our actors into their memory and their future?

These are not the masses, not whole groups of people thrown out by the millions—as it happened for example in 1948 with the Partition of India—from one part and the other with a slash of a knife on the map of a continent. These are individuals, escapees, in groups of one, two, ten or families, from one of the last infernal fireplaces lit by our time. And who have had the strength, the opportunity, enough money to go further than the makeshift camps where crowds of the disinherited pile up on the other side of a neighbouring nation's border.

These people, for whom the incredible desire to do more than just survive has arisen, to seek out freedom at the other end of the world, if that is where it might be found.

Iran, Iraq, Afghanistan, Kurdistan, sometimes Palestine, some of the former Soviet Bloc, these are the states or countries from which they flee.

Today our Ulysseses are without names and without the right of return.

Yesterday we were traders, teachers, engineers, doctors, farmers, IT specialists, billiard champions, boxing hopefuls, actors, playwrights or theatremakers, fathers, primary school teachers. Today: no one. No one, the name that Ulysses gives to Polyphemus.

Sometimes fate throws them towards the far south-east and, going by Karachi, Indonesia, they dream between the disjointed boards of stinking boats of arriving alive in a country so big, so wealthy, so under-populated, so new that its people will not fail to be delighted at the arrival of these great wanderers; but there they find themselves hardly even saved from the waters, thrown behind fences and bars by the cruel Australian government.

1. Cixous notes the dual paradoxical meaning of this term in the previous essay '*Hospitality?*' where she explains that, in French, '*l'hôte*' refers to either the host or the guest. The title in French—'*Nos hôtes*'—also sounds similar to '*nos autres*', meaning 'our others'. In her famous essay '*Sorties*' Cixous has written extensively about the idea of the other within the self, particularly the female self, what she calls the 'not-me within me' (1986: 90).

Nos hôtes

Qui sont ces réfugiés que nos acteurs accueillent dans leur âme et leur corps? Qui séjournent pour un temps éphémère dans un caravansérail ou un autre? Qui sont ceux qui accueillent nos acteurs dans leur mémoire et leur destin?

Ici ce ne sont pas des masses, pas des peuples entiers jetés par millions —comme il advint par exemple en 1948 à la Partition de l'Inde—de part et d'autre d'un trait de couteau sur la carte d'un continent. Ce sont des individus, échappés, par un, deux, dix ou par familles, d'un des derniers foyers infernaux allumés par notre époque, et qui ont eu la force, la chance, l'argent nécessaires à aller plus loin que dans les camps de fortune où s'entassent les foules déshéritées de l'autre côté d'une frontière voisine.

Ce sont des personnes en qui s'est levé l'incroyable désir de faire plus que survivre, d'aller chercher la liberté à l'autre bout du monde, si c'est par là-bas qu'elle est.

L'Iran, l'Irak, l'Afghanistan, le Kurdistan, parfois la Palestine, quelques pays anciennement soviétiques, sont les états ou pays qu'ils fuient.

Nos Ulysses sont aujourd'hui sans nom et sans retour.

Hier on était commerçant, professeur, ingénieur, médecin, agriculteur, informaticien, champion de billard, espoir de la boxe, comédien, auteur de théâtre, père de famille, institutrice. Aujourd'hui: personne. Personne le nom par lequel Ulysse se désigne à Polyphème.

Le sort les lance tantôt vers le lointain sud-est et, passant par Karachi, l'Indonésie, ils rêvent entre les planches disjointes des bateaux pourris d'arriver vivants dans un pays si grand si riche si peu peuplé si neuf qu'il ne pourra manquer de se réjouir de la venue d'errants de qualité; mais ceux-là se retrouvent à peine sauvés des eaux, jetés derrière grillages et barreaux par le très cruel gouvernement d'Australie. Là, au fond du désert sans herbe, sans arbre, ils sont appelés criminels et détenus pendant des années, hors droit et hors humanité. L'ONU peut toujours faire remontrance. L'Australie s'en balance.

Ceux qui vont vers l'ouest, après quatre mois, six mois, un an, deux ans d'odyssée, atteignent enfin le portillon qui s'appelait Sangatte. Une localité de 800 habitants. Inoubliable. Sur le front d'une colline le grand hangar

There, in the farthest reaches of the desert, without grass, without trees, they are called criminals and detained for years, outside law and outside humanity. The UN can always remonstrate. Australia doesn't give a damn.

Those who go westward, after four months, six months, a year, two years of odyssey, finally arrive at the gate called Sangatte. A village of 800 inhabitants. Unforgettable. On top of a hill, the large warehouse fitted out by the Red Cross in 1999, became, at the exact moment when we were drawing out so much of our humanity, that we found so many admirable and exasperating subjects there, and discovered that we were the ones hosted by these hostages of the misfortunes of history, the hosted, I mean the invited guests, those applying at the cabin doors—a ruin and a memory.

At the caravanserai, the travelers become (as they always were since Ulysses) storytellers.

In its turn, the tale becomes the main character in these times of distress.

So we tell. And the tale is embalming in both senses of the word. It preserves and it perfumes. Those who listen experience a strange enchantment. It's as if the haunting regret and the memories of bad treatment rip out tears, they float on disaster, the light of a smile: it is happiness that defends itself, which we've tasted in the past, that we refuse to lose.

Everyone agrees that they dare to want a free life and the enlightenment that comes with study.

And what they call: a destiny. They ask for the right to a destiny. A destiny, which is to say, a future.

They fled without a future. Now they are without identity papers and without definition. One day their story will be picked up again where it has been violently cut off. They hope.

'Take my story, tell it, make sure it doesn't die without a burial and that we have not lived our modest and precious existences without leaving a trace nor descendants'.

It is here that the magical accessory enters onto the stage, whose power and future role we had not counted on: the tape-recorder. We believed we were listening to the present and for several hours sharing the bread of exodus offered by these sudden friends. But the tape-recorder will have gathered together more than just the story. The tremulous music of voices, chants, messages from timbres and sighs, the story with all its breaths, its tears, its silences, its gusts of wind, its roaring waves, the story with its own actor and poet.

The story, both alive in the present moment and instantaneously eternal.

Program Extract

aménagé par la Croix-Rouge en 1999, devenu, pendant le temps même où nous y puisions tant de moments humains, que nous y trouvions tant de sujets d'admiration et d'exaspération, et que nous y étions les hôtes de ces otages du malheur dans l'histoire,—les hôtes, je veux dire les invités, les demandeurs à la porte des cabines—une ruine et un souvenir.

Au caravansérail, les voyageurs deviennent (comme il en fut toujours depuis Ulysse), des conteurs.

Le récit devient à son tour le personnage principal pour ce temps de détresse.

Alors on raconte. Et le récit embaume. En tous les sens. Il conserve et il fleure. Celui qui écoute éprouve un étrange enchantement. C'est que si la lancinance du regret et la trace des mauvais traitements arrachent des larmes, il flotte sur le désastre la lumière d'un sourire: c'est le bonheur qui se défend, celui qu'on a goûté, on refuse de le perdre.

Tous sont d'accord pour oser vouloir une vie libérée et les lumières répandues par les études.

Et ce qu'ils appellent: un destin. Ils demandent le droit au destin. Un destin, c'est-à-dire, un futur.

Ils ont fui le sans futur. Maintenant ils sont sans papiers et sans définition. Un jour leur histoire reprendra là où elle a été violemment sectionnée. Espèrent-ils.

'Prenez mon histoire, racontez-la, faites qu'elle ne soit pas une morte sans sépulture et que nous n'ayons pas vécu nos modestes et précieuses existences sans laisser trace ni descendance'.

C'est ici qu'entre en scène l'accessoire magique dont on n'avait pas calculé le pouvoir et le rôle ultérieur: le *magnétophone.* On croyait écouter au présent et pendant quelques heures partager le pain d'exode offert par ces amis soudains. Mais le magnétophone aura recueilli plus que le récit. La musique tremblée des voix, la psalmodie, les messages des timbres et des soupirs, le récit mais avec ses souffles, ses larmes, ses silences, ses rafales de vents, ses chahuts de vagues, le récit avec son acteur et son poète personnels.

Le récit, sur le vif, au présent instantanément éternel.

Extrait du programme du spectacle

Drums on the Dam

The play: *Drums on the Dam—In the form of an ancient puppet play performed by actors*
Creators: The Théâtre du Soleil
First performed: 11 September 1999 at the Cartoucherie of Vincennes, Paris
Director: Ariane Mnouchkine
Text: Hélène Cixous
Music: Jean-Jacques Lemêtre
Set: Guy-Claude François, Ysabel de Maisonneuve and Didier Martin
Costumes: Nathalie Thomas and Marie-Hélène Bouvet

Synopsis: *Drums on the Dam* echoed the events reported in the media in 1998 when the Chinese government breached the levees in Northern China in order to release water pressure from the over-swollen Yangtze River. The government failed to warn the local populations of the incoming inundation and consequently the flood claimed over 3500 lives and left 15 million citizens homeless. The play explores questions of unilateral power, environmental geopolitics and its effect on citizens. For the performance, the Théâtre du Soleil developed a unique hybrid aesthetic of different Asian performance traditions. In particular, the actors perform the characters of the play as if they were Japanese Bunraku puppets. The puppet-actors appear to be 'controlled' by puppet masters who were also played by actors.

Résumé de la pièce: Il y a mille ans peut-être ou bien avant-hier, dans les états du Seigneur Khang, l'inondation menace la ville et les champs. Les courtisans complotent, les paysans s'alarment, la digue devient l'enjeu de toutes les rivalités tandis que le pouvoir se fissure à mesure que les flots montent… Tambours sur la Digue fait echo aux évènements de 1998; quand le gouvernement chinois a ouvert une digue dans le nord de la Chine pour réduire la pression du fleuve Yangtsé. Le gouvernement n'avait pas prévenu les citoyens de l'inondation qui arrivait et le déluge fut responsable de 3500 morts et 15 millions de citoyens sans abri. La pièce soulève les questions du pouvoir unilatéral, de la géopolitique de l'environnement et de ses effets sur les citoyens. Pour le spectacle, le Théâtre du Soleil puise son esthétisme dans les traditions asiatiques. En particulier, le Bunraku: les comédiens jouent les personnages de la pièce comme s'ils étaient des marionnettes de théâtre japonais. Les marionnettes-acteurs ont ainsi l'air d'être 'dirigées' par les maîtres des marionnettes, joués eux aussi par des comédiens.

Striking Sticks

That's it. We're off again, says the captain. What luck! It was 1 August 1998. Me, who believed I'd be able to… I looked for a place to tether, a hole, a cave, a mine, a whale's antrum. Too late. The off-beat rhythm had begun. The jaws of a monstrous wave already gaping towards the tip of the sky, squatting on the tip of the tidal wave, soaked in foam, I was carried once again towards the Theatre.

– Where are we going, captain Li? I chirped.

– Further, higher, more over there, as usual, what do I know, Madame Li assured me.

Boarded! I wanted to flee. The departure had already taken me. It is a voyage of forced enchantment. And we don't even know what we are climbing onto. The take off/separation takes place. Which is to say, I peel off, I am unstuck but what carries me? Carriage? Horse? Horseplane? Old or modern means to fly over? Go figure/We will find out.

– Are you frightened?

– Terrorised, as usual

– At least you have something, to have fear is already to have something

– True! I cling to the terror. To have terror for earth and for error is not nothing.[1]

I comment on the sky: in the full light of day it was black and I couldn't see anything, not even the sky. I note: total catastrophe. I recognise the apocalyptic climate. It is an inquiry into the Heart, or a hunt at the Heart of the World, a course set towards the Interior continent in which we search for visible Transfiguration. The Theatre. What a God! Or rather, what Gods! All of us, we invoke it, we say its name, we comment on its traces, we invent its laws. Theatre thanks. Grant us mercy Theatre, we implore. What I know is that Theatre exercises two absolute authorities over me, one harsh, undoubtedly violent, the other a crazy tenderness stronger still than strength, with one hand Theatre slaps me and leads me by the stick, the famous fairy wand, a little thin and flexible stick which authors of enchantment use,

1. Cixous creates assonance between the words 'terror', 'earth' and 'error' in the French: *terreur, terre* and *erreur.*

Coups de baguettes

Ça y est, on repart, dit le capitaine. Quel coup! C'était le 1er Août 1998. Moi qui croyais pouvoir... Je cherchai où me terrer, un trou, une grotte, une mine, un antre de baleine. Trop tard. Le contretemps avait commencé. Les mâchoires d'une vague monstrueuse béaient déjà vers la pointe du ciel, accroupie sur la pointe du raz, trempée d'écume, j'étais emportée encore une fois vers le Théâtre.

– Où allons-nous, capitaine Li, piaillai-je.

– Plus loin, plus haut, plus par là-bas, comme d'habitude est-ce que je sais, m'assura Mme Li.

Embarquée! Je voulais fuir. Le départ m'avait déjà prise. C'est un voyage par enchantement forcé. Et on ne sait même pas sur quoi on est grimpé. Le décollement a lieu. C'est-à-dire je décolle, je suis décollée, mais qu'est-ce qui me porte? Char? cheval, chavion? Ancien ou moderne moyen de survoler? Va savoir.

– Tu as peur?

– Terrorisée, comme d'habitude.

– Au moins tu as quelque chose, avoir peur c'est déjà quelque chose.

– Vrai! Je m'accrochai à la terreur. Avoir la terreur pour terre et pour erreur, ce n'est pas rien.

Je remarquai le ciel: en plein jour il était noir et je ne voyais rien, pas même le ciel. Je notai: catastrophe totale. Je reconnus le climat d'apocalypse. C'est une quête du Cœur, ou une chasse au Cœur du Monde, une course vers le continent de l'Intérieur dont nous cherchons la Transfigure visible. Le Théâtre. Quel Dieu! ou bien Quels Dieux! Tous nous l'invoquons, nous disons son nom, nous commentons ses traces, nous inventons ses lois. Théâtre merci. Grâce Théâtre, supplions-nous. Ce que je sais c'est que Théâtre exerce sur moi deux autorités absolues, l'une sévère, redoutable violente, l'autre d'une tendresse folle encore plus puissante que la force, d'une main Théâtre me frappe et me mène à la baguette, la fameuse baguette fée, un petit bâton mince et flexible dont se servent les auteurs d'enchantements, Prospero, Shakespeare et bien d'autres. D'une main, est-ce la même, une autre, l'autre, une troisième, il me frôle le cœur, je pleure et tout d'un coup je suis un/e

Prospero, Shakespeare and others. On the one hand, is it the same, an other, the other, a third, it brushes against my heart, I cry and all of a sudden I am an other/another. How many hands/tomorrows does it have, we don't know, they are multiplied according to the beings upon which it strikes its marvelous blows.

The stick is itself an other, as a ring, it is a wedding ring, Ring-a-ding. So if it is both ring and baton simultaneously it is a ringlet. The good circonfusion[2] is instantly established.

A black wind was blowing. I saw myself already catapulted in one of these postmodern Asias, pushed into large computerised libraries, lost in airports, drowned in markets, clinging to my notebooks, peeling through Chinese newspapers, making my inquiries to find the present-day Phoenix. Pilgrim despite myself. A hopeless desire to desert, a weakness of spirit before continents in the process of globalisation.

– And if you wrote—no. If we rediscovered an ancient play that would have been written by the famous poet Hxshi-Xhou[3], an undated play, and in pieces, as for its origin we don't know exactly where it was born, some say in China, others in Korea? said the Captain and before my eyes he becomes Madame Li. He had had enough mollycoddling.

To be written by Xi-Xou! I was saved. I was relieved. Dislodged. Replaced. To what does life hold, the oeuvre, the door. A wave of the wand and everything is delivered.

Emotion made a concave night in me, everything empty and restless where a dream of the poet Xi Xou comes to play. I was visited, peopled and replaced.

It was an initiating scene. On the peak of a last dune, two passionate creatures were waltzing in a storm. I looked at their waltz because I was having trouble distinguishing one from the other rolled in the hurricane, and even distinguishing myself from them. It seemed to me that I was a father with a son or even my daughter with her mother or even this couple who whirl, the last one in the world, the survivors or the dying. We were saved but to see, without any future, the end of everything present. I lived through the climbing waters, the slow fall of the living sand, the slipping away of dead bodies, a yellow flag was slowly covering all those I hadn't had time to know, my characters were sinking at the exact moment that I was meeting

2. The translation is faithful to Cixous's neologism. '*Circonfusion*' is a neologism that evokes Derrida's neologism '*circumfession*' that puns on 'confession' and 'circumcision' in an essay and interview from *Augustine and Postmodernism: confession and circumfession* (2005). Cixous' neologism *circonfusion* appears to be made from the verb '*circler*', 'to circle' and the noun '*confusion*' meaning 'confusion' that seems to present a feminine alternative to *circumfession* by bringing together the circle with the pejorative '*con*' or '*cunt*' and the '*fusion*' or 'fusion' often associated with mother-child relations.

3. Cixous plays with the sound of her own unusual surname by turning it into various versions of invented Chinese-looking names that sound like 'Cixous'.

autre. Combien il a de mains, on ne sait, elles sont multipliées à la mesure des êtres sur lesquels il porte ses merveilleux coups.

La baguette est elle-même une autre, en tant que bague elle est anneau, Wage Bagge. Donc si elle est à la fois bague et bâtonnet c'est qu'elle est biguette. La bonne circonfusion est d'emblée établie.

Un vent noir soufflait. Je me voyais déjà catapultée dans une de ces Asies postmodernes, poussée dans de grandes bibliothèques computerisées, perdue dans des aéroports noyée dans des marchés, accrochée à mes cahiers, épluchant les journaux chinois, faisant mon enquête pour trouver le phénix actuel. Pélerine malgré moi. Une vaine envie de déserter, une faiblesse de l'esprit devant les continents en voie de globalisation.

– Et si tu écrivais—non. Si on retrouvait une pièce ancienne qui aurait été écrite par le fameux poète Hxshi-Xhou, une pièce non datée, et en morceaux, quant à l'origine on ne sait pas exactement où il est né, certains disent en Chine, d'autres en Corée? Dit le Capitaine et sous mes yeux il devint Mme Li. Il avait suffi d'une couche de fesses en plus.

Etre écrite par Xi-Xou! J'étais sauvée. Je fus allégée. Délogée. Remplacée. A quoi tient la vie, l'oeuvre, la porte. Un coup de biguette et tout est délivré.

L'émotion fit en moi une nuit concave, toute vide et remuante où vint jouer un rêve du poète Xi Xou. J'étais visitée, peuplée, et remplacée.

C'était une scène initiatique. Au sommet d'un sable dernier, deux créatures passionnées valsaient dans une tempête. Je regardais leur valse parce que j'avais du mal à distinguer l'un des deux, roulés dans l'ouragan et même à me distinguer d'eux. Il me semblait que j'étais le père avec le fils ou bien j'étais ma fille avec sa mère ou bien ce couple qui tourbillonne c'est le dernier du monde, les survivants ou expirants. On était sauf mais pour voir sans aucun futur la fin de tout présent. Je vécus la montée des eaux, la chute lente du sable vivant, le défilé des morts un drap jaune couvrait lentement tous ceux que je n'avais pas eu le temps de connaître, mes personnages sombraient à l'instant même où je faisais leur connaissance, à quoi bon voir si c'est pour perdre de vue. Au matin il ne restait plus que nous du périssement universel, j'avais perdu le seigneur le moine, le médecin, toute une cour et tout un peuple.

L'invisibilité des deux survivants se fit. Un deuil violent me combla. Quelle foule j'avais à pleurer et à raconter! J'étais submergée par l'émoi, c'est-à-dire par les moi de tous ces disparus dont j'avais reçu la garde. Je vois encore la danse sur la crête désolée, la valse de la vie avec la mort, du devin avec le destin, du porteur de prophéties avec Théâtre le dieu des fantômes et des résurrections. Je passai un coup de fil à Mme Li.

– C'est parti! criai-je à Madame Li.

Puis j'osai lui dire qu'il ne resta plus personne au matin à part elle et moi.

Vient l'automne.

Pendant que Mme Li capitaine Ariane et toute la troupe cinglent vers

them, what use is it to see well if it means losing the view. In the morning, there was only us left from the universal perishing; I had lost the master, the monk, the doctor, a whole court and a whole people.

The invisibility of two survivors was accomplished. A violent mourning overcame me. What a crowd I had to cry over and to tell! I was submerged in emotion, which is to say, by the egos of all those who disappeared whom I had received into my custody. I still see the dance on the sorry peak, the waltz of life with death, of the divine with destiny, of the carrier of prophesies with Theatre, the god of ghosts and resurrections. I ring Madame Li.

– We're off! I cried to Madame Li.

Then I dare to tell her that there will be no-one left tomorrow morning apart from her and me.

Autumn comes.

While Madame Li captains, Ariane and all the troupe make for Asia, I am going (I go) to my Asia/asylum here in bed where I read all the Noh theatre in the world.

When the travelers return, I don't know how, I see them, from the first day, changing into puppets under some stroke of genius or unconscious espionage, from the beginning they were metamorphosing and me, stupefied, it is not me who had blown this enchantment here, if I had not stopped playing with puppets it was in secret, it is a principle that what I desire I never confess to, and so, I will never know how they had guessed my secret.

During their Sanctuary,[4] what were the egos in me doing that were speaking to me?

As the poet Xi Xou I divine Dame Gigogne. Characters jump from my arms, my knees, the creases of my dresses, the fingers enter me through the ears and play all sorts of tricks on me, turning from one sex into the other. I am country, port, city, hostel and travelers. Each one of them is, at the same time, the future couple of the actor with the character and clandestine passenger, ready at my side. I am my own wise-woman. It appears that the birth of Dame Gigogne lasts the entire show, and now I understand it. I am there for her rehearsal. He who is the joker and the joke of the thing, is that all this progeny arrives in Xi Xhou's pregnancy, the poet of whom the cranial box is a womb/matrix that is half male, half sow, half female.

Who still remembers Gigogne, except the (Larousse) dictionary? And yet, what a woman and what a puppet!

(...)

Today Gigogne is listed in a big book flanked by Gigot. And yet, and yet...

They enter in clusters, in gusts, they were dancing furiously between themselves, they were cascading their angers, haste lifts them up, they were

4. In the French, Cixous uses the word '*Asie*' meaning 'Asia' but which is almost homophonous with '*asile*' meaning 'sanctuary' or 'refuge'.

l'Asie, je vais (j'allai) en mon Asie ici au lit où je lis tout le Nô du monde.

Au retour les voyageurs, je ne sais pas comment, je les vis dès le premier jour s'échangeant sous quelque coup de génie ou d'espionnage par inconscients en marionnettes, dès le début ils étaient en métamorphose et moi stupéfiée, ce n'est pas moi qui ai soufflé cet enchantement-là, si je n'avais cessé de jouer avec des marionnettes, c'était en secret, c'est un principe ce que je désire je ne l'avoue jamais, et voilà, je ne saurai jamais comment, qu'on m'avait deviné mon secret.

Pendant leur Asie que faisaient les moi qui me parlaient?

En tant que le poète Xi Xou je devins la Dame Gigogne. Des personnages me sortent des bras, des genoux, des plis de robes des doigts m'entrent par les oreilles me jouent tous les tours, se tournent d'un sexe à l'autre. Je suis pays, port, ville, auberge et voyageurs. Chacun d'eux est à la fois le futur couple du comédien avec le personnage et passager clandestin à mon bord qui s'y prête. Je suis ma sage-femme. Il paraît que l'accouchement de Dame Gigogne durait pendant tout le spectacle, et maintenant je le comprends. J'assiste à sa répétition. Ce qui est le plaisant et la plaisanterie de la chose c'est que toute cette progéniture arrive dans l'enceinte de Xi Xhou le poète dont la boîte crânienne est une matrice moitié mâle moitié femelle moitié femâle.

Qui se souvient encore de Gigogne, sinon le (Larousse) dictionnaire. Et pourtant, quelle femme et quelle marionnette!

(...)

Aujourd'hui Gigogne gît dans un gros livre flanquée de Gigot. And pourtant, et pourtant...

Ils entraient par grappes, par bourrasques, ils dansaient furieusement entre eux, ils cascadaient leurs colères, une hâte les soulevait, ils gigotaient en l'air, une vague les escamotait. Je n'avais jamais vu une telle moisson, les mois étaient Légion, ils ne se gênaient pas, il suffisait d'un fleuve d'une rivière du mot eau et aussitôt une brassée de bateliers, dehors mes propres forêts grondaient et tombaient sous la hache. Je me suis dit: mais ils n'arrêtent pas de s'épouser et de s'esquinter et de s'entretuer. Que va dire le public!? Il pleut, il meurt, à torrents. Ils passaient à l'acte avec une férocité légère, foin des convenances, une nudité des pulsions gouvernait mes côtes, ils ne se retenaient pas pour répondre aux injonctions du désir et de la nécessité. Les marionnettes sont sans détour. Elles oscillent mais ne tergiversent pas. Sous les apparences d'une passivité de poupée mue par un maître elles sont d'une activité sans pareille. C'est qu'elles ne tiennent pas en place. Ce sont des emportées. Si Hamlet avait été marionnette Claudius eût été trucidé acte 2 scène 1.

Mais pourquoi parlai-je ici maintenant à cette heure d'Asie au lit de marionnettes? C'est qu'il faisait Nô en moi. C'est-à-dire fantastique et très vite. Pendant les Nôs d'été les fantômes passent la porte de l'Oubli, ils viennent

wriggling in the air, a wave conjures them away. I had never seen such a harvest, the months were Legion, they weren't embarrassed, a stream, a river, the word 'water' suffices and, at the same time, an armful of boatmen, outside my own forests were moaning and falling under the axe. I said to myself: but they never stop marrying each other, tiring each other out and killing each other. What will the public say? He cries, he dies, in torrents. They passed through the act with a light ferocity, the devil take proprieties, a nudity of drives governed my sides, they didn't hold onto themselves in order to respond to the injunctions of desire and necessity. The puppets are without detour. They oscillate but don't prevaricate. Under the guises of a passive doll moved/stripped by a master, they are unparalleled activity. They never sit still. They are swept away. If Hamlet had been a puppet, Claudius would have been bumped off by act 2 scene 1.

But why do I speak here, now, at this hour of Asia/asylum, from my puppet bed? It is because Noh is working inside me. Which is to say fantastically and very quickly. During the Summer Nohs, the ghosts pass through the door of Forgetting, they come to repeat their unprecedented sadness, because, for them, never in the past, the present is their death and I was there. Nothing so natural in this country of characters than the supernatural. On the clock, the two hands drum the hour of revisitings and metamorphoses. It is utterly natural to meet your own dead mother on a country path, to eat with her and not to recognise her. In truth, the most discreet and ubiquitous specter is us, the public. We are (in secret) in the know. It smells like the blood. Of puppets.

And yet, and yet is a citation, and more exactly a symbolic phrase in the language spoken in *Drums on the Dam*, which is to say the language of puppets. The language of puppets has a speaking sound different from our own. I had to learn it, apply myself. Each language has the rhythm and melody of the body that houses it.

The first versions of *Drums* committed a sizable error, of amount, of breath. The characters were speaking like you and me, too long and heavy.

I had not yet moulted, streamlined. I spoke in long and literal enjambments.

To express the state of souls, I added to every modalisation its knowing commentary. I spoke in excess instead of in silence—voila—

But in a puppet, everything hangs by a thread. The speech is an escaped kite: it says, with one swish of a beribboned tail, 'all clouds and firmament'. The thin voice is immense. A little gives everything the scale of grandeur.

– Let go of the baggage, cried Madame Li.

– I wanted to see you there, I whined.

We are gripped from birth. Letting go is an art. Don't mistake us there, the puppet on strings is not a stitch up. It is the wife of the air. It has unclinging hands. The paws of a cat more exactly, it touches but doesn't hold

répéter leur malheur inouï, car pour eux jamais de passé, le présent est leur fatalité et j'y assistais. Rien de plus naturel dans ce pays de personnages que le surnaturel. Sur l'horloge les deux baguettes tambourinent l'heure des revenances et des métamorphoses. Il est tout à fait surnaturel de rencontrer sa propre mère morte sur un chemin de campagne, de souper avec elle et de ne pas la reconnaître. En vérité le spectre le plus discret et le plus ubiquiteux c'est nous, le public. Nous sommes (dans le secret) au parfum. Ça sent le sang. De marionnettes.

Et pourtant, et pourtant est une citation, et plus exactement une locution symbole de la langue parlée des Tambours sur la Digue, c'est-à-dire la langue des marionnettes. La langue des marionnettes a son parler autre que le nôtre. J'ai dû l'apprendre, m'y faire. Chaque langue a le rythme et la mélodie du corps qui la loge.

Les premières versions de *Tambours* commettaient une erreur de quantité, de mesure, de souffle. Les personnages parlaient comme des vous-et-moi, trop long et lourd.

C'est que je n'avais pas encore déplumé, effilé. Je parlais à longues et littérales enjambées.

Pour exprimer les états d'âmes, j'ajoutais à tout modalisateur son commentaire savant. Je parlais d'abondance à la place du silence—Voilà –

Mais en marionnette tout tient à un fil. Le discours est un cerf-volant échappé: il dit, d'un coup de queue enrubannée tous les nuages et le firmament. Le ténu fait l'immense. Le petit donne toute l'envergure du grand.

– Lâche les bagages, criait Mme Li.

– Je voudrais t'y voir, piaillai-je.

Nous sommes des agrippés de naissance. Larguer est un art. Ne nous y trompons pas, la marionnette à fils n'est pas une ligotée. Elle est l'épouse de l'air. Elle a des mains décramponnées. Des pattes de chat plus exactement, elle touche mais ne tient pas. Ce qu'elle agrippe c'est le courant de l'air, les ondes des passions, seulement ce qui passe, l'émeut, la lâche. Mains décrispées, tout juste aptes à se joindre en prière.

J'écrivis: et pourtant. J'allais dérouler un rouleau de méditations philosophiques qui n'oublierait ni Montaigne ni Lévinas ni les sages tibétains. Je m'y pris. Je coupai. J'écrivis: et pourtant, et pourtant. Et j'ouvris la fenêtre. Un héron s'envola.

Les manches du Seigneur flottaient. Seigneur flottant. Monde flottant.

Le vol, le mauvais vol, la physique des âmes: le Seigneur flotte, stagne, les eaux boueuses le charrient. Il n'aura pas pris l'air.

Je peins les hésitations désastreuses. Le chancelier balloté file d'abord vers la mère, balance, revient vers le père, tournoie, repart, rate la marche de l'histoire, embrouillé de désirs jusqu'à la dislocation mortelle. Sa marionnette ne fait pas exactement le poids, fétu qui saute par dessus la réalité, refoulée de toutes parts.

on. What it holds onto is the air current, the waves of passion, only that which passes, the riot, lets it go. Hands unclenched, barely apt for joining in prayer.

I was writing: and yet. I was going to unravel a roll of philosophical meditations that would not leave out Montaigne, Levinas, nor the wise Tibetans. I take myself there. I cut. I was writing: and yet, and yet. And I open the window. A heron flies by.

The sleeves of the Master were floating. The floating Master. The floating world.

The flight, the bad flight, the physical state of souls: the Master floats, stagnates, the muddy waters were carrying him. He will not have taken in air.

I paint the disastrous hesitations. The reeling person who runs firstly towards his mother, balances, returns to his father, turns, sets off again, misses the step of the story, tangled up in desire to the point of mortal dislocation. His puppet doesn't exactly have weight, weightless one who jumps over reality, driven back from everywhere.

Duan, the daughter of the Soothsayer who is also a son/strings[5] is the clear-cut excellence of detachment. She cuts, she goes, she takes the weather/time by the horns, the head of the troupe of drummers, she regulates the rhythms, nothing makes knots, not even love, not even happiness.

She even knows how to dodge the traps of polite pathos. She dares. It is she who dares to say: The goodbyes must be brief. Goodbye.

Me, I would not have dared (to join) to do what…

Up until the first performance I had to fight myself to not be weighed down by prosthetic flourishes.

A true puppet is precise, neither round nor soft nor hazy, but a sketched explanation. It draws its feelings, their angles, their twitches, it is versatile with all accuracy. It marks the pauses. The Steward makes a decision. He goes by this step to the Seigneur.[6] Gesture, speech, the thinking gesture. At the fourth step a thought stops short, his foot in full momentum. Thought turns the step/no into its opposite. Thinking foot, a thought that goes walkabout.

The puppet walks on sticks. For the first time, we see these ordinarily invisible sticks that make us act, these others, or these authors that move us, facilitate us or make each word hard for us, each turn, each resolution. To incarnate these sticks that command us in the indecipherable person but easily perceptible to the *shite*[7] (the puppeteers), it is a stroke of genius by the

5. Cixous uses the word '*un fils*' which means 'a son' but is also a homograph of '*fils*' meaning 'strings'.

6. The 'Seigneur' is both a character in the play and the word for the Lord, as in 'Lord God and master' in common parlance.

7. The *shite* is the main actor in Noh theatre. He commonly portrays several characters

Duan la fille du Devin qui est un fils aussi, est l'excellence nette du détachement. Elle coupe, elle va, elle prend le temps par les cornes, la tête de la troupe des tambours, elle règle les rythmes, rien ne fait des noeuds même l'amour même le bonheur.

Elle sait même esquiver les pièges du pathos de politesse. Elle ose. C'est elle qui ose dire: Les adieux doivent être brefs. Adieu.

Moi je n'aurais pas osé (joindre) faire ce que ...

Jusqu'à la première représentation je devais lutter contre moi pour ne pas alourdir d'une fioriture prothétique.

Une vraie marionnette est nette: ni ronde ni molle ni floue, mais expliquée dessinée. Elle dessine ses sentiments, leurs angles, leurs à-coups, elle est versatile avec toutes les précisions. Elle marque les arrêts. L'Intendant prend une décision. Il va de ce pas chez le Seigneur. Geste, parole, le geste pense. Au quatrième pas une pensée arrête sec son pied en plein élan. La pensée renverse le pas en sens contraire. Pied pensant, pensée qui marche.

La marionnette marche aux baguettes. Pour, la première fois nous les voyons ces baguettes d'ordinaire invisibles qui nous agissent, ces autres, ou ces auteurs qui nous meuvent, nous facilitent ou nous difficilitent chaque mot, chaque tour chaque résolution. Incarner les baguettes qui nous commandent dans la personne indéchiffrable mais bien perceptible des shités (dits les manipulateurs) c'est le coup de génie du maître-maîtresse des marionnettes. D'ailleurs son génie c'est toujours cela: à force d'invocations, que paraissent à nos yeux toutes ces puissances et dominations secrètes que nul n'a jamais encore vues, depuis les Erinyes jusqu'aux machinations de l'inconscient. Les invisibles lui font reddition.

Personne, dans le public, pour s'étonner sauf de voir pour la première fois ce que tous nous sentons plus ou moins obscurément: que nous sommes des êtres singuliers pluriels cohabités cohabitants cohantés cohantants, que nous sommes de ce fait non-coïncidents avec ces nous-mêmes, toujours freinés décalés, que nous sommes conduits quand nous croyons conduire, il y a toujours plus de demains deux mains sur le volant du présent, moi-même écartée de moi-même au moment où je vais m'affirmant

notre faute et notre mérite sont partagés

nous sommes une résultante endeuillée d'une autorité souveraine. Endeuillés de nous-mêmes pour toujours, dérapeurs de notre volonté. Dès que nous voyons ces compagnons attentifs et indissociables nous (nous) reconnaissons dans ces expropriés compliqués, mais comme toujours nous voyons les baguettes dans le dos des autres, mais la poutre dans notre oeil nous ne la voyons pas.

Qui sont donc ces baguettes qui paraissent démons, ombres, jumeaux? C'est l'autre *en* moi mon traître, mon mensonge ou ma vérité, mon opérateur ou mon opératrice qui prend la décision. Notre moitié celle qui nous permet d'être innocent dans le crime donc de pouvoir vouloir tuer car c'est

master-mistress of the puppets. Elsewhere, her genius is always that: due to invocations, that appear before our eyes in all their powers and secret dominations such that no one has ever yet seen them, since the Erinyes[8] until the machinations of the unconscious. The invisible ones make him surrender.

No-one in the public to surprise except to see, for the first time, everything that we feel, more or less obscurely: that we are singular plural beings, coinhabited coinhabitants cohaunting cohaunteds, that we are, by this non-coincidental fact with ourselves, always held back moving forward, that we are driven when we believe in driving, there are always more tomorrows, two hands[9] on the wheel of the present, myself isolated from myself at the moment when I am going to assert myself

our fault and our worth are shared/split

we are a bereaved result of sovereign authority. Bereaved of ourselves forever, robbers of our volition. As soon as we see these attentive companions and inseparable ones we recognise ourselves in these complicated expropriations, but as always, we see the sticks in the backs of others but we fail to see the beam in our own eye.

So who are these sticks that make demons, shadows and twins appear? It is the other *in* me, my traitor, my lie or my truth, my operator who makes the decision. Our half, which permits us to be innocent of the crime so as to be able to want to kill because it is the other, called It's-Not-Me that substitutes for us. That which doubles us and follows us and is us. That part which loves us in the dark, the indulgent half that forgives us the misdeeds that it makes us do. And also our self-pity.

In a pine forest beside a stream where lovers were dancing their destiny I was contemplating the turns of their love. It is a waltz. They are a good six or seven or even more those two-there, they spin-turn-change as they wrap themselves around their supports, their tendrils shed, entangled. To embrace one another is their impossibility, to make an 'or' or a 'for' from puppets is very hard. We see love lose the thread, there is danger, over there are bushes of roses, armfuls of caresses, threatened by emotion, the kisses are so quickly feasting on blood, the roses scratch, everything is going to be unraveled. As in life, like life itself.

But to kill is easier, to put in pieces, to separate, we take the scissors, the blade of a knife, we cut and—

---

throughout a performance and wears a different mask for each character.

8. The Erinyes are female deities from Ancient Greek mythology.

9. Cixous plays on the homophony between 'tomorrows' and 'two hands', in French: '*demains*' and '*deux mains*'. The passage also alludes to Shakespeare's *Macbeth* Act V scene V when Macbeth, after hearing that Lady Macbeth is dead, proclaims: 'Tomorrow, and tomorrow, and tomorrow, Creeps in this petty pace from day to day'. Cixous draws a link between *demains* and *mains* in the French translation of Shakespeare—between the repeated 'tomorrow' and Lady Macbeth's blood-stained hands.

l'autre, appelé C'est-Pas-Moi qui substitue pour nous. Celle qui nous double et nous suit et nous est. Celle qui nous aime au noir, l'indulgente moitié qui nous pardonne ce qu'elle nous fait méfaire. Et aussi la pitié que nous avons pour nous-même.

Dans une épineuse forêt au bord du fleuve où des amants dansaient leur destin je contemplais les tours de leur amour. C'est une valse. Ils sont bien six ou sept ou plus encore ces deux-là, ils roulent tournent changent en s'enroulant autour de leurs supports leurs vrilles mus emmêlés. S'étreindre est leur impossibilité, faire un ou une pour des marionnettes c'est très difficile. On voit l'amour perdre le fil, il y a danger, les voilà buissons de roses, brassées de caresses, menacés par l'émoi, les baisers ont si vite fait de mordre au sang, les roses griffent, tout va tourner au démêlé. Comme dans la vie, comme dans la vie même.

Mais tuer est beaucoup plus facile, mettre en pièces, séparer, on prend des ciseaux, la lame d'un couteau, on coupe et –

Mais qui *on*? Toujours ce On qui ne connaît pas ma honte. Ce Om, cet homme cette ombre de moi.

Je n'ai pas voulu cela dit Wang Po, véridique. Je voulais tuer mais pas toi. C'est mon épée qui a fourché, dit Wang Po, et il faut le croire. L'auteur de mes actes manqués, le fauteur de mes lapsus tragiques, c'est Pasmoi. La baguette a bien dérapé, et voici que *les choses* prennent le dessus. Les Choses, ces déesses ou dieux sans visage et sans nom qui mènent le monde que nous croyons mener et nous ôtent du doute. Qui sont ces hôtes noirs qui soulèvent nos bras et nous croquent les jambes? Certes nous les nommons vingt fois par jour et les conservons inconnus, société anonyme à capital illimité. Ce sont les *Choses*. Elles peuvent faire tout et n'importe quoi sans que nous y engagions notre responsabilité. Et pourtant. Sans nous elles ne sont pas. Elles sont notre face cachée montrée. Et notre face nue est bien noire. Peinte en voile noir par notre aveuglement forcené. C'est à Elles que la marionnette du Seigneur assigne le cours des événements une fois son fil de téléphone de sa main coupé.

Les Choses sont décidées. Ma main a signé.

Les Seigneurs marionnettes se regardent jouées. Actionnées. Jouets curieux de leur fonctionnement décapité. Ce n'est pas cela ce que le *je* voulais, mais l'autre je l'a fait. La Non-coïncidence syncopée de son rapport à soi aura été la dernière horlogerie observée par le Chef de l'Etat.

Qu'il y a un autre *ici* voilà ce que les Tambours auront fait paraître, en tapant sur la peau de la scène en cadence. Ici est divisé en cet ici et l'autre, ou bien Ici se divise en icis, entre y et ci ou si, qui sait. Cette complexicité on peut en jouer mais on en est aussi joué. On reconnaît sans peine la complexe complicité du Mentir d'Etat. La non-icité et la non-moiité n'empêchent pas, au contraire, l'exercice de l'autoricité, sur toutes les autres marionnettes. La dé/possession est un pouvoir masqué.

But who is *we*? Always this We that doesn't know my shame. This Om, this man[10] this shadow of me.

I didn't want that, said Wang Po, truthfully. I wanted to kill but not you. It is my sword that slipped, said Wang Po, and you must believe it. Lacking an author to my acts, the one to blame for my tragic lapses, is Notme. The stick skidded and thus *things* get the upper hand. Things, these goddesses or gods without face and without name that lead the world, the world that we believe we lead, and remove all doubt from us. Who are these black hosts who lift up our arms and crunch our knees? Certainly we name them twenty times a day and keep them unknown, anonymous society with unlimited capital. These are *Things*. They can do everything and anything without demanding responsibility from us. And yet. Without us, they don't exist. They are our hidden face revealed. And our naked face is very black. Painted in a black veil by our deranged blindness. It is to Them that the puppet of the Seigneur assigns the course of events once from the cut telephone line of his hand.

Things are decided. My hand signaled.

The Seigneur puppets watch one another being played. Put into action. Curious toys of their decapitated operation. It is not that the *I* wanted, but the other I did it. The syncopated Non-coincidence of its relation to self will have been the last watchmaking seen by the head of state.

There is an other/another *here* that the Drummers will make appear, by tapping on the skin of the stage in rhythm. Here is divided into this here and the other, or the Here divides into heres, between there and this or if, who knows. One can play this complexicity[11] but one is also played somewhat. We recognise, without difficulty, the complex complicity of the Liar of the State. The non-here-ness and the non-me-ness don't stop, on the contrary, the exercising of author-here-ness/authorised-ness, on all the other puppets. The dis/possession is a disguised power.

What is a Face? Over there we see it clearly. A Face is a borrowing. What is my Body? My body is in the body of someone else. Or perhaps it is my head. Who plays the Seigneur? asked a spectator. It's Madame Li who plays the Seigneur, I say. And yet. What if it was the nephew Hun who played him. But no. It is the Seigneur who plays Hun so that Hun can play him. But Hun has entered Wang Po by some flaw or fissure. Often we catch the strike of the other stick.

In the Sewing, I see a naked puppet. The naked breast of Duan. Suddenly I *see*, for the first time, Nakedness. I had never seen it before. As

10. Cixous plays on the homophony between 'Om' and 'man', in French: '*Om*' and '*homme*'.

11. The translation is faithful to Cixous's neologism. '*Complexicité*' is a neologism formed from the adverb '*complex*' and the noun '*cité*' and the sound of '*complicité*', hence drawing together notions of complexity, place (the city), a legal summons, citation and complicity.

Qu'est-ce qu'un Visage? Alors là on le voit bien. Un Visage est un emprunt. Qu'est-ce que mon Corps? Mon corps est dans le corps de quelqu'un d'autre. Ou bien c'est ma tête. Qui joue le Seigneur? demandait un spectateur. C'est Mme Li qui joue le Seigneur, dis-je. Et pourtant. Si c'était le neveu Hun qui le jouait? Mais non. C'est le Seigneur qui joue Hun pour que Hun le joue. Valse. Mais Hun est entré dans Wang Po par quelque faille ou fente. C'est que souvent on attrape un coup de l'autre baguette.

Dans la Couture, je vois une marionnette nue. Le sein nu de Duan. Soudain je *vois* pour la première fois la Nudité. Je ne l'avais jamais vue. Comme si j'avais vu le jour que l'on ne voit pas. La nudité de la marionnette est la seule nudité visible. Je vois le nu, en voile et en mousse, le sein peint. La nudité est de voile peint. Il n'y a pas plus nu qu'un sein en voile dévoilé. C'est par enchantement.

Et, de même, une marionnette meurt nette, jamais on n'aura vu de tels arrêts de mort. Voyez la mort du Chancelier: elle saisit l'homme en plein élan, et le fauche en vol. Je suis fauché meurt-il.—Oui, la voilà retrouvée la vérité antique de la mort, celle que l'on représentait avec des ciseaux ou une faux, avec raison. De nos jours nous la pallions, nous l'étirons, nous la couvrons d'un manteau de drap blanc et flou, nous ne voulons plus en voir le tranchant, la lame, nous ne supportons plus d'être la marionnette du temps que nous sommes pourtant. La vérité c'est ça: d'un instant à l'autre en pleine action un grand coup de baguette dans la gorge dans le flanc, pas de verbe, une phrase nominale barrée. Arrêt. C'est comme l'oiseau abattu en plein vol. Le vol lui-même est saisi, percé, métamorphosé en pierre. Chute. C'est fait. On meurt d'un coup d'aile. On n'a même pas le temps de mourir lorsqu'on est créature à fil. D'un coup: supprimé. Il n'y a pas de fin. C'est terrible, cette privation des consolations ultimes. Et pas de dernier mot.

'Coups de baguettes' in Au Théâtre au cinéma au féminin, textes réunis et présentés par Mireille CALLE-GRUBER et Hélène CIXOUS, Paris, L'Harmattan, 2001, pp. 44-51

if I had seen the day that one does not see. The nakedness of the puppet is the only visible nudity. I see it naked, veiled and in foam, the painted breast. Nudity is a painted veil. There is nothing more naked than a veiled breast unveiled. It is by magic.

And, even so, a puppet, fully dead, never has one seen such a finality of death. Look at the death of the Chancellor: it seizes the man in full momentum, and mows him down in flight. I am a dead loss he dies.—Yes, thus rediscovered of the ancient truth of death, that which we represented with scissors or a scythe, with reason. These days we overcome it, we stretch it, we cover it with a coat made of white and fuzzy material, we no longer want to see the cutting edge, the tear, we can no longer put up with being the puppet of time that we nevertheless are. The truth is that: from one moment to the next, in the middle of taking action, a big strike of the stick in the throat, in the flank, no verb, a nominal sentence crossed out. Stop. It's like a bird shot down in mid-flight. The flight itself is seized, perforated, metamorphosed into a rock. Fall. It is done. We die in the flap of a wing/blink of an eye. We don't even have time to die when we are creatures on strings. In one blow/suddenly: suppressed. There is no end. It is terrible, this deprivation of ultimate consolations. And no last word.

'Striking Sticks' was first published in French in Au Théâtre au cinéma au feminine *(texts complied by Mireille Calle-Gruber and Hélène Cixous), Paris, Harmattan, 2001, pp. 44-51*

Theatre Surprised by Puppets

The Spirited Author

'What if you were writing a play that would have been written by the poet Hsi-Xhou, an ancient play, that was performed long ago—sometimes by puppets, sometimes by female actors playing all the parts, sometimes by men playing all the parts, depending on whether the play was performed in such and such a kingdom under such and such a law and prohibitions?'

Thus said the director one day to the author.

So the author set about writing the play that had been written by her ancient predecessor and master, the poet Hsi-Xhou.

In the daytime, in the year 1998, the author was studying ancient texts such as those that had been brought to us when they went up the Silk Road and the Stage Road, from Japan, China, Korea, India, with jewelry, molten glass, musical instruments, banners, brushes, engravings. Brought back, set down in scholarly volumes, illustrated and taught.

At night time, the master puppeteer Hsi-Xhou arrived and gets the imagination of the author-puppet moving, pulling on all the strings.

If ever there was a text dictated and the author spirited away, this was it. This is such a play, transmitted as never before.

The playwright always dreams of being the skin of the stage, tight like silk on a drum, a sensitive stage upon which pass the characters of the play with puppet steps.

In brushing against the mental skin, those that pass by imprint their emotions, their hastes, their fevers. The playwright dreams of being this manuscript impregnated by the stamping of characters.

In the dream, the moved author is transformed and stripped[1] as the marvelously agitated puppet: the play comes to rest on the soul of her body with the precise lightnesses and shimmering of dragonflies and other butterfly-psyches. All that is left to do is faithfully restore the dream.

---

1. Cixous creates a homophony between 'ému' and '*mu*' and '*mue*' that is lost in the translation 'moved' 'transformed' and 'stripped'.

Le Théâtre surpris par les marionnettes

L'auteur soufflé

'Si tu écrivais une pièce qui aurait été écrite par le poète Hsi-Xhou, une pièce ancienne, qui fut jouée autrefois tantôt par des marionnettes, tantôt par des acteurs qui tantôt étaient des femmes jouant tous les rôles, tantôt étaient des hommes jouant tous les rôles, selon que la pièce était représentée dans tel royaume sous telle loi et tel interdit?'

Voilà ce que le metteur en scène dit un jour à l'auteur.

Alors l'auteur se mit à écrire la pièce qui avait été écrite par son antique prédécesseur et maître le poète Hsi-Xhou.

Le jour, pendant l'année 1998, l'auteur étudiait les textes anciens tels qu'ils nous ont été rapportés en remontant la route de la Soie et de la Scène depuis le Japon, la Chine, la Corée, l'Inde, avec bijoux, pâtes de verre, instruments de musique, bannières, pinceaux, estampes. Rapportés, déposés dans des volumes érudits, illustrés et enseignés.

La nuit, arrivait le maître marionnettiste Hsi-Xhou et il mettait en branle l'imagination de l'auteur-marionnette, en tirant sur tous les fils.

Si jamais il y eut texte dicté et auteur soufflé ce fut bien en ce cas. Ceci est donc une pièce transmise comme jamais encore.

L'auteur de théâtre rêve toujours d'être la peau du plateau tendue comme la soie d'un tambour, plateau sensible sur lequel passent à pas de marionnettes les personnages de la pièce.

En effleurant la peau mentale, les passants impriment leurs émotions, leurs hâtes, leurs fièvres. L'auteur de théâtre rêve d'être ce manuscrit imprégné par le piétinement des personnages.

En rêve, l'auteur ému est mu, et mue en marionnette merveilleusement agie: la pièce vient se poser sur l'âme de son corps avec des légèretés précises et chatoyées de libellules et autres papillons-psychés. Il n'a plus qu'à la restituer fidèlement.

Mais ceci, c'est le rêve de l'auteur.

Réveillée, c'est une autre affaire: l'auteur, debout, est traversée par les

But this, this is the dream of the author.

Woken up, it's quite another story: the author, standing, is crossed over by the large monumental texts that architexturise[2] her memory, with long and vast occidental dialogues, and it's not at all the nocturnal veils, nor the sliding step of Noh theatre.

So the author returned to the workshop to look among the rolls of texts, the tightly braided and very light fabric in which to cut out these characters that came from very far away, from the origins of theatre itself. The text needs to be almost transparent, and yet, of an extreme and dense solidity, a nothing in order to carry the weight of humanity.

Writing is comparable to the Korean couture that retains the translucent fabric by a triple fold so tightly woven that it vanishes: from rigour comes flexibility.

The Flood

For all eternity, from the beginning of the beginning and for ending a world, each Summer, and yet, despite the sediments of memory, we always say that the flood is the worst, and surely it is The Worst. In 2297 before our era, the Yellow River and the Blue River mixed their waters which rose above the mountain peaks and no-one survived to tell the tale.

The Emperors constructed piers nine times the size of man. But the Empire was suffering from internal floods against which we constructed no piers.

There is the word Inundation that we pronounce either with fear or indifference.

Because of saying the words in advance: water water water water, we finish by forgetting the horror. That is how it arrives.

We can replace the word 'water' with the word 'war' or another.

The Puppets

The author, the director, the actors, the stage, the dykes, the palace, the boat, the sheets of rain… everything is a puppet.

Everything is agitated. Each one is put into movement by its puppeteer. All the puppet receives are the motions transmitted by the gentle shocks of the puppeteer. There is nothing more animated, more carefully raised from inertia to emotion than a creature engineered by its mechanic: the heart beats all the way into the knees, the whole body articulates a feeling, from the elbow to the heel, the sentence of the soul runs and manifests itself.

The puppet is inside, it is the sublime spirit of the puppet. The

2 The translation is faithful to Cixous neologism '*architectent*' that turns the noun '*l'architecture*' into a verb and that creates a rhythm and assonance with the word '*textes*' or 'texts' that precedes it.

grands textes monumentaux qui architectent sa mémoire, par les longs et vastes dialogues occidentaux, et ce n'est pas du tout les voiles nocturnes, ni le pas glissé du nô.

Alors, l'auteur est retournée à l'atelier chercher parmi les rouleaux des textes le tissu tressé serré et très léger dans lequel tailler ces personnages venus de très loin, des origines mêmes du théâtre. Il faut un texte presque transparent et cependant d'une extrême et dense solidité, un rien pour porter le poids de l'humanité.

L'écriture est comparable à la couture coréenne qui retient le tissu translucide par un triple pli si serré qu'il va jusqu'à s'effacer: de la rigueur sort la souplesse.

L'inondation

De toute éternité, au commencement du commencement et pour finir un monde, chaque été, et cependant, malgré les sédiments de la mémoire, l'inondation on dit toujours que c'est la pire, et sûrement c'est La Pire. En 2297 avant notre ère, le Fleuve Jaune et le Fleuve Bleu mêlèrent leurs eaux qui montèrent jusque pardessus les têtes des montagnes et personne ne survécut pour raconter ce déluge.

Les Empereurs élevèrent des jetées de neuf fois la taille d'un homme. Mais l'Empire souffrait d'inondations intestines contre lesquelles on n'élevait point de jetées.

Il y a le mot Inondation que l'on prononce ou avec crainte, ou avec indifférence.

A force de dire à l'avance les mots: l'eau l'eau l'eau l'eau, on finit par oublier l'horreur.

C'est alors qu'elle arrive.

On peut remplacer le mot l'eau par le mot guerre ou un autre.

Les marionettes

L'auteur, le metteur en scène, les acteurs, le plateau, les digues, le palais, le bateau, les rideaux de pluie… tout est marionnette.

Tous sont agis. Chacun est mis en mouvement par son marionnettiste. Toute la marionnette reçoit les motions transmises par les légérissimes secousses du marionnettiste. Il n'y a pas plus animé, plus minutieusement soulevé depuis l'inertie jusqu'à l'émotion qu'une créature machinée par son mécanicien: le cœur bat jusque dans les genoux, tout le corps articule un sentiment, du coude au talon, la phrase de l'âme court et se manifeste.

Le marionnettiste est dedans, il est l'esprit sublime de la marionnette. La marionnette accomplie obéit absolument à son marionnettiste.

Elle ne connaît pas le doute, elle ne freine ni ne résiste.

Elle acquiesce. Elle se laisse. Elle est commandée, elle est accordée. Elle

accomplished puppet absolutely obeys its puppeteer.

It doesn't know doubt, it doesn't slow down nor resist.

It acquiesces. It abandons itself. It is commanded, it is amenable. It doesn't answer back. It doesn't plant itself in front of the director with its fists on its hips. It doesn't walk the earth tapping the ground with its foot. It has no authority.

It doesn't weigh down its feet. It advances on the floor—puppet who unrolls its transparent carpet two inches above the anchored ground. It doesn't have its feet on the ground, but just above it. Its breathing lifts it up.

The Face of the puppet is immobile. Innumerable expressions of our desires pass through this mirror. The Face is immobile, the space which is no larger.

Ecstasy seizes the Face upon which we catch a glimpse of the immensity of the Gods.

The director asks the actor for the puppet. The actors must avoid the pedestal, noise, commentary, realism, heavy objects, the floor, images—supports—props. Upon attaining purity, the limbs will move and not ideas. The puppet is suspended. The actor is suspended for the benefit of action.

The director asks the actor to be two. Don't go faster than what you can as two. Time in double time: order and execution. Unfold: to explain. The body of the puppet explains itself. What is more manifest and more theatrical than a puppet in the process of playing a character?

The puppet is the exteriorisation of the interior puppet that we are. Inside we are multiple, complicated, articulated beings. The social people that we are obliged to be are identifiable and unreadable simplifications, opaque screens, shields.

The puppet is an open book. The puppet is absolutely innocent, no matter what deeds or misdeeds it has done: it is shown, readable to the naked eye. It is nothing more than consent.

It lets everything be done, everything imprinted, it is so abandoned to the motilities and movements of its puppeteer that it no longer bangs at the edges, it does not moor at rigid mast.

The Secret is in the Imbalance

It does not conceal our essential throwing of the dice.

Here is the human being: unstable, uncertain, exposed to mental storms and worldly upheaval, never assured, battling all its life against the hostile elements that one creates and that one flees.

Life, as it is seen from the seat of the spectator, is a theatrical play with which we try in vain to familiarise ourselves, but it remains at the mercy of unexpected events of which we are the sorcerer-apprentices. We cause what

ne discute pas. Elle ne se plante pas en face du metteur en scène avec les poings sur les hanches. Elle ne marche pas sur terre en tapant le sol du pied. Elle n'a aucune autorité.

Elle ne fait pas peser son poids. Elle avance sur un sol—marionnette qui déroule son tapis transparent à deux pouces au-dessus du sol ancré. Elle n'a pas les pieds sur terre mais juste au-dessus. Sa respiration la soulève.

Le Visage de la marionnette est immobile. Sur ce miroir passent les innombrables expressions de nos passions. Le Visage immobile, l'espace n'en est que plus grand.

C'est à l'extase qui saisit le Visage qu'on aperçoit l'immensité des Dieux.

Le metteur en scène demande à l'acteur la marionnette. L'acteur doit ôter le socle, le bruit, le commentaire, le réalisme, les objets lourds, le sol, les images—supports—soutiens. Une fois atteinte la pureté, ce qui bougera ce sont les membres et non les idées. La marionnette est en suspension. L'acteur est suspendu au profit de l'agi.

Le metteur en scène demande à l'acteur d'être deux. Ne va pas plus vite que ce que tu peux faire en étant deux. Temps à deux temps: ordre et exécution. Déplier: expliquer. Le corps de la marionnette s'explique. Quoi de plus manifeste donc de plus théâtral qu'une marionnette en train de jouer un personnage?

La marionnette est extériorisation de la marionnette intérieure que nous sommes. Intérieurement nous sommes des êtres démultipliés, compliqués, articulés. Les personnes sociales que nous nous obligeons d'être sont des simplifications identificatoires et illisibles, des écrans opaques, des boucliers.

La marionnette est un livre ouvert. La marionnette est innocente absolument, quels que soient ses faits ou méfaits: elle est montrée, lisible à l'œil nu. Elle n'est qu'aveu.

Elle se laisse tellement faire, tellement imprimer, elle est si abandonnée aux mobiles et mouvements de son marionnettiste, qu'elle ne cogne plus aux limites, elle ne s'amarre pas aux rigides mât.

Le secret est dans le déséquilibre

Elle ne dissimule pas notre essentielle chancelance.

Voilà l'être humain: instable, incertain, soumis aux intempéries mentales et mondiales, jamais assuré, débattant toute sa vie contre les éléments hostiles que l'on suscite et que l'on fuit.

La vie vue depuis le banc du spectateur, est une pièce de théâtre qui, ayant beau nous être familière, reste à la merci des événements inattendus dont nous sommes les apprentis-sorciers. Nous causons ce que nous espérons ne jamais voir arriver. Et même la mort. Nous ne connaissons qu'elle. Et pourtant, quelle surprise!

Voyez la marionnette du Seigneur: totalement écaillée, vieille, fragile,

we hope to never see happen. And even death. We know only that. And yet, what a surprise!

See the puppet of the Seigneur: completely flaking, old, fragile, shaking. 'Each time we perform this show, we are more and more careful because it has already been repaired several times', remarks the director. To repair. To repair. The human being damages and repairs, until the day when the irreparable enters—all of a sudden—and it's the play, its end and its beginning.

Everything is held by a thread, isn't it? The blows dealt by fate, unintentionally, we carry them.

The puppet of the Seigneur is shaking. The word 'shaking', still a puppet! Which is to say, a metaphor. Several years ago, an old goat woke up in the Seigneur. We don't see it but we feel it and listen to it. Obstinate, trembling, pigheaded, capricious, kicking out its elegant but scaled hooves.

The puppet, the soul, the genius, the ambiguous gender of the puppet wins out, spreads through the river's course like flowing/fluent language.

The spirit of indecision. The swaying. Why do we have two legs if not to think of one foot on top of the other. A play filled with puppets represents the truth that society would like us to deny: at what point do we go backwards in advancing, and in threatening we flee and in fleeing we threaten, the back is our other face, and from one moment to the next we can change our destiny, choice, faith, faithfulness, gender, direction, parties and even sex!

What remains unchangeable is sadness.

The Puppet is Naked

Everything about this creature is naked: the eyes, the hair, the costume, the ankle, the gait.

Naked? Evident, exposed. Tiny. Fragile. Breakable. Angular. Solid but worn. It had already been played a lot. We feel that they have been lived through a lot, the puppets, and well-travelled.

Suddenly, we feel like crying out that it is us: when the figure is so eternal and the body so fragile that it cannot tense up without breaking, it is us, the human creature surrounded by the winds of time, miniscule in the History of Forces and Powers, shrunk before the enormity of a flood, confronted by very powerful cosmic things, but, by the same token, atom in the immensity and cosmic particle.

There is nothing greater than the miniscule creature, against whose smallness all outbursts are measured.

The Rhythm of the Puppet

Be two-but-one. One, but inhabited. Make the crossing, draw-it. A puppet enters. Stop. Go forward. No jerking. But the precise unfolding, the

chevrotante. 'Chaque fois qu'on joue ce spectacle, on fait encore plus attention parce qu'elle a déjà été réparée plusieurs fois' remarque le metteur en scène. Réparer. Réparer. L'être humain endommage et répare, jusqu'au jour où l'irréparable entre—tout d'un coup—et c'est la pièce, sa fin et son commencement.

Tout tient toujours à un fil, n'est-ce pas? Les coups du sort, sans faire exprès, nous les portons.

La marionnette du Seigneur est chevrotante. Le mot 'chevrotante', encore une marionnette! C'est-à-dire une métaphore. Il y a quelques années, une vieille chèvre s'est réveillée dans le Seigneur. On ne la voit pas mais on la sent et on l'entend. Obstinée, tremblante, entêtée, capricieuse, ruant de ses sabots élégants mais écaillés.

La marionnette, l'esprit, le génie, le genre ambigu de la marionnette gagne, se répand dans le cours du fleuve comme dans le langage courant.

L'esprit d'indécision. Le balancement. Pourquoi avons-nous deux jambes sinon pour penser d'un pied sur l'autre. Une pièce peuplée de marionnettes joue la vérité que dans la société nous voudrions dénier: à quel point nous reculons en avançant, et en menaçant nous fuyons et en fuyant nous menaçons, le dos est notre autre face, et d'un instant à l'autre nous pouvons changer de destin, de choix, de foi, de fidélité, de genre, de direction, de parti et même de sexe!

Ce qui demeure inchangeable c'est la douleur.

La marionnette est nue

Tout de cette créature est nu: les yeux, les cheveux, le costume, la cheville, la démarche.

Nue? Evidente, exposée. Toute petite. Fragile. Cassable. Anguleuse. Solide mais usagée. Elle a été beaucoup jouée déjà. On sent qu'elles ont beaucoup été vécues, les marionnettes, et beaucoup voyagées.

Soudain, nous sentons à pleurer que c'est nous: quand la figure est si éternelle et le corps si fragile qu'il ne peut pas se crisper sans se briser, c'est nous, la créature humaine environnée par les vents du temps, minuscule dans l'Histoire des Forces et des Pouvoirs, rétrécie devant la géance d'une inondation, confrontée aux choses cosmiques très puissantes mais, par là même, atome dans l'immense et parcelle cosmique.

Rien de plus grand que l'infime créature, à la petitesse de qui se mesurent tous les déchaînements.

Rythme de la marionnette

Sois deux-mais-une. Une, mais habitée. Fais le passage, dessine-le. Une marionnette entre. Arrête. Avance. Pas de saccade. Mais le déroulé précis, l'exactitude de la danse. Une marionnette qui fait dix choses à la fois

exactitude of the dance. A puppet who does ten things at once muddles everything up and loses the puppet.

Be two: it is the same as writing. The puppet writes with time, in full intervals, in (invisible) whites, separating and tying together the regular full stops, the sentences, the lines, the bonds of passion, drawing the space from which will burst forth the shout, the crisis, the access, disjoining, cutting, flawless painting, for that sudden outburst in tension, spark or light, like the jump of the *shité* in Noh. Like the leap of the cat crouching for a long time in the vibrating body and only letting fly when it is mature.

Thus we see the boatman, reached by the blow of dishonour, running around the dykes like a gutter cat, holding the head of the puppet between his hands. We see that the soul of the boatman is this gutter cat. And on his immobile face, we believe we see, we see, a scrolling through of all the great tragic grimaces painted on the masks of silent films. Mirage, magic, miracle, through puppetisation.

Everything will have been de-re-composed and transposed, as if soaked in the dyes of humanity's essence, hair transposed, dyed like a puppet, skin, gesture, breathing, voice.

The voice! Ah! This is what gave us the most string to twist again. It is the voice that is the foreigner in the puppet. Poignant mystery of this creature composed of two spread out beings, the body and the voice that came from outside, came from the singer sitting on the side, impassive, who lends it. As if one needed to be two in order to express the enormity of the interior combat. From now on in this theatre, the puppet and its puppeteer will have been played by a single person in the end. It's the actress or actor who has to lend her/his foreign/strange voice to the puppet to which the actress actor gives their body. And for that, you will have had to renounce your voice, that which is the most inextricated within you, that which you renounce with the most difficulty, and go to look for one, entirely other, in the vocal music of the puppets. Even the breath, you transpose it and you blow the music of voice into the throat of the puppet—puppet, of which the flesh, the timbre, the volume, are your creation.

To be a puppet is very tiring: it requires being both mother and child, double childbirth, from scene to scene.

The Horizon in Silk

To the puppets who worry about it, the world responds here in prophetic silks: they are twenty-two skies that open and fall shaking, all overrun by the imminence of catastrophes. Clouds, messages, peaks, promised terrors, extending their living fabric above the small, stubborn and anxious creatures.

Rare are the puppets who lift their head looking to scrutinise the consequences. For the most part, they are lazy like us, and impatient like us, they

brouillonne et perd la marionnette.

Sois deux: c'est l'écriture même. La marionnette écrit avec des temps, des intervalles nets, des blancs (invisibles), séparant et liant par des points réguliers les phases, les traits, les bonds des passions, dessinant l'espace d'où jaillira le cri, la crise, l'accès, disjoignant, coupant, peignant sans bavure, pour que soudain éclate dans la tension, l'étincelle ou l'éclair, comme le bond du shité dans le nô. Comme le bond du chat se ramasse longuement dans le corps vibrant et ne se décoche que lorsqu'il est mûr.

On voit alors le batelier, atteint par le coup du déshonneur, courir comme un chat de gouttière autour des digues, se tenant la tête entre les mains de marionnette. On voit que l'âme du batelier est ce chat de gouttière. Et sur son visage immobile, on croit voir, on voit, défiler toutes les grandes grimaces tragiques peintes sur les masques des films muets. Mirage, magie, miracle, par marionnettisation.

Tout aura été dé-re-composé et transposé, comme trempé dans la teinture humaine essentielle, le cheveu transposé, teint en marionnette, la peau, le geste, la respiration, la voix.

La voix! Ah! C'est elle qui nous a donné le plus de fil à retordre. C'est qu'elle est l'étrangère dans la marionnette. Mystère poignant de cette créature composée de deux êtres éloignés, le corps et sa voix venue du dehors, venue du chanteur assis sur le côté, impassible, et qui la prête. Comme s'il fallait être deux pour exprimer l'énormité du combat intérieur. Or voici que dans ce théâtre la marionnette et son marionnettiste auront finalement été joués par une seule personne. C'est l'actrice ou l'acteur qui doit prêter sa voix étrangère à la marionnette à laquelle l'actrice acteur donne son corps. Et pour cela, tu auras dû renoncer à ta voix, ce qu'il y a en toi de plus indissocié, ce à quoi tu renonces le plus difficilement, et aller en chercher une, toute autre, dans la musique vocale des marionnettes. Même le souffle, tu le transposes et tu insuffles dans la gorge de la marionnette une musique de voix—marionnette, dont la chair, le timbre, le volume sont ta création.

Etre une marionnette c'est très fatigant: il s'agit de faire la mère et l'enfant, double accouchement, de scène en scène.

L'horizon en soie

Aux marionnettes qui l'inquiètent, le monde répond ici en soies prophétiques: ils sont vingt-deux les cieux qui s'ouvrent et tombent en frissonnant, tout parcourus par les imminences des catastrophes. Nuages, messages, cimes, terreurs promises, étendant leur tissu vivant au-dessus des petites créatures têtues et angoissées.

Rares sont les marionnettes qui lèvent la tête en cherchant à scruter les conséquences. Pour la plupart, elles sont paresseuses, comme nous, et comme nous impatientes, elles préfèrent ne pas tenir le compte de leurs actes. Mais

prefer not to take their actions into account. But the spectators see the trembling weather that changes behind the inhabitants of the City. In vain the book of the sky unfurls its magnificent warnings.

However, below in the workshop, the mistress of indigo, with her fellow artists, has done everything to be able to listen to the fateful messages. Lopsided on the sloping sky, you must see them listening to the nuances, dye, dip, repaint, talk about greys, golds, crimsons, trembling with delicate fervour, hoping that certain ones among them will receive the text of the message spread in silk. Silk also has a voice that comes from far away. Ah! If only we were listening.

For the Ground, Music

A floating world, piping music. One must imagine, says the musician, the relationships that have not yet existed, and verbs that say pictures that are practically impossible: to listen to an image, to look at a sound.

It's also that music plays itself and goes from self or from silk, seeping, listening, escaping.[3] Lengthening the gait of the puppet, carrying, without effort, the weight of that which doesn't rest, accompanying without holding back, never was it such a mother, music: it goes, asking itself if there exists a rhythm that is not square but flowing, and it is exactly from this questioning that it surges, keeping itself from imposing and simultaneously from leaving everything to chance.

This music here lends an ear, listens to the hesitations of the puppet, translates them into a polyphony, then, upon turning the soul, changes rhythm, obeying the spiritual gasps, receives and returns the variations of emotion. Music is also broken and raised from one shore of continents to the other, having only the fluctuations of drama as its laws.

With a gifted step, it paints with candour, without hesitation, with elegance, meticulousness, violence, serenity, particularly submissive to surprise.

Such is what moves forward without ever returning to the strong weather/temporal moment, that which doesn't hurry, doesn't follow the urgency of staccato, is without doubt the music of grace, a (force) vigour without spine that accords in counterpoint (with the great bell), with the interior pulsation of the puppet.

'Le théâtre surpris par les marionnettes' was first published in French in Tambours sur la digue, sous forme de pièce ancienne pour marionnettes jouée par des acteurs, *Théâtre du Soleil, 1999, pp. 115-124*

3. Cixous creates assonance and alliteration between the words 'va de soi ou de soie, s'écoulant s'écoutant s'échapper' that is somewhat lost in the translation 'from self or from silk, seeping, listening, escaping'.

les spectateurs voient trembler le temps qui s'altère derrière les habitants de la Ville. En vain le livre du ciel déploie ses somptueux avertissements.

Cependant en bas dans l'atelier, la maîtresse de l'indigo a tout fait, avec ses compagnons artistes, pour faire entendre les messages fatidiques. Penchés sur le ciel couché, il faut les voir écouter les nuances, teindre, tremper, repeindre, faire parler les gris, les ors, les pourpres, trembler de ferveur délicate, espérer que quelques-uns recevront le texte du message répandu dans la soie. La soie a aussi sa voix venue des lointains. Ah! si on l'écoutait.

Pour sol, la musique

A monde flottant, musique fluée. Il faut imaginer, dit le musicien, des relations qui n'ont pas encore existé, et des verbes pour dire des figures presque impossibles: écouter une image, regarder un son.

C'est que la musique aussi joue d'elle-même et va de soi ou de soie, s'écoulant s'écoutant s'échapper. Longeant le pas de la marionnette, portant sans effort le poids de celle qui ne se pose pas, accompagnant sans retenir, jamais elle ne fut aussi mère, la musique: elle va se demandant si ça existe un rythme qui n'est pas carré mais flué, et c'est justement de ce questionnement qu'elle surgit, se gardant d'imposer et se gardant simultanément de laisser aller au hasard.

Cette musique-là prête l'oreille, écoute les hésitations de la marionnette, les traduit en une polyphonie, puis, au tournant de l'âme, change de rythme, obéissant aux halètements spirituels, reçoit et rend les variations de l'émotion. La musique aussi est mue et soulevée d'une rive à l'autre des continents, n'ayant pour lois que les fluctuations du drame.

A pas de don elle peint avec franchise, sans hésitation, avec élégance, minutie, violence, sérénité, pointilleusement soumise à la surprise.

Alors ce qui s'avance sans jamais retourner au temps fort, ce qui ne presse pas, ne talonne pas dans l'urgence du staccato, c'est sans doute la musique de la grâce, une (force) vigueur sans arête qui s'accorde en contrepoint (au bourdon) à la pulsation intérieure de la marionnette.

'Le théâtre surpris par les marionnettes', in Tambours sur la digue, sous forme de pièce ancienne pour marionnettes jouée par des acteurs, *Théâtre du Soleil, 1999, pp. 115-124*

And Suddenly Nights of Awakening

The play: *And Suddenly Nights of Awakening*
Creators: The Théâtre du Soleil
First performed: 26 December 1997 at the Cartoucherie of Vincennes, Paris
Director: Ariane Mnouchkine
Collective Creation: with Hélène Cixous
Music: Jean-Jacques Lemêtre
Set: Guy-Claude François
Masks: Erhard Stiefel
Paintings: Danièle Heusslein-Gire
Costumes: Nathalie Thomas and Marie-Hélène Bouvet

Synopsis: *And Suddenly Nights of Awakening* addresses the theme of militarism and the Chinese oppression of Tibet. A Tibetan delegation occupies the theatre, protesting against the French government selling aircraft to China. The plot of the play was inspired by the occupation of foreigners in the Church of Saint-Bernard, Paris, as well as at the Cartoucherie, which housed the protests against French immigration policies under the government of President Jacques Chirac. The play considers the obstacles to Tibetan independence and the difficulties encountered by aid organisations in their attempts to improve the plight of Tibetans. The performance featured a mixture of Commedia dell'arte and Tibetan choreography with an emphasis on the diaspora of the Tibetan people in the world and the complex political relations between East and West.

Résumé de la pièce: *Et soudain des nuits d'éveil* aborde le theme du militantisme et de l'oppression chinoise au Tibet. Une délégation thibétaine occupe un théâtre, protestant contre la vente d'avions de la France à la Chine. Le scenario de la pièce a notamment été inspiré par l'occupation des étrangers en situation irrégulière de l'Église Saint-Bernard, ainsi qu'à la Cartoucherie, qui a donné lieu, à Paris, aux manifestations contre la politique d'immigration menée en France sous le gouvernement de Jacques Chirac. La pièce montre les obstacles à l'indépendance tibétaine et les difficultés pour les organisations d'aide à améliorer les conditions des Tibétains. Le spectacle qui mèle commedia dell'arte et danses tibétaines met l'accent sur la diaspora tibétaine à travers le monde, en soulignant les relations politiques complexes entre l'Est et l'Ouest.

A Moment of Conversion

From the outside, from the exterior world, from the stage of the world, the 'World Stage' that Shakespeare spoke to us about, look what arrives in theatre, a fragment of wandering people, whipped by the violent Chinese storm. The tribe enters quickly and gets under cover.

Thus it is that the theatre, this one, (or perhaps another), no longer makes theatre, no longer even thinks of it. There is urgency: the threat of death, exile, the annihilation that accompanies the Tibetan people has come to camp out on our doorstep. Imminence mobilises us. Suddenly we have the pain of a whole people before our eyes, who, up until yesterday we were thousands of kilometres from our awareness. As soon as all the roles revolt against themselves: theatre is no longer the place of representations. So it becomes the house of the present. And what a present! A tense present, fragile, threatened by the interruption of mortality.

We smell time. Days are granted one by one, like those of condemned prisoners. It's because the Tibetans who were taken in dared to place a tough bet—on the understanding or the spirit of justice.

From their provisionary ark, they throw an insistent call for recognition at the indifferent nation states of the world: 'Admit finally, once and for all, that Tibet exists'.

The great political ear pretends to be deaf, of course.

Each section of every camp, tenacious, stands its ground. The war is wearing out. It might persist for a long time. But it cannot continue eternally. The end approaches.

However, inside, under the welcoming roof structure, we live. It is this life, rapidly improvised, that we recount. It is neither more nor less extraordinary than those improvised survivals that we dreamed of as children, since Robinson Crusoe. We patch together, we return to the nomadic experience. As if we were under the tent. Or in a besieged citadel. We know the problems of supplies. We wait.

We wait. We despair/hope for.

All that without heroism. There is neither tenor nor diva. People. Us you.

Un moment de conversion

Du dehors, du monde extérieur, de la scène du monde, le 'World Stage' dont nous parlait Shakespeare, voilà qu'arrive dedans un Théâtre une parcelle d'un peuple errant, fouetté par le violent ouragan chinois. La tribu entre vite se mettre à l'abri.

Voilà que ce Théâtre, celui-ci, (ou bien un autre), ne fait plus de théâtre, on n'y pense même plus. Il y a urgence: la menace de mort, d'exil, d'anéantissement qui accompagne le peuple tibétain, est venue camper chez nous. L'imminence nous mobilise. Soudain nous avons sous les yeux la peine de tout un peuple qui jusqu'à hier se tenait à des milliers de kilomètres de notre attention. Aussitôt tous les rôles font une révolution sur eux-mêmes: le théâtre n'est plus le lieu des représentations. Le voilà qui devient la maison du présent. Et quel présent ! Un présent tendu, fragile, menacé d'une interruption mortelle.

On sent le temps. Les jours sont accordés un à un, comme à des condamnés. C'est que le peuple des hébergés tibétains a osé faire un redoutable pari—sur la compréhension ou l'esprit de justice.

Depuis leur arche provisoire ils lancent aux Etats du monde indifférent un appel insistant à la reconnaissance: 'avouez enfin, une fois pour toutes, que le Tibet existe'.

La grande oreille politique fait la sourde, bien entendu.

Chaque partie du tout campe, tenace, sur ses positions. La guerre est d'usure. Ça peut durer longtemps. Mais ça ne peut pas durer éternellement. La fin approche.

Cependant, dedans, sous la charpente accueillante on vit. C'est cette vie, rapidement improvisée, que nous racontons. Elle n'est ni plus ni moins extraordinaire que ces survies improvisées dont nous rêvions enfants depuis Robinson Crusoe. On bricole, on revient à l'expérience nomade. Comme si on était sous la tente. Ou dans une citadelle assiégée. On connaît les problèmes d'approvisionnement. On attend.

On attend. On dés-espère.

Tout cela sans héroïsme. Il n'y a ni ténor ni diva. Des gens. Nous vous.

Ce dépouillement collectif ne fut pas calculé. La surprise acceptée a

This collective stripping away was not calculated. The accepted surprise disarmed everyone. The pretentions, the presumption, the satisfaction, are left outside for some time. We have the courage to hang up, abandon the posts. Without heroism. That's enough. No drums and no trumpets. We surpass ourselves a little. All at once, these unexpected phenomena appear in lightly jostled destinies: thanks manifest, little revelations of the heart, grumpy people let a hidden tenderness escape.

As you see, it doesn't only concern Tibet. But a modest, unexpected occasion to be human beings, provoked by a chance intrusion, that of the great Tibetan martyr. These are the envoys from mythical countries who, without having counted on anything, come to carry out a conversation in our country, but so transparent that even the word 'conversation', justified as it is, is too heavy for the thing, too weighed down.

Words exactly, I ought not to forget to speak of them. Words also, of course, come from the same pervading modesty. At home—because we are 'in the house'—between us—because it is a question of an 'us' simple and domestic—we speak to one another in half-words, by interjections, signs, moreover this 'us' is half Tibetan. Thus, under our roof, circulates a language of bric-a-brac and of '*tashi delek*'[1], light, gay, economical, urgent, allusive. The author herself is suspended and 'improvised'. She keeps a diary, but really in hiding.

How much time and until when is this brief and minimal humanity going to hold itself together? A day, three nights, six nights? From outside, the echoes arrive from the skiff, commentaries from newspapers, screaming silences from governments, choir of associations.

What rarely comes is sleep. At nine hundred we sleep with difficulty. Little by little this insomnia, a little calamity, takes another more serious face: would it not act, under the familiar and irritated look of disturbed sleepers, using the approach of what Buddhism calls: awakening? Without anyone deciding or knowing, a light wisdom spreads over the stage.

Compassion wins out. For a moment.

It is a moment of sharing and of recognition.

From the performance program pamphlet

---

1. A Tibetan greeting.

désarmé tout le monde. La prétention, la présomption, la satisfaction, sont laissées dehors pour quelque temps. On a le courage de décrocher, d'abandonner des postes. Sans héroïsme. Cela se fait. Pas de tambours et de trompette. On se dépasse un peu. Du coup se produisent des phénomènes imprévus dans les destins légèrement bousculés: des grâces se manifestent, des petites révélations des cœurs; des personnes grincheuses laissent échapper une tendresse cachée.

Comme vous le voyez, il ne s'agit pas simplement du Tibet. Mais d'une modeste occasion inattendue d'être humains, provoquée par la chance d'une intrusion, celle du grand Tibet martyr. Ce sont les envoyés du pays fabuleux qui sans avoir rien calculé, viennent opérer chez nous une conversion, mais si transparente que même le mot 'conversion', si juste soit-il, est trop lourd pour la chose, trop chargé.

Les mots justement, je ne dois pas oublier d'en parler. Les mots aussi, bien sûr, sont de la même modestie ambiante. A la maison—car on est 'à la maison'—entre nous—car il s'agit d'un 'nous' simple et domestique—on se parle à demi-mots, par interjections, signes, d'ailleurs ce nous est à moitié tibétain. Alors circule sous notre toit une langue de bric de broc et de tashi delek, légère, gaie, économe, urgente, allusive. L'auteur elle aussi est suspendue et 'improvisée'. Elle tient bien un journal, mais vraiment en cachette.

Combien de temps et jusqu'à quand cette brève et minime humanité va-t-elle tenir ensemble? Un jour, trois nuits, six nuits? Du dehors les échos arrivent dans la nacelle, commentaires des journaux, criants silences des gouvernements, chœur des associations.

Ce qui se fait très rare, c'est le sommeil. A neuf cents, on dort difficilement. Peu à peu cette insomnie, une petite calamité, prend un autre visage plus sérieux: ne s'agirait-il pas, sous la mine familière et agacée des dormeurs dérangés, de l'approche de ce que le bouddhisme appelle: l'éveil? Sans que personne ne le décide ou sache, une légère sagesse se répand sur le plateau.

La compassion gagne. Un moment.

C'est un moment de partage et de reconnaissance.

Fiche-programme du spectacle

Our Bad Blood

'Blood (...), once on the ground,
It is very difficult to make it rise up again, alas!
The rapid liquid which is spilled on the earth goes away!'
The Eumenides, v. 261-263

Spilled blood cannot be un-spilled. Irreversible is the loss of blood spread by the assassin.

It's this irreversibility that Aeschylus was singing and denouncing.

Non-reversible for the victim. Nor erasable for the assassin. No, all the perfumes of Arabia will not soothe the little hand that killed. The hands of the Macbeths will no longer ever be purified. Today they still smell of innocent blood.

Along the red river of agonising fate, all the poets are leaning over, powerless to hold onto the life that passes by, and they were watching it run, century after century, the thread of tragic horror. They hear the shameful hymn moaning, Aeschylus, Shakespeare, Balzac, Hugo, horribly fascinated by the carnages of which man is the author, with the city. In the streets, we sink up to the ankles in red mud.

Blood, how it freezes over, boils, turns, goes to the head, floods, blackens.

Blood, we take it for a substantial soul, the vital principle that does the rounds of our interior country, the part of us that must remain hidden and that can be ripped from us.

Blood with religious properties, that which has a price, that which, spilled on the alter according to rites, has the power to redeem crimes and sins.

Blood that was called pure, that we pretended was blue and cannot lie, blood that it was necessary to preserve on the borders and not mix up.

Blood today, there it is, always discoloured and recoloured and a carrier of bad thoughts and bad memories. We say: 'blood', and to our misfortune, there it is—the first word of racism.

Poor blood, your shape links to the worst fantasies of our century. We say 'blood' and quickly the word 'contaminated' sticks to the old word of life.

Nos mauvais sangs

« Le sang (...), une fois sur le sol,
Il est bien difficile de le faire remonter, popoï!
Le rapide liquide qui est versé à terre s'en va! »
Les Euménides, v. 261-263

Le sang versé ne se reverse pas. Irréversible est la perte du sang répandu par l'assassinat. C'est cette irréversibilité qu'Eschyle chantait et dénonçait.

Non réversible pour la victime. Ni effaçable pour l'assassin. Non, tous les parfums d'Arabie n'adouciront point la petite main qui a tué. Les mains des Macbeths plus jamais ne seront purifiées. Aujourd'hui encore elles sentent le sang innocent.

Au bord de la rouge rivière au destin angoissant se sont penchés tous les poètes impuissants à retenir la vie qui s'en va, et ils regardaient courir, de siècle en siècle, le fil de l'horreur tragique. Entendez-les gémir l'hymne indigné, Eschyle, Shakespeare, Balzac, Hugo, affreusement fascinés par les carnages dont l'homme est l'auteur, avec la cité. Dans les rues on enfonce jusqu'aux chevilles dans la boue rouge.

Le sang comme il se glace, bout, tourne, monte à la tête, inonde, noircit.

Le sang nous le prenons pour l'âme substantielle, le principe vital qui fait le tour de notre pays intérieur, la part de nous qui doit rester cachée et que l'on peut nous arracher.

Le sang aux religieuses propriétés, celui qui a un prix, celui qui, versé sur l'autel selon les rites, a le pouvoir de racheter crimes et péchés.

Le sang que l'on appelait pur, que l'on prétendait bleu et ne pouvoir mentir, le sang qu'il fallait préserver dans ses frontières et ne pas mêler.

Le sang aujourd'hui toujours le voilà décoloré et recoloré et porteur de mauvaises pensées et de mauvais souvenirs. On dit: « le sang », et pour notre malheur, voilà le premier mot du racisme.

Pauvre sang, ta figure communique avec les pires fantasmes de notre siècle. On dit « sang » et aussitôt s'agglutine au vieux mot de vie le mot « contaminé ». D'une part le sang est contaminateur, d'autre part le sang est

On the one hand, blood is a contaminant, on the other hand, blood is contaminatable and contaminated. Through blood, wild, moves our love and our hate. Certain blood is declared hateable in advance, it could infect the blood of noble races. Thereupon, to crown the history of precious liquid, such that by it the curse of AIDS comes to us.

Here, we remember that a certain Mr Machin associated AIDS with Jews. The fear of contamination by AIDS is, we know, an anti-Semitic reflex. Who touches upon the myth of the purity of blood? AIDS, the Jew, the black person… We leave on a crusade against the crossings! Each one to his blood!! Such is the fear of contamination of blood by blood widely spread and insidious!

But, by contrast, the same frightened ones are not very afraid of the contamination of the soul by bad examples and bad associations. Against the moral plague we don't take many precautions. We see these people driven by the taste of poisons, which they are mad about—I'm talking about gold and power—hurrying to banquets where an abundance of dishes are served that drug their ambitions.

But there is a sour odour in the curtains of these palaces,—do you recognise it? It is the 'decay of kingdoms.' That which we smelled in the Kingdom of Denmark. Such a stench is a cry. It's this cry that wakes up the characters in our play. Certain characters, like the Erinyes, were sleeping under the earth for five thousand years, others for eight days at least. A cry of horror, alarm, revolt.

We are witnesses, we can reduce millions of human creatures to dust over tens and tens of years, and the earth stuffed with assassinated people doesn't shake. We don't hear the millions of cries. Until the day when suddenly, a cry pierces the heavy layers of silence. That of an overwhelmed child perhaps? Or of a mother hit by an incredible misfortune. And it's the crack in the wall.

Such is history: one day, the sheep learn from their defenceless bodies that their shepherds were the wolves. Injured, losing blood, they are dying. What, those who cared for them killed them? No?! Yes! Who can imagine that? Even us who see the victims die one by one, it's with fear and stupefaction that we are hard-pressed to admit the worst: the cutthroat shepherds.

And how and why is such a crime so unthinkable? Especially in our proudly advanced country, and where the fashion is to repeat the word 'ethics' all day?

And if this strange and monstrous crime was only born of this epoch? So are the numerous injustices and inaccuracies1 tangled up in our own time? Isn't it the symptom of the new sickness of the kingdom?

---

1. Cixous creates an assonance between '*injustices et injustesses*', 'injustices and inaccuracies', by creating the neologism '*injustesses*', a word that suggests the negative of '*justesse*', 'accuracy'.

contaminable et contaminé. Par le sang passent, sauvages, notre amour et notre haine. Certains sangs sont déclarés d'avance haïssables, ils pourraient infecter les sangs des nobles races. Là-dessus, pour couronner l'histoire du liquide précieux, voilà que par lui nous arrive le fléau du Sida.

Ici, on se rappelle qu'un certain Monsieur Machin a associé le Sida aux juifs. La peur de la contamination par le Sida est, on le sait, un réflexe antisémite. Qui touche au mythe de la pureté du sang? Le Sida, le juif, le noir... On part en croisade contre les croisements! Chacun son sang!! Comme elle est largement répandue et insidieuse la peur de la contamination du sang par le sang!

Mais par contre, les mêmes effrayés n'ont pas très peur de la contamination de l'âme par les mauvais exemples et les mauvaises fréquentations. Contre la peste morale on ne prend pas beaucoup de précautions. On voit ces gens pressés par le goût des poisons, dont ils raffolent,—je veux parler de l'or et du pouvoir—se presser aux banquets où sont servis à foison les mets qui droguent leurs ambitions.

Mais il y a une odeur aigre dans les rideaux de ces palais,—vous la reconnaissez? C'est la « pourriture des royaumes ». Celle que l'on sentait au royaume de Danemark. Une telle puanteur c'est un cri. C'est ce cri qui réveille bien des personnages de notre pièce. Certains, comme les Erinyes dormaient sous la terre depuis cinq mille années, d'autres depuis huit jours à peine. Un cri d'horreur, d'alarme, de révolte.

Nous en sommes témoins, on peut réduire en poussière des millions de créatures humaines pendant des dizaines et des dizaines d'années, et la terre bourrée d'assassinés, ne tremble pas. On n'entend pas des millions de cris. Jusqu'au jour où soudain un cri perce les lourdes couches de silence. Celui d'un enfant terrassé peut-être? Ou d'une mère frappée par un malheur inouï? Et c'est la fente dans la muraille.

Voici l'histoire: un jour, des agneaux apprennent à leur corps défendant que leurs bergers étaient des loups. Blessés, perdant leur sang, ils agonisent. Quoi, ceux qui les soignaient les ont tués? Non?! Si! Qui peut imaginer cela? Nous mêmes qui voyons les victimes s'éteindre une à une, c'est avec crainte et stupéfaction que nous sommes contraints d'admettre le pire: des bergers égorgeurs.

Et comment et pourquoi un crime si impensable? Surtout dans nos pays fièrement avancés, et où la mode est à répéter le mot « éthique » toute la journée?

Et si ce crime étrange et monstrueux était justement né de notre époque? Justement des nombreuses injustices et injustesses enchevêtrées de notre propre temps? N'est-il pas le symptôme de la nouvelle maladie du royaume?

Tous les parfums de l'Arabie n'adouciraient pas les blanches mains souillées. Mais dans nos royaumes certains ont peut-être inventé les moyens de dévitaliser les nez.

All the perfumes of Arabia would not soothe their sullied white hands. But in our kingdoms certain people have perhaps invented the means by which to devitalise the nose.

But this is not a fable.

GLOSSARY

Athena

(*Bonnard*): 'The Virgin warrior doesn't have a mother, or hardly. Zeus having one day swallowed one of his wives, Metis—whose name means Wisdom—came down with a strong headache. He brought over his son the blacksmith and begged him to relieve him by splitting his forehead with a blow of the axe. Hephaestus obeyed, raising with two hands his tool and striking with all his might. So from the immortal head of Zeus burst forth a big impetuous girl who, pushing forth an almighty cry, began to dance fully armed with weapons (…)

Athena-Pallas resides in the acropolis. Her Palladium—talisman fallen from the sky—makes the fortresses invincible. When the people of Athens have to yield to force, only the enemy takes possession of the ground, it's to the guardian Athena, not to the occupant, that they hand over the territory of the republic by decree. Athena is the goddess of cities and federations. She guides political communities. She inspires the State's councillors, the assemblies of citizens, the courts. Persuasion is on her lips and governs in concord. Her justice is humane. She requires all legal forms. She repudiates vendetta and the law of retaliation. She makes the penalty equal to the offense.

On a hill of Athens, she founded the first court where citizens, in the name of the city, judged a citizen. She presided over the jury. Orestes, will he be tied to the Erinyes for having, under the order of a god, avenged his father by spilling the blood of his mother, who had assassinated his wife? The voices of the court are equally divided. Athena votes for Orestes' acquittal (…)'

The Chorus of the Erinyes

And in my song for this earth
What must I invoke?

Athena

Everything that leads to victory which is not bad,
Things that come from the earth, and from the marine dew,
And from the sky. And the breaths of winds.
That blow with a good sun

Mais ceci n'est pas une fable.

GLOSSAIRE

Athéna

(Bonnard): « La Vierge guerrière n'a pas de mère, ou à peine. Zeus ayant un jour avalé l'une de ses femmes, Métis—dont le nom veut dire Sagesse—en conçut un grand mal de tête. Il fit venir son fils le forgeron et le pria de le soulager en lui fendant le front d'un coup de hache. Héphaistos obéit, levant à deux mains son outil et frappant de toute sa force. Alors, de la tête immortelle de Zeus, jaillit une grande fille impétueuse qui, poussant un cri formidable, se mit à danser toute en armes (…)

Athéna-Pallas réside dans les acropoles. Son Palladium—talisman tombé du ciel—rend invincibles les forteresses. Quand le peuple d'Athènes doit céder à la force, que l'ennemi prend possession du sol, c'est à la gardienne Athéna, non à l'occupant, qu'il remet par décret le territoire de la république. Athéna est la déesse des cités et des fédérations. Elle guide les communautés politiques. Elle inspire les conseils de l'État, les assemblées de citoyens, les tribunaux. La Persuasion est sur ses lèvres et gouverne dans la concorde. Sa justice est humaine. Elle impose à tous des formes légales. Elle répudie la vendetta et la loi du talion. Elle proportionne la peine à la faute.

Sur une colline d'Athènes, elle a fondé le premier tribunal où des citoyens, au nom de la cité, jugèrent un citoyen. Elle présidait le jury. Oreste sera-t-il livré aux Erinyes pour avoir, sur l'ordre d'un dieu, vengé son père en versant le sang de sa mère, qui avait assassiné son époux? Les voix du tribunal se partagent également. Athéna vote pour l'acquittement d'Oreste (…) »

Le Choeur des Erinyes

Et dans mon chant pour cette terre
Que dois-je invoquer?

Athéna

Tout ce qui veille à une victoire qui ne soit pas mauvaise,
Les choses qui viennent de la terre, et de la rosée marine,
Et du ciel. Et les souffles des vents
Qui soufflent avec un bon soleil
En approchant de ce pays.
Que le fruit débordant de la terre et du bétail
Ne se lasse pas avec le temps à force de fleurir pour les citoyens,
Que les semences des hommes soient préservées.
Quant aux impies, puisses-tu les emporter au loin,

When approaching this country.
That the overflowing fruit of the earth and of livestock
Don't grow weary with time due to flowering for the citizens,
That the seeds of men are preserved.
According to the godless, you can bring them from afar,
Because I love, in the manner of a gardener,
That the race of the just ones, because of them, is not afflicted.
Such will be your invocations.
Aeschylus, *The Eumenides*

Conscience

(Littré)[2] 1. Feeling of oneself or mode of general sensibility that permits us to judge from our existence. *Rousseau:* 'The conscience is the intimate, immediate feeling, acknowledgement of the activity of myself in each phenomenon of one's moral life.'

Philosophy of Science Dictionary: One could define the conscience as the feeling of myself in all domains of moral life.

2. Witnessing or secret judgement of the soul that gives approval to good actions and that reproaches bad ones: or, alternately, form of emotion for the group of benevolent and disinterested instincts, the whole of which also carries the name moral sense. The voice of the conscience.

Bossuet: 'She pardoned him for his crime, handing him over to his conscience as punishment.'

On my honour and on my conscience: oath that the head of the jury pronounces before reading the verdict.

On my conscience, in my conscience, in all conscience: sort of familial oath.

To have on one's conscience: to answer from.

To have clean hands and clear conscience: to be irreproachable.

To be a man of conscience: to be incapable of forfeiting honour, with integrity.

To have no conscience, to be without conscience: to have no scruples about anything.

To do something as a matter of conscience: to see it as an obligation.

3. Religious term. The feeling of faults committed. To take a test of conscience.

4. The region of the heart considered the seat of the conscience, only to be employed in this sense in the following phrases: to put one's hand on one's conscience, to examine one's self with good will.

Etymology (Gaffiot): Conscientia, cum—scientia. Knowledge of something shared

2. In this glossary Cixous cites a range of lexicographers, philosophers and authors to compile definitions of her key words. In this case she cites Émile Littré who compiled the famous *Dictionnaire de la langue française* in 1863–72.

Car j'aime, à la façon d'un jardinier,
Que la race des justes, à cause d'eux, ne soit pas affligée.
Telles seront tes invocations.
Eschyle, *Les Euménides*

Conscience

(Littré) 1. Sentiment de soi-même ou mode de la sensibilité générale qui nous permet de juger de notre existence. *Rousseau*: « La conscience est le sentiment intime, immédiat, constant de l'activité du moi dans chacun des phénomènes de sa vie morale. »

Dictionnaire des Sciences Philosophiques: On pourrait définir la conscience comme le sentiment du moi dans tous les domaines de la vie morale.

2. Témoignage ou jugement secret de l'âme qui donne l'approbation aux actions bonnes et qui fait reproche des mauvaises; ou, autrement, mode d'émotion de l'ensemble des instincts bienveillants et désintéressés, ensemble qui porte aussi le nom de sens moral. La voix de la conscience.

Bossuet: « Elle lui pardonna son crime, le livrant pour tout supplice à sa conscience. »

Sur mon honneur et sur ma conscience: serment qui prononce le chef du jury avant de lire le verdict.

Sur ma conscience, en ma conscience, en conscience: sorte de serment familier.

Avoir sur la conscience: répondre de.

Avoir les mains pures et la conscience nette: être irreprochable.

Etre homme de conscience: être incapable de forfaire à l'honneur, à la probité.

N'avoir point de conscience, être sans conscience: ne se faire scrupule de rien.

Se faire une affaire de conscience: regarder comme un devoir.

3. Terme de religion. Le sentiment des fautes commises. Faire son examen de conscience.

4. La région du cœur considéré comme le siège de la conscience, ne s'emploie en ce sens que dans les locutions suivantes: mettre la main sur la conscience, s'examiner de bonne foi.

Etymologie(Gaffiot): Conscientia, cum—scientia. Connaissance de quelque chose partagée avec quelqu'un, connaissance en commun. Claire connaissance qu'on a au fond de soi-même, sentiment intime. Au sens moral: sentiment intime de quelque chose, claire connaissance intérieure. Sentiment, avec idée de bien, de mal.

> *« Chacune de ces voix prenait à son tour la parole, et chacune à son tour disait vrai. Comment choisir? Chacune à son tour semblait trouver le point de sagesse et de justice, et disait: Fais cela. Etait-ce cela qu'il fallait faire? Oui. Non. Le raisonnement disait une chose. Le sentiment en disait une autre; les deux conseils étaient contraires. Le raisonnement n'est que la raison, le*

with someone, common knowledge. Clear conscience that one has, at the base of oneself, intimate feeling. In the moral sense: intimate feeling of something, clear interior knowledge. Feeling, with the idea of good, of bad.

> *Each one of these voices took its turn to speak, and each one in its turn said true. How to choose? Each one in its turn seemed to find the point of wisdom and of justice, and said: Do that. Was it that which had to be done? Yes. No. Reasoning said one thing. Feeling said another; the two pieces of advice were contrary. Reasoning is only reason, feeling is often the conscience. One comes from man, the other from higher up.*
>
> Victor Hugo, 1793

Contamination
(Littré) 1. To touch in a physical and a moral sense. 2. To sully from contact, employed above all in the moral sense. 3. Who touches upon, to properly touch upon. 4. Contact. 4. Contagion.

Etymology (Gaffiot): Tangere: 1. To touch, touch upon: to take, to taste, to eat. To attain. To hit: to take a hand to, to seduce a young girl. To impregnate, to water down. 2. (*Fig.*) To dupe, to trap. To touch, to be provoked by a taunt.
Contaminare: To mix up, to mix together. To sully by contact. To corrupt.
Cicero: 'Contaminare veritatem mendacio.' 'To replace the truth with a lie.'
Contingere: To touch, to attain. To infect, to contaminate.
Contagio: Contact. Contagion, infection. Pernicious influence.

Cynicism, Cynical
(Littré) 1. Little used medical term, cynical spasm: convulsive movement of cheeks by which the lips spread in the manner of showing one's teeth like an irritated dog. 2. Cynical philosophy. *Descartes:* 'The cynics were biting and without modesty' (...) They reproached others with their faults without keeping anything back, even adding to their reproaches an air of contempt and insult; it is this which, according to some, caused them to be given the name of cynics, because they were biting and barking at everyone like dogs.' *From Holbach:* 'Often under the guise of the cynic and the stoic, under the appearance of disinterestedness, of contempt for grandeur, praise, pleasure, we find only easily upset souls, gnawed at by envy, devoured by ambition, held by a vain desire for a usurped glory every time that one doesn't owe it to the real advantages that one procures from society.' *Condillac:* 'The taunts, satires, invectives were their weapons and they didn't help anyone. Such was the character of the spirit common to all cynics.' *Condillac*: 'Everything degenerates and, above all, the virtues carried to excess; elsewhere it is easier to counterfeit them, this sect seemed to appeal to those, all of those who, without merit, were ambitious to make themselves a name; the cynics thus passed from contempt of vices to contempt of

sentiment est souvent la conscience. L'un vient de l'homme, l'autre de plus haut. »
Victor Hugo, 1793

Contamination
(Littré) 1. Toucher au sens physique et au sens moral. 2. Souiller par contact, employé surtout au sens moral. 3. Qui touche à, proprement toucher à. 4. Contact. 5. Contagion.

Etymologie (Gaffiot): Tangere: 1. Toucher, toucher à: prendre, goûter, manger. Atteindre. Frapper: porter la main sur, séduire une jeune fille. Imprégner, mouiller. 2. *(Fig.)* Duper, attraper. Toucher, piquer par une raillerie.

Contaminare: Mélanger, mêler. Souiller par contact. Corrompre.

Cicéron: « Contaminare veritatem mendacio ». « Altérer la vérité par un mensonge. »

Contingere: Toucher, atteindre. Infecter, contaminer.

Contagio: Contact. Contagion, infection. Influence pernicieuse.

Cynisme, Cynique
(Littré) 1. Terme de médecine peu usité, spasme cynique: mouvement convulsif des joues par lequel les lèvres s'écartent de manière à laisser voir les dents comme un chien irrité. 2. Philosophe cynique. *Descartes*: « Les cyniques étaient mordants et sans pudeur. » (...) Ils reprochaient aux autres leurs défauts sans garder aucun ménagement, ajoutant même à leurs reproches un air de mépris et d'insulte; c'est ce qui, selon quelques-uns, leur fit donner le nom de cyniques, parce qu'ils étaient mordants et qu'ils aboyaient contre tout le monde comme des chiens. » *D'Holbach*: « Souvent sous le manteau du cynique et du stoïcien, sous les apparences du désintéressement, du mépris des grandeurs, de la louange, des plaisirs, nous ne trouverons que des âmes bileuses, rongées par l'envie, dévorées d'ambition, embrasées du vain désir d'une gloire usurpée toutes les fois qu'on ne la doit point aux avantages réels qu'on procure à la société. » *Condillac*: « Les railleries, les satires, les invectives furent leurs armes et ils ne ménagèrent personne. Voilà le caractère d'esprit qui était commun à tous les cyniques. » *Condillac*: « Tout dégénère et surtout les vertus portées à l'excès; d'ailleurs comme il est plus aisé de les contrefaire, cette secte parut appeler à elle tous ceux qui, sans mérite, furent ambitieux de se faire un nom; les cyniques passèrent donc du mépris des vices au mépris des mœurs et des bienséances; ils devinrent impudents, ils mirent la sagesse à ne rougir de rien. »

Étymologie: du grec *kunikos, kuôn, kunos*: chien.

customs and proprieties; they became imprudent, they reflect the wisdom to not blush at anything.'

Etymology: from the Greek *kunikos, kuôn, kunos*: dog.

Erinyes

The Erinyes, also called the Eumenides (which is to say the 'Benevolent ones', from a nickname destined to flatter them, and, by consequence, to avoid bringing on oneself, by calling them an odious name, their undoubtable anger) are violent goddesses, that the Romans identified with their Furies. They are born in drops of blood from which the mutilation of Uranus impregnated the earth. They therefore belong to the oldest divinities of the Hellenic Pantheon. These are primitive forces that don't recognise the authority of the gods of the younger generation. (…) Originally, they are of an indeterminate number. Then their number becomes precise, like their names: one generally recognises them from three, Alecto, Tisiphone and Megaera. In hand they hold torches or whips. Often, they are compared to 'bitches' (…). Their essential function is the vengeance of a crime, particularly crimes committed against the family. (*Grimal*)

Aeschylus tells in *The Eumenides* the story of Orestes, the matricide, that the Erinyes pursued with their anger in order to avenge the murder of his mother Clytemnestra. Athena, the young goddess, will change forever the course of history and Law in founding the first court. It is thus that Orestes has the right to the first trial before a real court. From this trial, the Erinyes are dismissed and Orestes acquitted. Athena calms the anger of the ancient goddesses. They consent to reside from that moment onwards under the earth. Henceforth, we will live in a community of rights, Athena above, below the Erinyes became benevolent…

Hippocrates

Hippocrates is born on the Dorian island of Kos, in Asia Minor, in 460 BC, he is a contemporary of Socrates. His father, Heraclides, was a doctor and belonged to a family of Asclepiads, which is to say, a family that pretended to be real descendants of Asclepius, the heroes of Trikala, who became the god of medicine. Son of Apollo, he, says one reliable tradition, had learned the medical art from his father himself and from the centaur Chiron, and after the expedition against Troy, Machaon and Podalirius, his two sons, served as doctors in the Greek army. As it was thus the rule, it is in his family that Hippocrates learned medicine, before traveling like so many itinerant Greek doctors. Hippocrates lived out his last years in the north of Greece and he would die in Larissa, very old.

He acquired from his living an exceptional renown, which came from

Érinyes

Les Erinyes, appelées aussi les Euménides (c'est-à-dire les « Bienveillantes », d'un surnom destiné à les flatter, et par conséquent à éviter d'attirer sur soi-même, en les nommant d'un nom odieux, leur redoutable colère) sont des déesses violentes, que les Romains identifièrent avec leurs Furies. Elles sont nées des gouttes du sang dont la mutilation d'Ouranos imprégna la terre. Elles appartiennent par conséquent aux plus anciennes divinités du panthéon hellénique. Ce sont des forces primitives, qui ne reconnaissent pas l'autorité des dieux de la plus jeune génération. (...) Primitivement, elles sont en nombre indéterminé. Puis, leur nombre se précise, ainsi que leurs noms: on en connaît généralement trois, Alecto, Tisiphoné et Mégère. A la main, elles tiennent des torches ou des fouets. Souvent, on les compare à des « chiennes » (...). Leur fonction essentielle est la vengeance du crime, tout particulièrement ceux commis contre la famille. *(Grimal)*

Eschyle raconte dans *Les Euménides* l'histoire d'Oreste, le matricide, que les Erinyes poursuivaient de leur colère afin de venger le meurtre de sa mère Clytemnestre. Athéna, la jeune déesse, changera à jamais le cours de l'histoire et de la Loi en fondant le premier tribunal. C'est ainsi qu'Oreste a droit au premier procès devant un vrai tribunal. Lors de ce procès, les Erinyes sont déboutées et Oreste acquitté. Athéna calme la colère des antiques déesses. Celles-ci consentent à demeurer désormais sous la terre. Dorénavant, on vivra dans une communauté de droit, en haut Athéna, en bas les Erinyes devenues bienveillantes...

Hippocrates

Hippocrate est né dans l'île dorienne de Cos, en Asie Mineure, en 460 av. J.-C., il est contemporain de Socrate. Son père, Heraclidès, était médecin et appartenait à une famille d'Asclépiades, c'est-à-dire, une famille qui prétendait descendre réellement d'Asclépios, le héros de Tricca, devenu dieu de la médecine. Fils d'Apollon, celui-ci, dit une tradition constante, avait appris l'art médical de son père lui-même et du Centaure Chiron, et lors de l'expédition contre Troie, Machaon et Podalire, ses deux fils, servirent comme médecins dans l'armée grecque. Comme c'était alors la règle, c'est dans sa famille qu'Hippocrate apprit la médecine, avant de voyager comme tant de médecins itinérants grecs. Hippocrate vécut ses dernières années en Grèce du Nord et il serait mort à Larissa, très âgé.

Il acquit de son vivant une exceptionnelle renommée, qui lui vint de ses succès thérapeutiques, d'une certaine vision philosophico-médicale de l'homme dans le monde, mais aussi de ses œuvres écrites pour lesquelles il utilise le dialecte ionien, celui des savants, et non son dialecte maternel. Il comprit que le rire de Démocrite d'Abdère n'était pas celui de sa folie. Il sût reconnaître le mal d'amour dont souffrait Perdiccas; il repoussa la maladie pestilentielle qui menaçait l'ensemble de la Grèce, Athènes comprise.

his successful treatments, from a certain philosophico-medical vision of man in the world, but also from his written works for which he utilises the Ionic dialect, that of the scholars, and not his maternal dialect. He understood that the laugh of Democritus was not madness. He knew how to recognise the evil of love from which Perdiccas was suffering; he pushed away again the pestilential sickness that was threatening the entirety of Greece, including Athens. Hippocrates' treatment is quite a complicated application of several relatively simple principles: act at the appropriate moment and with a minimum of violence: restore the equilibrium of the body in its entirety, put the individual in harmony with its setting.

> 'Keep two things in mind with sicknesses: be useful or at least don't harm.' (Introduction by Danielle Gourevitch, Mirko Grmek and Pierre Pellegrin, *De L'Art Médical*, Hippocrates)

Shame

(Littré) 1. Dishonour, disgrace, humiliation. *Corneille*: 'The glory of a death that covers us with shame.' *Voltaire*: 'Go, shame would be to betray what I love.' *La Chaussée*: 'The shame is in the offence and not in the excuse.' 2. Painful feeling that stirs up in the soul the thought or fear of dishonour. *Bourdaloue*: 'Shame is a passion that reasonable nature excites in us and that turns us away from, without us noticing neither how nor why, all excesses and all impurities of vice.' *Bourdaloue*: 'The shame of good, says Saint Bernard, is in us the source of all evil and the shame of evil is the principle of all good.' *Rousseau*: 'Shame, friend of the conscience against evil, was widowed with years.'

To have lost all shame: to be insensible to dishonour. The reproaches of the conscience cause shame.

Justice

(Rey) The conformity to law, the moral feeling of equity, laws and judgements and precepts, the power of justice.

Justitia (*Grimal*): Roman personification of Justice. She is not altogether equivalent to the Greek Themis, but rather to Dike and also Astraea who plays her role in the legend of the Golden Age. When the crimes of humanity put Justitia into flight, and was forced to leave the earth where she was living amongst Mortals, she took refuge in the Sky and became the constellation of the Virgin.

> *Justice is what makes injustice acceptable. Upon what piles of injustice was Justice raised! Justice wasn't made to be fair. It is made to arrest/stop. Justice, between men, there must be. To cut short the sadnesses that are interminable. To divide up everything that exceeds, to repress the sobs. The victims are scandalised, they never stop complaining. Justice is there to regulate the cries and cut the course/courts of complaints.*

La thérapeutique d'Hippocrate est une application assez compliquée de quelques principes relativement simples: agir au moment propice et avec un minimum de violence: restaurer l'équilibre du corps dans son ensemble, mettre en accord l'individu et son milieu.

« Avoir dans les maladies deux choses en vue: être utile ou du moins ne pas nuire. » (Introduction de Danielle Gourevitch, Mirko Grmek et Pierre Pellegrin, *De L'Art Médical*, Hippocrate)

Honte

(Littré) 1. Deshonneur, opprobre, humiliation. *Corneille*: « La gloire d'une mort qui nous couvre de honte. » *Voltaire*: « Va, la honte serait de trahir ce que j'aime. » *La Chaussée*: « La honte est dans l'offense et non pas dans l'excuse. » 2. Sentiment pénible qu'excite dans l'âme la pensée ou la crainte du deshonneur. *Bourdaloue*: « La honte est une passion que la nature raisonnable excite en nous et qui nous détourne, sans que nous remarquions même ni comment ni pourquoi, de tous les excès et de toutes les impuretés du vice. » *Bourdaloue*: « La honte du bien, dit Saint Bernard, est en nous source de tout mal et la honte du mal est le principe de tout bien. » *Rousseau*: « La honte, compagne de la conscience du mal, était veuve avec les années. » *Avoir perdu toute honte*: être insensible au deshonneur. Les reproches de la conscience causent de la honte.

Justice

(Rey) La conformité au droit, le sentiment moral d'équité, les lois et les jugements et préceptes, le pouvoir de justice.

Justitia (Grimal): Personnification à Rome de la Justice. Elle n'est toutefois pas équivalente de la Thémis grecque, mais de Diké et aussi d'Astrée qui joue son rôle dans la légende de l'Age d'or. Lorsque les crimes de l'humanité eurent mis en fuite Justitia, et l'eurent contrainte à quitter la terre où elle vivait familièrement avec les Mortels, elle se réfugia au Ciel et devint la constellation de la Vierge.

> *La justice c'est ce qui rend l'injustice convenable. Sur quels tas d'injustice s'élève la Justice! La Justice n'est pas faite pour être juste. Elle est faite pour arrêter. La Justice, entre hommes, il la faut. Pour couper court aux douleurs, qui sont interminables. Trancher tout ce qui dépasse, refouler les sanglots. Les victimes sont scandaleuses, elle ne cessent de se plaindre. La Justice est là pour régler les cris et couper le cours des plaintes.*
>
> *La Justice est la bonne gestion de l'Injustice.*
>
> *La Justice est notre tragédie nécessaire.*
>
> Hélène Cixous, *Le Coup*

Justice is the smooth management of Injustice.

Justice is our necessary tragedy.

Hélène Cixous, *The Blow*

DIKE (Graves): **Greek goddess of justice.**

Themis: goddess of Law belonged to the race of Titans. She is the daughter of Uranus, and of Gaia and sister Titanides. Like the goddess of eternal laws, she figures among the divine wives of Zeus, the second after Metis. With Zeus, Themis engenders the three Hours: Eunomia (Discipline), Dike (Justice) and Eirene (Peace). Three names that evoke the idea of growth, augmentation and bearing fruit. The Hours have a double aspect: divinities of nature, they preside over the cycle of vegetation. They assure the maintenance of society. *Empedocles*: 'Everywhere expands with ample powerful ether and in the immense flame of light, the Universal Law of Dike.'

Etymology (Bailly): *Dike: dikh*: rule, hence: manner of being or acting. What serves as rule, law, justice.

Judiciary action, hence: court action, the court of the trial, debate, the court that judges the trial, advocacy, judicial decision, judgement, consequence of a judgement, pain, punishment, rule, law.

Doctor

(Littré) 1. He who practices medicine. *Pascal*: 'If they (the magistrates) had true justice, if doctors had the true art of healing, they would only make square caps:[3] the majesty of these sciences would be rather venerable towards itself.' 2. Doctors of all arts, were once called doctors who, without medical studies, pretended to be in possession of secrets and recipes. 3. (*Fig.*) What is appropriate to restore or conserve health. 4. The doctor of souls, the priest, the confessor.

Etymology: (Bailly) Greek: *Medesthai, medeo*: to take care, to protect, therefore: who reigns over, therefore: protector.

(Gaffiot) Latin: *medicus*: fit to heal, who cares, heals.

Medeor: to heal, to treat (when speaking of remedies: to be good).

Night (Nyx)

(Graves) Is the personification and the goddess of the Night. She is the daughter of Chaos in Hesiodic theogony. She engendered two elements, the aether and the day and a whole series of abstractions. Some say that at the

3. A kind of hat worn by clergymen.

DIKÉ (Graves): **déesse grecque de la justice.**
Thémis: déesse de la Loi appartient à la race des Titans. Elle est fille d'Ouranos, et de Gaïa et sœur des Titanides. Comme déesse des lois éternelles, elle figure parmi les épouses divines de Zeus, la seconde après Métis. Avec Zeus, Thémis engendra les trois Heures: Eunomia (Discipline), Diké (Justice) et Eirine (Paix). Trois noms qui évoquent l'idée de pousser, de croître et de fructifier. Les Heures ont un double aspect: divinités de la nature, elles président au cycle de la végétation. Elles assurent le maintien de la société. *Empédocle*: « Partout s'étend par l'ample puissant éther et dans l'immense flamme de la lumière, la Loi Universelle de la Diké ».

Étymologie (Bailly): *Diké: dikh*: règle, d'où usage, manière d'être ou d'agir. Ce qui sert de règle, droit, justice. Action judiciaire, d'où procès, cours du procès, débat, tribunal qui juge le procès, le plaidoyer, décision judiciaire, jugement, conséquence d'un jugement, peine, châtiment, la règle, le droit.

Médecin
(Littré) 1. Celui qui exerce la médecine. *Pascal*: « S'ils (les magistrats) avaient la véritable justice, si les médecins avaient le vrai art de guérir, ils n'auraient que faire de bonnets carrés: la majesté de ces sciences serait assez vénérable d'elle-même. » 2. Médecins de tous arts, se disait autrefois des médecins qui, sans études médicales, prétendaient être en possession de secrets et de recettes. 3. *(Fig.)* Ce qui est propre à rendre ou à conserver la santé. 4. Le médecin des âmes, le prêtre, le confesseur.
Étymologie (Bailly) Grec: *Medesthai, medeo*: prendre soin de, protéger, par suite: qui règne sur, par suite: protecteur.*(Gaffiot)* Latin: *medicus*: propre à guérir, qui soigne, guérit. *Medeor*: soigner, traiter (en parlant de remède: être bon).

Nuit (Nyx)
(Graves) Est la personnification et la déesse de la Nuit. Elle est la fille du Chaos dans la théogonie Hésiodique. Elle-même engendra deux éléments, l'aether et le jour et toute une série d'abstractions. Certains disent qu'au début était l'obscurité et que de l'obscurité naquit le Chaos. De l'union de la Nuit et de l'Erèbe naquirent le Destin, la Vieillesse, la Mort, le Meurtre, la Continence, le Sommeil, les Rêves, la Discorde, la Souffrance, la Tyrannie, Nemesis, la Joie, l'Amitié, la Compassion, les Parques et les trois Hespérides.

Selon les Orphiques, la Nuit aux ailes noires, déesse que Zeus lui-même redoute, fut courtisée par le Vent et déposa un œuf d'argent dans le sein de l'Obscurité. Eros, que certains nomment Phanès, sortit de cet œuf et mit en marche l'Univers. Eros avait des ailes, deux sexes et quatre têtes, et parfois sifflait comme un serpent ou bêlait comme un bélier. La Nuit vivait avec lui dans une caverne et se manifestait sous trois aspects: Nuit, Ordre et Justice.

beginning there was obscurity and that, from obscurity, Chaos was born. From the union of Night and Erebus was born Destiny, Old Age, Death, Murder, Continence, Sleep, Dreams, Discord, Suffering, Tyranny, Nemesis, Joy, Friendship, Compassion, the Fates and the three Hesperides.

According to the Orphics, the Night with black wings, goddess that Zeus himself feared, was courted by the Wind and laid a silver egg in the breast of Obscurity. Eros, who some call Phanes, came out of that egg and put the Universe into motion. Eros had wings, two sexes and four heads, and sometimes whistled like a snake or bleated like a ram. Night lived with him in a cave and manifested under three guises: Night, Order and Justice. In front of this cave was sitting the inevitable mother Rhea; hitting a bronze drum, she was forcing man to pay attention to the oracles of the goddess.

Strophe
'O Night my mother, mother who gave birth to me
To be the punishment of those who no longer see the light
Like those who still see it,
Listen to me because the child of Leto dishonours me
By ripping from me this flattening fear,
This expiation to offer to the mother
Who has the power of purification by this murder'
Aeschylus, *The Eumenides*

Pardon

(Littré) 1. Remission of a fault, of an offence. The pardon of injuries. *Hamilton*: 'We don't have much spirit when we ask for pardon, only when we offend.' 2. Letters of pardon, letter that the prince granted in a small chancellery to excuse certain offenses less large than those that require letters of grace. 3. The day of pardon, day that the Jews celebrate on the tenth of their month of Tishri, which corresponds to our month of September; they abstain from work, as on the day of the Sabbath, fast till the evening, and make it their business on that day to pardon all the injuries that they have received.

Etymology (Gaffiot): *Per-donare*: to give completely.

Perjury

(Rey) Parjure employed as noun and adjective,[4] refers to and qualifies a person who, by false oath, doesn't make good on his promises, on his commitments (to be perjured to). Perjury also refers to false oath, in particular, false

4. This is only true in the French language. In English, the noun 'perjury' describes the offense, 'perjurer' describes the person who has committed the offense and the adjective is 'perjurious'.

Devant cette caverne se tenait assise l'inévitable mère Rhéa; frappant sur un tambour de bronze, elle contraignait l'homme à prêter attention aux oracles de la déesse.

Strophe
« o Nuit ma mère, mère qui m'a enfantée
Pour être le châtiment de ceux qui ne voient plus la lumière
Comme de ceux qui encore la voient,
Ecoute-moi car l'enfant de Léto me met en déshonneur
En m'arrachant cet aplati de peur,
Cette expiation à offrir à la mère,
Qui sur ce meurtre a le pouvoir de purification. »
Eschyle, *Les Euménides*

Pardon
(Littré) 1. Remision d'une faute, d'une offense. Le pardon des injures. *Hamilton*: « On n'a pas tant d'esprit quand on demande pardon, que quand on offense. » 2. Lettres de pardon, lettre que le prince accordait en petite chancellerie pour remettre la peine de certains délits moins grands que ceux qui exigent des lettres de grâce. 3. Le jour du pardon, jour que les juifs célèbrent le dix de leur mois tisri, qui correspond à notre mois de septembre; ils s'abstiennent du travail comme le jour du sabbat, jeûnent jusqu'au soir, et font profession ce jour-là de pardonner toutes les injures qu'ils ont reçues.

Étymologie (Gaffiot): *Per-donare*: donner complètement.

Parjure
(Rey) Parjure employé comme nom et adjectif, désigne et qualifie une personne qui, par un faux serment, manque à ses promesses, à ses engagements (être parjure à). Parjure désigne aussi le faux serment, en particulier le faux témoignage devant les tribunaux. Il est alors emprunté au neutre latin *perjurium*: action de se parjurer.

Se parjurer: violer son serment, affirmer sous serment ce que l'on sait faux.

Étymologie (Rey): Parjurus: « qui manque à ses engagements », d'où: « imposteur », « menteur ». Mot formé de *per*, exprimant ici une idée de « déviation », et de *jus, juris*: droit.

Prophète
(Littré) 1. Celui qui, chez les hébreux, inspiré de Dieu, prédisait l'avenir. *Deutéronome XXXIV 10*: « Il ne s'éleva plus en Israël de prophète semblable à Moïse, à qui le Seigneur parlât comme à lui face à face. » *Pascal*: « On n'entend les prophètes que quand on voit les choses arriver. » Les quatre

witness in court. It is thus taken from the neutral Latin *perjurium*: action of perjuring oneself.

Se parjurer: to violate oath, to affirm under oath what one knows is false.

Etymology (Rey): *Parjurus:* 'who reneges on his commitments', hence: 'impostor', 'liar'. Word formed from *per*, expressing here an idea of 'deviation', and from *jus, juris:* law.

Prophet

(Littré) 1. He who, among the Hebrews, inspired by God, predicted the future. *Deuteronomy XXXIV 10*: 'There will never be in Israel a prophet comparable to Moses, to whom the Lord speaks as if he were face to face.' *Pascal*: 'One only hears prophets when one sees things happening.' The four great prophets, Isaiah (*in Hebrew* 'Yahweh is deliverance'), Jeremiah (*in Hebrew* 'Yahweh raises up'), Ezekiel (*in Hebrew* 'that God makes the child strong'), Daniel (*in Hebrew* 'God has brought justice'), said thus because they left a greater number of writings. The prophet-king, the king-prophet, the royal prophet: David. The false prophets, those who called themselves prophets without having divine inspiration. 2. Title given to Muhammad by Muslims.

Etymology (Bailly): Greek: *Pro:* before; *phêmi*: I speak. 1. To make visible, hence: to manifest his thought through speech, hence: to say. 2. To say one's position, hence: to have an opinion, to think, to believe.

Phenidzo: 1. To phophesi, to announce. 2. To spread a noise, to divulge.

Islands, listen to me,
people from afar, be attentive:
Yahweh called me, from the maternal stomach;
from the bowels of my mother, he made mention of my name.
He made my mouth like a sharp double-edged sword,
he sheltered me in the shadow of his hand,
he made a barbed arrow of me,
he concealed me in his quiver,
he said to me: 'You are my servant,
Israel, you through which I will gloriously appear.'
(*The book of Isaiah*, Ch. XLIX)

Responsibility

1. Legal term a) To solemnly promise in prescribed forms; for someone, to pledge as security, guarantor, to answer for someone. b) In the name of the State. c) This term is sacred in the terminology of marriage: it even instructs the terms *sponsus, sponsa* 'husband', 'wife'. *Plautus: 'Piliam tuam sponden mihi uxorem dari?'* 'So, you promise me your daughter in marriage?' 2. To engage in

grands prophètes, Isaïe (*en hb.* « Yahvé est délivrance »), Jérémie (*en hb.* 'Yahvé élève'), Ézéchiel (*en hb.* 'Que Dieu rende l'enfant fort'), Daniel (*en hb.* 'Dieu a rendu justice'), ainsi dits parce qu'ils ont laissé un plus grand nombre d'écrits. Le prophète-roi, le roi-prophète, le prophète royal: David. Les faux prophètes, ceux qui se disaient prophètes sans avoir l'inspiration divine. 2. Titre donné à Mahomet par les musulmans.

Étymologie (Bailly): Grec: *Pro:* avant; *phêmi*: je parle. 1. Rendre visible, d'où manifester sa pensée par la parole, d'où: dire. 2. Dire son avis, d'où avoir un opinion, penser, croire.

Phenidzo: 1. prophétiser, annoncer. 2. Répandre un bruit, divulguer.

Iles, écoutez-moi,
peuplades au loin, soyez attentives:
Iahvé m'a appelé, dès le ventre maternel;
dès les entrailles de ma mère, il a fait mention de mon nom.
Il a rendu ma bouche semblable à un glaive tranchant,
il m'a abrité dans l'ombre de sa main,
il a fait de moi une flèche acérée,
il m'a dissimulé dans son carquois,
il m'a dit: « Tu es mon serviteur,
Israël, toi par qui je me manifesterai glorieusement ».
(*Le livre d'Isaïe*, Ch XLIX)

Responsabilité

1. Terme de droit. a) Promettre solennellement dans les formes prescrites; pour quelqu'un, promettre à titre de caution, de répondant, se porter caution. b) Au nom de l'État. c) Ce terme est consacré dans la terminologie du mariage: c'est ce qu'enseignent les termes mêmes de *sponsus, sponsa* « époux », « épouse ». *Plaute: « Piliam tuam sponden mihi uxorem dari? »* « Alors, tu me promets ta fille en mariage? » 2. S'engager à faire la paix, prendre l'engagement que. 3. En général, promettre sur l'honneur, assurer, garantir, se porter fort. *Etymologie: (Gaffiot) Spondere*: Terme de droit: promettre solennellement, dans les formes prescrites, promettre à titre de répondant, se porter caution. Au nom de l'État, s'engager à faire la paix, prendre l'engagement. En général, promettre sur l'honneur, assurer, garantir, se porter fort.

(Benveniste) Respondeo, responsum: se dit des interprètes des dieux, des prêtres, notamment des haruspices, donnant en retour de l'offrande la promesse, en retour du cadeau la sécurité; c'est la « réponse » d'un oracle, d'un prêtre. Ceci explique une acception juridique du verbe: *respondere de iure* « donner une consultation de droit ». Le juriste, avec sa compétence, garantit la valeur de l'avis qu'il donne. »

« Si la loi de la responsabilité ne s'étendait pas sur tous les agents subalternes du

peace making, to make a commitment to. 3. In general, to promise on one's honour, to assure, to guarantee, to answer for.

Etymology: (Gaffiot) Spondere: Legal term: to solemnly promise, in the prescribed forms, to pledge as security from the guarantor, to answer for someone. In the name of the State, to engage in peace making, to make a commitment. In general, to promise on one's honour, to assure, to guarantee, to answer for.

(Benveniste) Respondeo, responsum: said of the interpreters of the Gods, the priests, including notably the soothsayers, giving in return for the offering of the promise, in return for the gift of safety; it's the 'response' of an oracle, a priest. This explains the legal sense of the verb: *respondere de iure* 'to give a consultation of law.' The judge, with his jurisdiction, guarantees the worth of the opinion that he gives.'

> *'If the law of responsibility didn't spread over all the subaltern agents of despotism, if it didn't exist above all among us, there wouldn't be a nation on earth more made than us for slavery. (...) Every subaltern is responsible, and you will only ever be slaves if, from the first vizier to the last minion, responsibility is not established.'*
> Mirabeau, 22 August 1789,
> Meeting of the Constituent Assembly

Blood

(Littré) 1. Quite thick liquid, of a red colour, sometimes clear and bright red, sometimes dark and like blackness, that fills the entire system of arterial and venous vessels. *Deuteronomy XII 21*: 'Only beware of eating the blood of these beasts, because their blood is their life, and thus you don't have to eat with their flesh what is their life.' 2. Said of different physical states defined by a certain state of blood. Heated blood. To refresh the blood. *Bossuet*: 'One is sick in the blood and in the bowels before breaking out in a fever.' 3. *(Fig.)* It is said of different states of the soul defined by a certain state of the blood. *Racine*—Esther: 'All my blood of anger and shame is enflamed.'

Rousseau—Confessions: 'I have no doubt that the bad blood that I had during this absence contributed to the sickness that I fell into after his return.' 4. *(Fig.)* The life of men when speaking of death, murder, carnage. *Isaiah XXCI21*: 'The earth will no longer hide the blood that had been spilled.' 5. Blood money: the price paid to a man who delivered a condemned person to death. *St. Math. XXVII 6*: 'We are not allowed to put it (the money paid to Judas) in the treasury because it is blood money.' *Psalms LVIII 3*: 'Save me from all these men of blood.' 6. Blood, the substance of a people, the poor. To suck the blood from people. *Rousseau*: 'One almost regrets being a man when one dreams of the unfortunate ones from whom one must eat blood.' 7. Blood, feelings of affection between members of the same family. *Corneille:*

despotisme, si elle n'existait pas surtout parmi nous, il n'y aurait pas une nation sur la terre plus faite que nous pour l'esclavage. (…) Tout subalterne est responsable, et vous ne serez jamais que des esclaves si, depuis le premier vizir jusqu'au dernier sbire, la responsabilité n'est pas établie ».

Mirabeau, 22 août 1789, Réunion de l'Assemblée Constituante

Sang

(Littré) 1. Liquide assez épais, d'une couleur rouge tantôt claire et vermeille, tantôt foncée et comme noire, qui remplit le système entier des vaisseaux artériels et veineux. *Deutéronome XII 2I*: « Gardez-vous seulement de manger du sang de ces bêtes, car leur sang est leur vie, et ainsi vous ne devez pas manger avec leur chair ce qui est leur vie. » 2. Se dit des différents états physiques définis par un certain état du sang. Sang allumé. Rafraîchir le sang. *Bossuet*: « On a le mal dans le sang et dans les entrailles avant qu'il éclate par la fièvre. » 3. *(Fig.)* Il se dit de différents états d'âme définis par un certain état du sang. *Racine*—Esther: « Tout mon sang de colère et de honte s'enflamme. » *Rousseau* - Confessions: « Je ne doute point que le mauvais sang que je me fis durant cette absence n'ait contribué à la maladie où je tombais après son retour. » 4. *(Fig.)* La vie des hommes en parlant de mort, de meurtre, de carnage. *Isaïe XXCI2I*: « La terre ne cachera plus le sang qui a été répandu. » 5. Le prix du sang: le prix payé à un homme qui a livré un condamné à mort. *St. Math. XXVII 6*: « Il ne nous est pas permis de le mettre (l'argent payé à Judas) dans le trésor parce que c'est le prix du sang. » *Psaumes LVIII 3*: « Sauvez-moi de tous ces hommes de sang. » 6. Le sang, la substance du peuple, des pauvres. Sucer le sang du peuple. *Rousseau*: « On a presque regret d'être homme quand on songe aux malheureux dont il faut manger le sang. » 7. Le sang, les sentiments d'affection entre les membres d'une même famille. *Corneille*: « Elle est mère et le sang a beaucoup de pouvoir. » *Bossuet*: « Les larmes que Saint Augustin appelle si élégamment le sang de l'âme. »

Étymologie (Gaffiot): Sanguis: sang qui coule, par opposition à: Cruor: sang coagulé, sang rouge, sang qui se répand. a) force vitale, vie. b) meurtre, carnage.

Cicéron: « nisi cruor apparet, vis non est facta » (« A moins qu'il n'y ait trace de sang répandu, il n'y a pas eu de violence. »)

Virgile: « atri cruores » (« Flots d'un sang noir. »)

Cruentus: sanglant, ensanglanté, inondé de sang.

Cruentare: 1. mettre au sang (par le meu tre, en tuant). *(Fig.)* blesser, déchirer. 2. teindre en rouge.

Crudelis: dur, cruel, inhumain. En grec: *Haima*: sang, hématome, hémorragie, hémophilie.

'She is the mother and blood has a lot of power.' *Bossuet*: 'The tears that Saint Augustine calls, so elegantly, the blood of the soul.'

Etymology (Gaffiot): Sanguis: blood that flows, in comparison to:

Cruor: coagulated blood, red blood, blood that spills. a) vital force, life. b) murder, carnage.

Cicero: 'nisi cruor apparet, vis non est facta' ('At least if there is no trace of spilled blood, there has been no violence.')

Virgil: 'atri cruores' ('Rivers of black blood.')

Cruentus: bloody, bloodied, inundated with blood.

Cruentare: 1. To put to sword (by murder, in killing). *(Fig.)* to injure, to tear up. 2. To dye red.

Crudelis: hard, cruel, inhuman.

In Greek: *Haima*: blood, hematoma, haemorrhage, haemophilia.

Oath

(Littré) 1. Affirmation or promise in calling God to witness or what one considers a saint, as divine. *Rollin*: 'He who tricks by false oath overtly declares by doing that that he fears his enemy but that he despises God.' *Rousseau*: 'It is a secondary crime to take a criminal oath.' 2. Oath, imprecation. *Vertot*: 'After having made horrible oaths, he pursued this affair until death.'

(Benveniste) The oath in Greece is the solemn affirmation placed under the guarantee of a non-human power charged to chasten perjury. In Greek notably, one can recapture in the already Homeric turn *horkon omnunai*, especially significant 'to take oath', its concrete origin: 'to seize the *horkons*', object charged with evil power ready to release itself in the case of a lack of oath. The old sacramental formula *isto Zeus* is a call to the divinities as ocular witnesses and thus irrecusable judges.

Etymology (Gaffiot): *Sacramentum: 1. The stake (consigned to the hands of Pontiffs by the parties that were pleading).*

2. Military oath. 3. General oath. 4. Mystery, sacrament.

THIS PLAY HAD BEEN WRITTEN BETWEEN
DECEMBER 1992 AND SEPTEMBER 1993.
THE EVENTS OF THIS STORY TOOK PLACE
BETWEEN 3500 YEARS BC AND THE YEAR 1993.
FOLLOWING THEM ARRIVED,
IN REALITY, FACTS THAT RESSEMBLED THEM.
THE SPEECH OF THEATRE,
PROFEREED TO THE PRESENT AND TO THE INTEMPORAL,
IS BY DEFINITION PROPHETIC.

Serment

(Littré) 1. Affirmation ou promesse en prenant à témoin Dieu ou ce que l'on regarde comme saint, comme divin. *Rollin*: « Celui qui trompe par un faux serment déclare ouvertement par là qu'il craint son ennemi mais qu'il méprise Dieu. » *Rousseau*: « C'est un second crime de tenir un serment criminel. » 2. Serment, imprécation. *Vertot*: « Après avoir fait des serments horribles qu'il poursuivrait cette affaire jusqu'à la mort. »

(Benveniste) Le serment en Grèce est l'affirmation solennelle placée sous la garantie d'une puissance non humaine chargée de châtier le parjure. En grec notamment, on peut ressaisir dans le tour déjà homérique *horkon omnunai*, signifiant spécifiquement « prêter serment », son origine concrète: « saisir le *horkons* », objet chargé de puissance maléfique prête à se déclencher en cas de manquement au serment. La vieille formule sacramentaire *isto Zeus* est un appel aux divinités comme témoins oculaires et par suite juges irrécusables.

Etymologie (Gaffiot): *Sacramentum*: 1. Enjeu (consigné entre les mains des Pontifes par les parties qui plaidaient).

2. Serment militaire. 3. Serment en général. 4. Mystère, sacrement.

CETTE PIÈCE A ÉTÉ ÉCRITE ENTRE
DÉCEMBRE 1992 ET SEPTEMBRE 1993.
LES ÉVÉNEMENTS DE CE RÉCIT SE SONT PRODUITS
ENTRE 3500 ANS AVANT J.C. ET L'ANNÉE 1993.
PAR LA SUITE SONT ARRIVÉS,
DANS LA RÉALITÉ, DES FAITS QUI LEUR RESSEMBLAIENT.
C'EST QUE LA PAROLE DU THÉÂTRE,
PROFÉRÉE AU PRÉSENT ET À L'INTEMPOREL,
EST PAR DÉFINITION PROPHÉTIQUE.

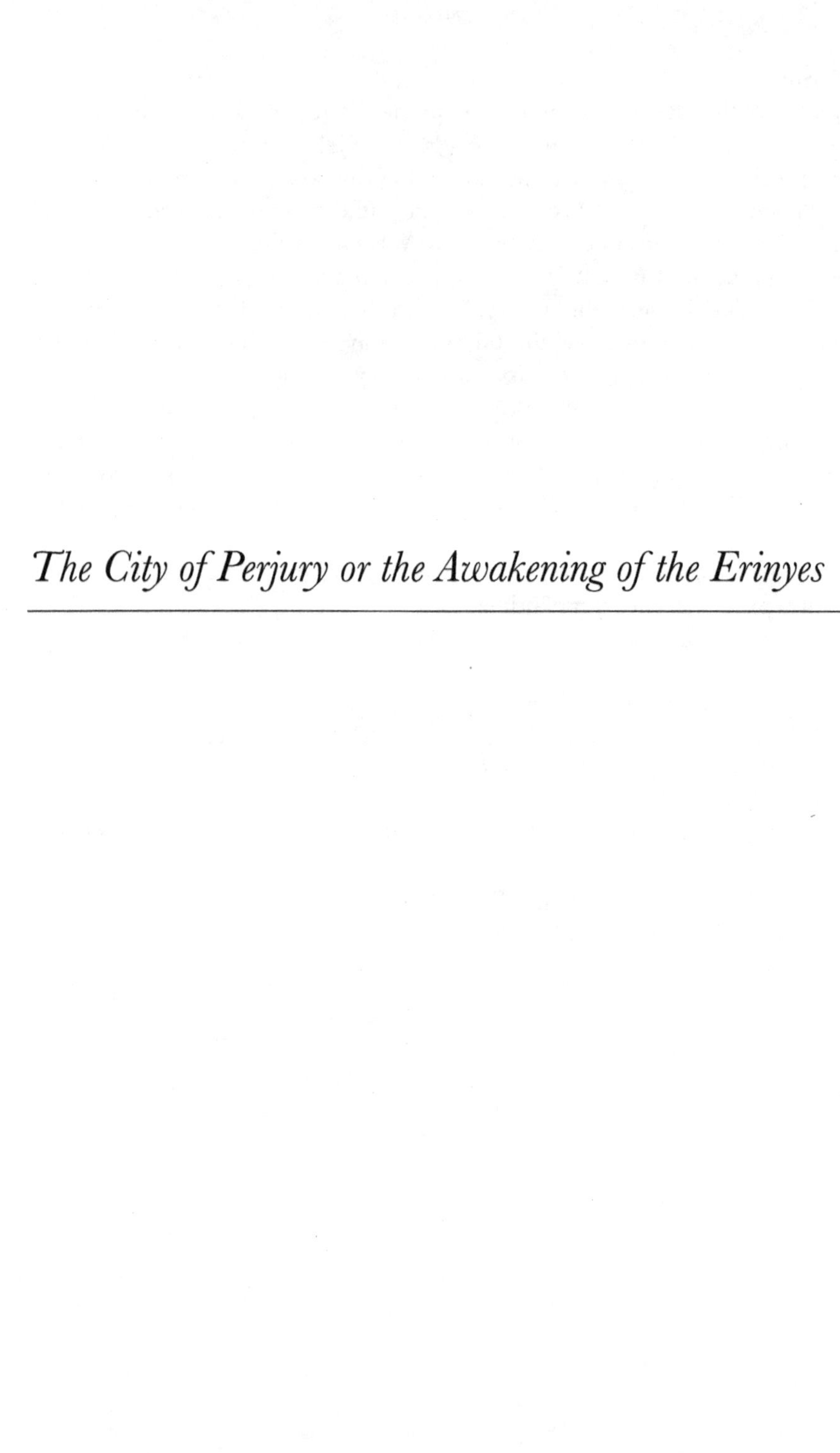

The City of Perjury or the Awakening of the Erinyes

The play: *The City of Perjury or the Awakening of the Erinyes*
Creators: The Théâtre du Soleil
First performed: 18 May 1994 at the Cartoucherie in Vincennes, Paris
Director: Ariane Mnouchkine
Text: Hélène Cixous
The playtext (editions du Théâtre du Soleil) appeared in 1994 but was updated with the new preface by Hélène Cixous 'Recognising Debts' in 2010
Music: Jean-Jacques Lemêtre
Set: Guy-Claude François
Costumes: Nathalie Thomas and Marie-Hélène Bouvet

Synopsis: *The City of Perjury or the Awakening of the Erinyes* was inspired by the drama that came to be known as 'The contaminated blood affair' in the 1980s and early 1990s when the French government knowingly distributed blood contaminated with HIV and Hepatitis C to thousands of haemophiliacs. The play takes the form of an Ancient Greek tragedy with characters from Greek mythology: the 'infernal goddesses' of vengeance, the Erinyes. *The City of Perjury or the Awakening of the Erinyes* tells the story of a mother who searches, not for ways to avenge injustice, but rather for ways to pardon the doctors responsible for the death of her two children. The play exhorts the audience to demand that corrupt political and business leaders are brought to justice. In a climate of corruption, it interrogates notions of responsibility and justice. It is also a metatheatrical reflection on the role of theatre and of strong heroines in raising public awareness of current and urgent social and political concerns.

Résumé de la pièce: *La Ville parjure ou le Réveil des Érinyes* est une pièce inspirée du drame qui prit le nom de 'l'Affaire du sang contaminé': dans les années 1980 et 1990 quand le gouvernement français distribue sciemment du sang contaminé (SIDA et Hépatite C) à des milliers d'hémophiles. La pièce prend la forme d'une ancienne tragédie grecque avec des personnages issus de la mythologie grecque: les 'déesses infernales' de la vengeance, les Érinyes. *La Ville parjure* est le combat d'une mère qui cherche non pas à se venger mais à faire dire "pardon" aux médecins responsables de la mort de ses deux enfants. La pièce demande aux spectateurs d'insister que les dirigeants politiques soient traduits en justice. Dans un climat de corruption, elle interroge les notions de responsabilité et de justice. Elle est aussi une réflexion méta-théâtrale sur le rôle du théâtre et de ces héroïnes fortes qui sensibilisent le public à une conscience active des injustices politiques et sociales brulantes d'actualité.

Acknowledging Debts

1. The Genesis of The City of Perjury

On the way, the first god of theatre is the *event*. The event happening at the theatre, the theatre as open to event, which is to say, to the *unforeseen* or the unforeseeable. 'We are going to make theatre', we say. It is always Ariane who invites me on this adventure: are you coming to make theatre? Naturally I say yes. Where are we going? We are going—we set out—towards. What will happen to us? Exactly what we are not expecting. It always begins in the same way: we set off, which is to say that a desire takes us and sets us in motion.

The funny thing about this expedition is that, in order to put the machine to work, we give ourselves a goal. We take it seriously. Until the event produces itself. It is a question of a meeting that creates a *deviation* in our path. It is a question of a sudden *deviance* in the country that gives us a shock and then a setback. Were we going straight? The road divides, and also our soul. We have fallen on a death, or death, in our path. We would recognise, if we thought about it, the outline of all tragedies, for example that of Oedipus. We didn't see destiny coming, it falls on top of us. We are thwarted. Pushed in the opposite direction. We are intercepted. Seized. Me, I didn't want to hear this story spoken about, this story that would control *The City of Perjury*. It was 1992, we had decided that the aim would be 'the fall of the Soviet Empire'. It was a good three or six months that we ferreted about. When suddenly: the meteor falls. An accident. 'The contaminated blood affair' as it would later come to be known. As always, it is Ariane who receives the stroke of inspiration—the telephone call of theatre. She speaks to me. The horrible 'thing' is taking hold of her. It marks a stopping point. I resist. No, no, I say, we were not going near the Berlin wall? No, no! In truth the first echoes were so dark, *atrocities* is the exact word, the bitter colour of blood, I could not believe it. And straight after, here we are before another wall, that of the Berlin wall, a high wall, very steep, that which encloses *The City of Perjury*, a triple wall: three walls of denial, of cruelty, of deafness, in

Reconnaissance de dettes

1. Genese de la La Ville Parjure

En cours de route, le premier dieu du théâtre c'est *l'événement*. L'événement advenant au théâtre, le théâtre comme ouvert à l'événement, c'est-à-dire à *l'imprévu* ou l'imprévisible. « On va faire du théâtre » se dit-on. C'est toujours Ariane qui m'invite à cette aventure: Tu viens faire du théâtre? Naturellement je dis oui. Où allons-nous? On va—on se met en route—vers. Qu'est-ce qui va nous arriver? Eh bien justement, ce à quoi nous ne nous attendons pas. Cela commence donc toujours de la même façon: voilà qu'on prend un départ, c'est-à-dire qu'un désir nous prend et nous met en mouvement. Le trait amusant de cette expédition c'est que, afin de mettre la machine en marche, on se donne un but. Et on le prend, au sérieux. Jusqu'à ce que l'événement se produise. Il s'agit d'une rencontre qui cause à notre chemin une *déviation*. Il s'agit d'une *déviance* soudaine dans le pays, qui nous cause un choc et puis un contretemps. Nous allions tout droit? La route se divise, notre esprit aussi. C'est que nous sommes tombés sur un mort, ou la mort, dans notre chemin. On reconnaîtrait, si on y pensait, le schéma de toute tragédie, par exemple celle d'Œdipe. On n'a pas vu venir le destin, il nous tombe dessus. Nous sommes contrecarrés. Poussés en direction opposée. Nous sommes interceptés. Saisis. Moi, de cette histoire qui commandera *La Ville Parjure*, je ne voulais pas entendre parler. C'était en 1992, nous avions donc pris pour but « la chute de l'Empire Soviétique ». Cela faisait bien trois mois ou six que nous furetions. Quand soudain: tombe le météore. Un accident. « L'affaire du sang contaminé » comme cela serait désigné plus tard. Comme toujours c'est Ariane qui reçoit le coup—de téléphone du théâtre. Elle m'en parle. La « chose » affreuse la saisit. Elle marque un arrêt. Je résiste. Non, non, dis-je, n'allions-nous pas vers le mur de Berlin? Non, non! En vérité les premiers échos étaient si noirs, *atroces* est le mot exact, couleur sang amer, je ne pouvais pas y croire. Et tout de suite après, nous voilà devant un autre mur que celui de Berlin, une muraille très haute, très épaisse, celle qui enclôt *La Ville Parjure*, un triple mur: trois murs de déni, de cruauté, de

the enclosure that was shutting in the Palace of the King without faith, the paradigm of so many presidents, heads of governments, princes concerned with power, who set the example of an indifference of the heart for their viziers and transmit gall and deathly coldness along the hierarchical ladder of the political body.

The theme of *Contamination* was contaminating all circles of society. An accident? But theatre, isn't its motor and its reason for existing, the task of watchman? Wasn't it invented to interrogate accidents and to pull out the secrets of such 'accidents'? To reveal to us that those of us who believe we see are blind. Theatre, this large ocular globe, this open Eye, that humans pass through with their eyes blindfolded. These irresponsible inhabitants of Life. We live by credit, we neglect to pay our debts. We think we have paid our debts, spared from sorrow, pain, fault, crime. And we consider the evils of the City as natural catastrophes. The divinities send us plagues. It is an accident, we say. In an obscure niche, at the bottom of the soul, Conscience, the guard dog, has plunged into a narcotic sleep. It's tiring to be vigilant. The accident, is it a *pure* accident? Or an *impure accident*, an act of bad will?—Come and see 'that', says Ariane. I went beyond my own incredulity, right up to the edge of horror.

2. *Where?*

It is the decisive question for the visionary director that Ariane is. Firstly there is the empty space that we make. There must be two empty spaces: the matrix of empty space, without precondition, where we are going to be able to believe, materialise, the animated place of the stage. And the interior emptiness of the author, the willing desert, suitable for receiving the unknowns, strangers, people, beasts, the living and the dead, a whole world of self-othering. The internal inactivity is the first moment of gestation for the author. For Ariane, nothing takes place before finding a place. So where? We will never say enough about the extent to which the place that arrives is the secret character, the most determining character there is for a theatrical creation. The place speaks.

Give place. The place—says Theatre—makes me act. Trace the unthinkable limit between inside and outside. Sign Theatre which by definition is inside outside, whip all the curtains outside the belt of the city, as does the Théâtre du Soleil which is located, we know, at the edge/the ear (of the city, the forest, the crossroads, of centuries)[1]. Fruit of chance, son of necessity. The place works. I imagine, in the future, attentive research and studies around the places in the whole oeuvre of shows by the Soleil. Soon, in the

1. The Cartoucherie, a former munitions factory, today functions as the rehearsal and performance spaces of the Théâtre du Soleil and is located on the outskirts of Paris, in the Bois de Vincennes.

surdité, dans l'enceinte desquels s'enfermait le Palais d'un Roi sans foi, paradigme de tant de présidents, chefs de gouvernement, princes soucieux de pouvoir, qui donnent à leurs vizirs l'exemple de l'indifférence du cœur et transmettent tout au long de l'échelle hiérarchique ou du corps politique le fiel et la froideur mortels.

Le thème de la *Contamination* contaminait tous les cercles de la société. Un accident? Mais le théâtre n'a-t-il pas pour moteur et pour raison d'être une mission de veilleur? N'a-t-il pas été inventé pour interroger l'accident, pour tirer les secrets de « l'accident »? Pour nous révéler que nous sommes des aveugles qui se croient voyants? Le Théâtre, ce grand globe oculaire, cet Œil ouvert, dans lequel passent ces humains aux yeux bandés. Ces habitants irresponsables de la Vie. Nous vivons à crédit, nous omettons de payer nos dettes. Nous nous croyons quittes, épargnés par la peine, la douleur, la faute, le crime. Et nous considérons les maux de la Cité comme des catastrophes naturelles. Les divinités nous envoient des pestes. C'est un accident, disons-nous. Dans une niche obscure au fond de l'âme, Conscience, le chien de garde, est plongé dans un sommeil narcotique. C'est fatigant d'être vigilant. L'accident est-il un *pur* accident? Ou un *accident impur*, un acte de mauvaise volonté?—Viens voir « ça », dit Ariane. Je me suis rendue au delà de ma propre incrédulité jusqu'aux bords de l'horreur.

2. *Où?*

C'est la question décisive pour le metteur en scène visionnaire qu'est Ariane. D'abord il y a le vide, que l'on fait. Il faut deux vides: le vide matriciel de l'espace, sans préalable, où va pouvoir croître, se matérialiser, le lieu animé de la scène. Et le vide intérieur de l'auteur, le désert volontaire, propre à recevoir des inconnus, des étrangers, des gens, des bêtes, des vivants et des morts, tout un monde à moi étranger. L'inoccupation du for intérieur est le premier temps de la gestation pour l'auteur. Pour Ariane, rien n'a lieu avant le lieu. Alors où? On ne dira jamais assez à quel point le lieu qui vient est le personnage secret le plus déterminant qui soit pour une création théâtrale. Le lieu parle. Donne lieu. Le lieu—dit le Théâtre—m'agit. Trace l'impensable limite entre le dedans et le dehors. Signe le Théâtre qui, par définition est dedans dehors, cingle tous rideaux dehors à la ceinture de la ville, comme le fait le Théâtre du Soleil qui est sis, on le sait, à *l'orée* (de la ville, de la forêt, des carrefours, des siècles). Fruit du hasard, fils de la nécessité. Le lieu travaille. J'imagine à l'avenir des études attentives et chercheuses portant sur les lieux à l'œuvre dans l'ensemble des spectacles du Soleil. Bientôt, dans l'élaboration de l'œuvre, la musique viendra à son tour faire « lieu » flexible, cosmos pensant, mer invisible porteuse des personnages et de leurs voyages, et langue universelle. Ce qu'aura dit la musique créée par Jean-Jacques Lemêtre pour *La Ville Parjure*, m'a inépuisablement tiré des

expansion of the oeuvre, music will, in its turn, create the flexible 'place', thinking cosmos, invisible sea, carrier of the characters and their journeys, and universal language.

What the music created by Jean-Jacques Lemêtre for *The City of Perjury* will have said, drew tears from me inexhaustibly. If I went twenty-five times to a performance, twenty-five times I responded with tears to the same question-meditation posed by the music: who is the child that dies in me each time I lose a life? In the frailest zones of the heart, thought only speaks musically. It doesn't know, it feels. And the place was created, very quickly. What Ariane lived, was the City of the Dead, this cemetery-city, this outside-mortuary-city that adds to Cairo's heart an additional capital, giant cemetery peopled under, above, shelter for more of the living than the deceased, where the debris of society makes a compost-human population. Mythical model of cohabitation. City of the Dead in internal exclusion from the City of the living. Death in Life, Life after Death.

The City of Perjury is also and in the first place the vision of the City-outside-the-City, the Shadow of the City, of the City at the door of the City, the City of scum and waste, the anti-city, that which stands up to the head-City, the site where the expelled people camp, excluded, banished, without-shelter, all these rejected—of which the species multiplies in contemporary civilization, this great producer of repulsed and forbidden people—from the beggars of the past or the 'miserable ones', those without identity papers, the exiled, migrants, clandestine people, refugees without refuge, condemned innocents, displaced populations, mistreated people make an interminable succession of oppressed and pursued.

To this destitute are added those exiled internally, those sacrificed to profit, the victims of the unbridled greed of the Money-Society, who sometimes even belong to the ranks of Society. Profit, Accumulation, Insatiability, the Stock Exchange in place of the heart, governs the actions of a Greedy World. The value of the human is hardly comparable to financial interests. There must be blind sacrifices for them not to see their own image in these human beings. To not-see and not-know are the mental acrobatics expertly practiced by the contemporary profiteers: all the plutocratic institutions, all the powers, executive, judiciary, legislative, medical, etc. are infiltrated, won, by Blindness. *The City of Perjury* is a city surrounded, threatened, unmasked, contradicted, denounced by this other city that these dead, who are not yet functioning, populate.

3. The Causes

The creations of the Théâtre du Soleil are the Causes. They are caused. They look for causes. They are inspired, caused, by a sort of bleak curiosity that is both infantile and philosophical, pushed to the point of not being

larmes. Si j'ai assisté vingt-cinq fois à une représentation, vingt-cinq fois j'ai répondu en larmes à la même question-méditation posée par la musique: qui est l'enfant qui meurt en moi, chaque fois que je perds une vie? Dans les zones les plus frêles du cœur, la pensée ne parle que musicalement. Elle ne sait pas, elle sent.

Et le lieu fut, et très vite. Ce qu'Ariane vit, c'était la Cité des Morts, ce cimetière-ville, cette extracité mortuaire qui ajoute au cœur du Caire une capitale supplémentaire, cimetière géant peuplé dessous dessus, abri pour plus de vivants que de défunts, où les débris de la société font une population composthume. Modèle fabuleux d'une cohabitation. Cité des morts en exclusion interne à la Cité des vivants. La Mort dans la Vie, la Vie après la Mort.

La Ville Parjure, c'est aussi et en premier lieu la vision de la Ville-hors-de-la-Ville, de l'Ombre de Ville, de la Ville à la porte de la Ville, la Cité des rebuts et des refus, l'antiville, celle qui tient tête à la Ville-en-chef, le site où campent les expulsés, exclus, bannis, sans-abri, tous ces rejetés dont les espèces se multiplient dans la civilisation contemporaine, cette grande productrice des refoulés et interdits: aux clochards d'autrefois ou aux « misérables », sans-papiers, exilés, migrants, clandestins, réfugiés sans refuge, condamnés innocents, populations déplacées, personnes maltraitées, font une interminable suite d'opprimés et pourchassés. A ces démunis s'ajoutent les exilés de l'intérieur, les immolés au profit, les victimes des cupidités effrénées de la Société-Argent, qui parfois appartiennent aux rangs mêmes de la Société. Le Profit, l'Accumulation, l'Insatiabilité, la Bourse à la place du cœur, gouvernent les actions du Monde Avide. La valeur de l'humain est nulle comparée aux intérêts financiers. Il leur faut de sacrées cécités pour ne pas voir dans ces êtres humains leurs semblables. Ne-pas-voir et ne-pas-savoir sont les acrobaties mentales pratiquées en experts par les profiteurs contemporains: toutes les institutions ploutocratiques, tous les pouvoirs, exécutif, judiciaire, législatif, médical, etc., sont infiltrés, gagnés, par la Cécité. *La Ville Parjure* est une ville bordée, menacée, démasquée, contredite, dénoncée par cette ville autre que peuplent des morts pas encore en fonction.

3. Les Causes

Les créations du Théâtre du Soleil sont des Causes. Elles sont causées. Elles cherchent les causes. Elles sont inspirées, causées, par une sorte de grave curiosité à la fois enfantine et philosophique, poussées à ne pas laisser en repos, à poser les questions insupportables, à demander raison aux insensés, à vouloir savoir pourquoi tant de gens ne veulent pas savoir. Ces *créations* se situent donc toujours aux racines, aux racines du bien et du mal mêlés, racines fendues, blessées, de la vie toujours déjà assiégée par son contraire. Par définition, ces récits-causes épousent la cause de la vie, rêvent

able to let it rest, to pose unbearable questions, to ask the insane to be reasonable, to want to know why so many people don't want to know. These *creations* situate themselves thus always at the roots, at the roots of good and bad mixed together, cracked roots, damaged from life always already besieged by its contradictions. By definition, these stories-causes embrace the cause of life, dream of births and inventions and seeing themselves forced to defend their skin at a high price. Because kingdoms are subject to rot/rottenness, as Aeschylus, the Bible, or Shakespeare know, or Montaigne, who has so many essays that deal with the symptoms of politics. In the *City of Perjury*, the illness is at the same time reality and metaphor. Now the contagious are not those who suffer in their bodies but those whose soul reeks without conscience.

4. Genealogy—Hauntology[2]

The City of Perjury is a descendant and inheritor of plays that came before it at the Théâtre du Soleil. Seen from close up, it carries the indelible traces of *Sihanouk*, *l'Indiad*, *The Atreides*, of Shakespeare. We could easily show a 'hauntology' of these different moments of the same, all too human, tragicomedy. 'The Author' that I am/follow[3] is not conscious of the moment when I write. It is when I wake up that I return to the previous works, and thus, that I discern, with a light trembling, the commonalities that return, the returning-apparitions, the insistencies. And that, in all the levels and circles of the City. Thus the *Elements:* after the fact, in the plays I perceive a tempestuous activity, inseparable from the action, indissociable from the desires and destinies of the characters. Tidal wave, deluges, storms, telluric movements, natural earthquakes are the symmetries and doubles of psychic agitations: just as the columns of fire that accompany the displacements of great Biblical figures, or the tempests of salt or behemoth whales, similar to the forests that walk in *Macbeth*, like the men who recreate between and against themselves the catastrophes and floods in each of my fables since *The Terrible But Unfinished Story of Norodom Sihanouk*. A story brings its own incompletion differently, in place of the story that seems to repeat itself and anticipate itself. Evil is a great inventor of new destructions.

A foreboding makes the play tremble from its beginnings, roused by hope until the last battle. Us, the public, we are there in the hope that this time it will not end badly. At the verdict, which is always death, this time,

2. '*Hauntologie*' is a term coined by Jacques Derrida that in French is homophonous with '*ontologie*' meaning 'ontology'. Hauntology plays with the idea that ontology or being and its inextricable relationship to non-being is always inflected, or haunted by the spectres of the past and of history.

3. The phrase '*je suis*' that figures here means both 'I am' and 'I follow' and this play on words is also employed by Derrida, particularly in his book *L'animal donc que je suis* (2006) where the pun describes the hauntology of human-animal relations in the contemporary world.

de naissances et d'inventions, et se voient contraints de défendre chèrement leur peau. Car les royaumes sont sujets à la pourriture, comme Eschyle, la Bible, ou Shakespeare le savent, ou Montaigne, dont tant d'essais traitent des symptômes en politique. Dans *La Ville Parjure*, la maladie est à la fois la réalité et la métaphore. Or les contagieux ne sont pas ceux qui souffrent dans leur corps mais ceux dont l'âme sans conscience empeste.

4. Généalogie—Hantologie

La Ville Parjure est descendante et héritière des pièces qui l'ont précédée au Théâtre du Soleil. Vue de près, elle porte les traces, indélébiles, de *Sihanouk*, de *l'Indiade*, des *Atrides*, des Shakespeare. On pourrait aisément dégager une « hantologie » de ces moments différents d'une même tragique Comédie trop humaine.

« L'auteur » que je suis n'en est pas consciente au moment où j'écris. C'est lorsque je me réveille et que je me retourne vers les ouvrages précédents, c'est alors, que je discerne, avec un léger tremblement, des traits qui reviennent, des réapparitions, des insistances. Et cela dans tous les étages et cercles de la Ville. Ainsi des *Éléments*: après coup, j'aperçois dans les pièces une activité tempestueuse inséparable de l'action, indissociable des passions et des destins des personnages. Raz-de-marée, déluges, orages, mouvements telluriques, les séismes naturels sont les symétries et les doubles des agitations psychiques: de même que des colonnes de feu accompagnent les déplacements des grandes figures de la Bible, ou des tempêtes de sel, ou des baleines béhémoths, de même des forêts marchent dans *Macbeth*, de même les hommes reproduisent entre et contre eux-mêmes les catastrophes et les déluges dans chacune de mes fables depuis *L'Histoire Terrible mais Inachevée de Norodom Sihanouk*. Une histoire vient s'inachever différemment, à la place de l'histoire qui semble la répéter et l'anticiper. Le mal est un grand inventeur de nouvelles destructions.

Un pressentiment fait trembler la pièce depuis ses commencements soulevés par l'espoir jusqu'à la dernière bataille. Nous, le public, nous sommes là dans l'espoir que cette fois cela ne finira pas mal. Qu'au verdict qui est toujours de mort, cette fois, d'une façon ou d'une autre, nous survivrons.

« L'auteur », moi en l'occurrence, fait tout ce qu'elle peut pour contourner l'échéance. Que la vie soit un plus ou moins long détour vers la mort, comme le rappelle Freud, je n'en doute pas. Notre chance de vie est dans la durée et les charmes du détour; et aussi dans notre aptitude à vivre au présent, car le présent ne connaît pas la mort. Le théâtre est une puissante négociation avec la vie et la mort. Sous son toit supraréel s'opère ce que Coleridge appela « a willing suspension of disbelief », une suspension provisoire volontaire de la résistance à la croyance.

En vérité notre récit est bien une succession de détours, de retards et de

one way or another, we will survive.

'The author', me in this instance, does all that she can to bypass expiration. That life is more or less a long detour towards death, as Freud reminds us, I do not doubt it. Our fortune in life is in the duration and the charms of the detour; and also in our aptitude to live in the present, because the present doesn't know death. Theatre is a powerful negotiation with life and death. Beneath its super-real roof, what Coleridge calls 'a willing suspension of disbelief', a voluntary and provisionary suspension of resistance to belief, takes effect.

In truth, our story is a succession of detours, lateness and delays, of suspensions of misfortune and sadness. But it is also a series of blows, theatrical coups, which is to say, stabbings. The battle is tight. And we don't know who, what, will triumph, in the end.

But when we go to the theatre (which we all do, spectators, actors, officials, assembled in the same House of Fate), we *operate* a displacement, we get out of habit. It is an act of affirmation, it is a gesture of solidarity with others and with the forces of life, it is always because we betted on Life triumphant that it is *already* a triumph of Life: we are going—or we come—*to see, to see ourselves not seeing, and to believe.* We *are going to* believe. *To believe* that we die at the end and that even still *Life* is stronger than our death. At least, for a moment we survive/we are on top of life and, looking at humanity with the naked eye, we oversee/see on.

5. *Saved by* The Eumenides

When Ariane felt the need to stage *The Atreides* play-cycle, the lot given to me was the task to translate *The Eumenides* by Aeschylus—chance among chances. The Eumenides, you remember, are not the main characters of the great play by Aeschylus. During the play of this name are the Erinyes, who are unleashed in sublime songs. The Eumenides are *the rest.* What is left over at the end of the play, after the capture, the execution, the surrender of the powerful persecuting furies from Orestes' matricide, when they have finally agreed to go under the earth to the level where forgotten grandmothers reside, those who became 'benevolent' through repulsion and relegation. Those here before us. Silenced, forbidden to say the truth.

It is there, under the earth that I went to solicit their return and their help. I was utterly distraught. I asked myself how to *transform* a sad story that had endured the misfortune of 'making number one' in the French newspapers for a year, that had become the object of columns of paper, how could I rip from the media pillory the breath of so many real people, for lots of children, who were about to die, even here, in the neighbourhood. How, *in theatre,* can we 'show' the tragedies that temporal or geographic distance was not protecting from the violence of reality. This time I didn't have the help

retardements, de suspensions du malheur et de la douleur. Mais il est aussi une série de coups, de coups de théâtre, c'est-à-dire de coups de poignard. La lutte est serrée. Et on ne sait pas qui, ce qui, à la fin, triomphera.

Mais quand on va au théâtre (ce que nous faisons tous, spectateurs, acteurs, agents, rassemblés dans la même Maison du Sort), on *opère* un déplacement, on sort de l'habitude. C'est un acte d'affirmation, c'est un geste de solidarité avec les autres et avec les forces de la vie, c'est toujours parce qu'on a parié pour un triomphe de la Vie, c'est *déjà* un triomphe de la Vie: on va—ou on vient—*voir, se voir ne pas voir, et croire.* On *va* croire. *Croire* qu'à la fin on meurt et que cependant *la Vie* est plus forte que notre mort. Au moins pour un temps on sur-vit et, regardant l'humanité à l'œil nu, on sur-voit.

5. *Sauvée par* les Euménides

Lorsqu'Ariane a eu besoin de monter le cycle des *Atrides*, à moi le lot m'a attribué la tâche de traduire les *Euménides* d'Eschyle, chance parmi mes chances. Les Euménides, vous vous en souvenez, ne sont pas les personnages principaux de la géniale pièce d'Eschyle. Pendant la pièce de ce nom, ce sont les Erynies qui sont déchaînées dans des chants sublimes. Les Euménides sont des *restes.* Ce qui reste à la fin de la pièce, après la réduction, l'exécution, la reddition des puissantes furies persécutrices du matricide Oreste, lorsqu'elles ont finalement consenti à se laisser descendre sous la terre jusqu'à l'étage où séjournent les grandmères oubliées, les devenues « bienveillantes » par refoulement et relégation. Les ci-devantes. Tues, interdites de dire la vérité. C'est là, sous la terre, que je suis allée solliciter leur retour et leur aide: j'étais en désarroi. Je me demandais comment *transfigurer* une douloureuse histoire qui avait eu le malheur de « faire la une » des journaux français pendant un an, d'être devenue l'objet de colonnes de papier, comment arracher au pilori médiatique le souffle de tant de personnes réelles, pour beaucoup des enfants, qui étaient en train de mourir, ici même, dans le voisinage. Comment, *au théâtre,* « montrer » des tragédies que la distance temporelle ou géographique ne protégeait pas des violences de l'actualité. Cette fois-ci je n'avais pas le secours de l'Asie ou l'écart d'un siècle. Pendant que j'écris, me disais-je, des hémophiles pâtissent et périssent, peut-être dans le quartier. La conscience de l'imminence et de la proximité de tant de deuils ne me quittait pas. Jamais je n'avais eu un si fiévreux sentiment de responsabilité. Jamais « écrire sur » ne m'avait semblé si difficile à « opérer » avec la délicatesse requise. Comment ne pas parler? Comment parler en ne heurtant pas? Comment frapper fort les bourreaux sans faire tressaillir les victimes? Sans le secours des Erinyes, ces furies qui ont toujours gardé cachée une bienveillance secrète, je ne m'en serais pas tirée. Il faut garder à l'horreur sa grandeur et à la pitié sa profondeur de pur cristal, et cela ne peut se faire que dans les airs mythologiques qui soufflent sous le

of Asia or the gap of a century. While I was writing, I was saying to myself: hemophiliacs suffer and perish, perhaps even in this suburb.

Awareness of the imminence and closeness of so much mourning wouldn't leave me. Never had I experienced such a feverish feeling of responsibility. Never had the words 'write on' seemed so difficult to 'operate' with the required delicateness. How not to speak? How to speak and not offend? How to forcefully strike the hangmen without making the victims wince? Without the help of the Erinyes, the furies who have always kept a benevolent secret hidden, and I wouldn't let myself be drawn in. One must maintain the grandeur of horror and the pure crystal depth of pity, and only that can make itself in the mythological airs that blow under the canopy of the theatre of the unconscious. There remain figures of humanity and of inhumanity. Far from the mummified agitations of newspaper and television, pity, when Shakespeare saw it go by, was a stark naked new-born, mounted on the gust of wind and blowing the horrible deed into everyone's faces, so well that tears flow. This furious cherub, it is always the child that we have lost and that we are. Pity is neither weak nor resigned, but the child of anger. To his call, enraged grandmothers get up with voices like bronze. Nothing will shut them up. Their choir turns in furious circles on all the places where mourning refuses to let assassins sleep and forget. In our epoch, indignation no longer dares to shriek. I borrowed the voices of prehistoric mourners.

6. The Ferryman

I had finished by remarking that, after several years and journeys, the slightly spectral and vital presence in all my theatrical fables, of one character other, the additional character, the magical and necessary being, active, discreet, the transparent choirmaster, who always appears in different guises, had long drawn all my curiosity. I saw that this character was *detached*, without affiliation to any 'houses' that share the territory of the stage/scene, but always *in circulation*, between the parts, the kingdoms, the communities, the camps—and being 'detached' by the play, able to make the junction or the corridor between these 'houses', often in a state of hostility in their relations with one another. I noted that he could also 'pass beyond' sexual difference, be man or woman equally, have nomadic powers: power like that of king Suramarit, dead father of Sihanouk, to move by bike from Phnom Penh to Peking although dead; or like the Baule Haridasi, power to be anywhere in India at the moment when Gandhi would greatly need a disinterested witness. These without-attachments could also move over and under the ground, and from death to survival. Similar to the *Ghost* of Hamlet, but with more freedom, longevity and cheerfulness, being emancipated from all heritage, from all intrigue, and without membership to either a world nor its opposite. I will soon call him/her *the ferryman*. It seems to me that he/she was

dais du théâtre de l'inconscient. Là demeurent les figures de l'humanité et de l'inhumanité. Loin des émois momifiés par le papier journal et la télévision, la pitié, quand Shakespeare l'a vue passer, était un nouveau-né tout nu, à cheval sur la rafale et soufflant l'acte horrible au visage de tous, si bien que les larmes ruissellent dans le vent. Ce chérubin furieux, c'est toujours l'enfant que nous avons perdu et que nous sommes. Pitié n'est ni faible ni résigné mais l'enfant des colères. A son appel se lèvent les grand-mères enragées aux voix d'airain. Rien ne les fera taire. Leur chœur tourne en ronde furieuse sur toutes les places où le deuil refuse aux assassins le sommeil et l'oubli. A notre époque l'indignation n'ose plus hurler. J'ai emprunté les voix des pleureuses préhistoriques.

6. Le Passeur

J'avais fini par remarquer, après quelques années, et voyages, la présence un peu spectrale et vitale, dans toutes mes fables théâtrales, d'un personnage autre, le personnage-supplément, l'être magique et nécessaire, actif, discret, le transparent meneur de chœur, dont la réapparition, toujours sous une figure différente, avait à la longue requis toute ma curiosité. Je voyais que ce personnage était *détaché*, sans lien avec aucune des « maisons » qui se partagent le territoire de la scène, mais toujours *en circulation* entre les partis, les royaumes, les communautés, les camps,—et comme « détaché » par la pièce à faire la jonction ou le passage entre ces « maisons » souvent en état d'hostilité les unes par rapport aux autres. Je notais qu'il pouvait aussi « passer » la différence sexuelle, être homme ou femme également, disposer de pouvoirs nomades: pouvoir, comme le roi Suramarit, père mort de Sihanouk, de circuler, à vélo de Phnom Penh à Pékin quoique mort; ou comme la Baoule Haridasi, pouvoir d'être n'importe où en Inde à l'heure où Gandhi aurait grand besoin d'un témoin désintéressé. Ce sans-attaches pouvait aussi passer sur et sous la terre, et de trépas à survie. Comme le *Ghost* de Hamlet, mais avec plus de liberté, de longévité et d'enjouement, étant affranchi de tout héritage, de toute intrigue, et sans appartenance ni à un monde ni à son contraire. Je l'appelai bientôt *le passeur*. Il me sembla qu'il était un double, ou peut-être l'esprit de la pièce, et quelqu'un toujours qui était du parti de la vie plutôt que de la mort. En tout cas un personnage d'une autonomie absolue, qui ne m'a jamais demandé de lui faire un destin. Comme s'il avait toujours été là. Et serviable, hospitalier, prêt à toute éventualité, sans aucune inhibition, il pouvait sortir de derrière un rideau, se faire un lit dans la cavité d'une tombe, ou faire passer le public d'une rive à l'autre du temps, si la pièce le demandait. On ne peut imaginer un acolyte plus généreux et plus puissant pour l'auteur par définition toujours-en-difficulté. Or, dans *La Ville Parjure*, cette incarnation de la magie du théâtre se présenta sous les traits de Monsieur Eschyle, employé à cette époque comme gardien

a double, or perhaps the soul of the play, and always someone who was more a part of life than death. In any case, a character with absolute autonomy, who never asked me to invent a future for him/her. As if he/she had always been there. And helpful, hospitable, ready for every contingency without any inhibition, he/she could come out from behind a curtain, make a bed for him/herself in the crack of a tomb, or move the public from one bank to the other in time, if the play called for it. One cannot imagine a more generous or powerful acolyte for the author by definition always-in-difficulty. Now, in *The City of Perjury,* this incarnation of theatrical magic presents itself in Monsieur Aeschylus, employed in this epoch as the caretaker of the municipal cemetery. What is charming about the ferryman is that he/she holds the absolute privilege of non-limits. He/she is present and extra-temporal. He/she has an ageless memory, he/she remembers the dawn of Greek democracy as much as the democracy yet to come, and being a caretaker, he/she remembers extra-temporally what Shakespeare was thinking as much as what Heidegger was philosophising. In short, I cannot do without the ferryman. Everything that surpasses me, he/she recollects it and takes it beyond. What an incalculable fantasy! I never know who will be in the next episode of the Great Series. I trust him/her. He/she has the strength and necessity of the captain of Dreams. And as if in a dream, he/she gives form to the most intense preoccupations, the most conflicted and thus the most complex, in an absolutely admirable economy of signs. The ferryman has a sober language, efficient, load-bearing. He/she speaks Theatre. What am I doing on this page? I am trying to say to what point the author of Theatre is happily indebted. It owes its creation to ghosts, predecessors, the director, to so many people, actors, characters. Happily haunted. Happily indebted.

January 2010 *'Reconnaissance de dettes' was first published in French in* La Ville parjure ou le Réveil des Érinyes, Théâtre du Soleil/Theatrical editions/ BNF, 2010, pp. 9-16

du cimetière municipal. Ce qui est délicieux avec le passeur c'est qu'il détient le privilège absolu du sans-limite. Il est présent et extratemporel. Il a une mémoire sans âge, il se souvient de l'aube de la démocratie grecque comme de celle de la démocratie à venir, en tant que gardien il se souvient extratemporellement de ce que pensait Shakespeare comme de ce que philosophait Heidegger. Bref, je ne peux pas me passer du passeur. Tout ce qui me dépasse il le recueille et le porte au delà. Et quelle fantaisie incalculable! Je ne sais jamais qui il sera dans le prochain épisode du Grand Feuilleton. Je lui fais confiance. Il a la force et la nécessité du commandant du Rêve. Et comme dans le rêve, il donne forme aux préoccupations les plus intenses, les plus conflictuelles et donc les plus complexes, dans une économie de signes tout à fait admirable. Le passeur a une langue sobre, efficace, porteuse. Il parle le Théâtre. Que fais-je sur cette page? J'essaie de dire à quel point l'auteur de Théâtre est heureusement endetté. Il doit la création à des fantômes, à des devanciers, au metteur en scène, à tant de personnes, d'acteurs, de personnages. Heureux hanté. Heureuse endettée.

Janvier 2010 'Reconnaissance de dettes' in La Ville parjure ou le Réveil des Érinyes, *Théâtre du Soleil/éditions Théâtrales/BNF, 2010, pp. 9-16*

The Atreides

The play: *The Atreides*
Creators: The Théâtre du Soleil
First performed: 1990-1992 at the Cartoucherie of Vincennes, Paris
16 November 1990: *Iphigenia in Tauris*
24 November 1990: *Agamemnon*
23 February 1991: *The Choephori*
26 May 1992: *The Eumenides*
Director: Ariane Mnouchkine
Text: Euripides (*Iphigenia in Tauris*), Aeschylus (*Agamemnon, The Choephori, The Eumenides)*
Translators: Jean Bollack (*Iphigenia in Tauris*), Ariane Mnouchkine (*Agamemnon, The Choephori*) and Hélène Cixous (*The Eumenides*)
Music: Jean-Jacques Lemêtre
Set: Guy-Claude François with sculptures by Erhard Stiefel
Costumes: Nathalie Thomas and Marie-Hélène Bouvet

Synopsis: Between 1990 and 1992, the Théâtre du Soleil staged the Euripides' play *Iphigenia in Tauris* and Aeschylus' trilogy of plays, the *Oresteia* (458 BC). The trilogy includes *Agamemnon*, *The Libation Bearers* (*Choephoroi*), and *The Eumenides. Iphigenia in Tauris* was translated by Jean Bollack, *Agamemnon* and *The Libation Bearers* (*Choephoroi*) were translated by Ariane Mnouchkine and *The Eumenides* was translated by Hélène Cixous. These plays recount the lives of the family members of the House of Atreus, the Atreides. Cixous' essays respond predominantly to *The Eumenides* in which the Erinyes goddesses appeal to Athena and 11 other judges to decide whether Orestes is guilty of matricide.

Résumé de la pièce: Entre 1990 et 1992, le Théâtre du Soleil monte *Iphigenie* à *Aulis* d'Euripide, et la trilogie dramatique d'Eschyle, *L'Orestie* (458 av. J-C). Après le sacrifice d'*Iphigénie*, *Agamemnon* met en scène le retour du roi de Mycènes après la Guerre de Troie, et son meurtre par Clytemnestre. À la vengeance d'Oreste (*Les Choéphores*), s'ensuit son procès (*Les Euménides*) où s'affrontent, devant un tribunal composé pour l'occasion: les Érinyes, Apollon et Athéna, ainsi que 11 autres juges, pour décider si Oreste est coupable de matricide.

No Response or the Call of Death

Where do these Choephori happen? These Eumenides? They happened a very long time ago, in rocky lands where we have never been. And yet, for our trouble, we endure these hardships, this blackness fills us with gloom, these poisons intoxicate us today, even this year. On the one hand, these are events that took place thousands of years ago, before our culture, before our history. On the other hand, these terrors have similarities in us. They are still in us and close to us, these violent states of the soul, that shatter us, throw us into disorder, are stronger than us, make exiles of us from our own selves, terrified people, obsessed people, these are those awful unknowns that, in our distraction, we call mourning, melancholy, hate, vengeful thirst, as if, with words to name them, we hope to restrain their unthinkable outbursts.

But what does it mean 'hate'? Hate is when Electra and her slaves cannot stop themselves for a minute to think about the person who hurts them the most, it is black love, it is such desire, a hunger that devours us, a mad attachment to death. We don't know what would make him happy. Would appease him. Each one has different rituals, each according to their culture, time, history, quirks. But the falling of the heart in the abyss of the chest, the burnings and the magical freezing of the flesh, the vertigos, the torrents of tears, all of us human beings, we know them as if we didn't have an individual body, a singular scene of flesh for suffering.

Listen! Who is shouting there? It is the call of death. Who is shouting there? The survivors—the supplicants—the masters of death. The coachmen: they whip and whip, the tomb doesn't move. The person who you call on this tomb doesn't respond. Telephone cut off. And yet, they call, we call. There is the call. From whom? From death. On behalf of death. We cannot do otherwise. We must call and without cutting off. Not drop the line, of the call—of death—pull, pull, it's why we have to be at least two, relays of breaths in twos, the call is continued, at the least interruption, it's clear, death would slip away, son and daughter are united, we will not let death fly by!

What a cruel scene, unbearable, hallucinating chase scene—Orestelectra pursuing Agamemnon. They cajole, insult, demand, provoke, beg, cause

Pas de réponse ou l'Appel du Mort

Où se passent ces Choéphores? Ces Euménides? Elles se passent il y a très longtemps, dans des pays de pierres où n'avons jamais été. Et cependant, pour notre peine, nous subissons ces duretés, ces noirceurs nous assombrissent, ces poisons nous enivrent aujourd'hui, cette année même. D'une part, ce sont des événements qui ont eu lieu il y a des millénaires, avant notre culture, avant notre histoire. D'autre part, ces terreurs ont en nous leurs pareilles. Ils sont encore en nous ou tout près de nous, ces violents états de l'âme, qui nous bouleversent, nous désordonnent, sont plus forts que nous, font de nous en nous-mêmes des exilés, des affolés, des obsédés, ce sont ces affreux inconnus, que, dans notre égarement, nous appelons deuil, mélancolie, haine, soif de vengeance, comme si, avec des mots pour les nommer nous espérions brider leurs impensables déchaînements.

Mais qu'est-ce que ça veut dire 'haine'? La haine c'est quand Electre et ses esclaves ne peuvent pas s'arrêter une minute de penser à la personne qui leur fait le plus mal, c'est l'amour noir, c'est un tel désir, une faim, qui nous dévore, un attachement fou à la mort. Nous ne savons pas ce qui lui ferait plaisir. L'apaiserait. Chacun ses rites différents, chacun selon sa culture, son temps, son histoire, ses manies. Mais les chutes du cœur dans le gouffre de la poitrine, les brûlures et le gel magique de la chair, les vertiges, les torrents de larmes, nous tous les êtres humains, nous les connaissons, comme si nous n'avions qu'un seul corps, une seule scène de chair pour souffrir.

Ecoutez! Qui crie là? C'est l'appel du mort. Qui crie là? Les survivants—les suppliants—les maîtres du mort. Des cochers: ils fouettent et fouettent, la tombe ne bouge pas. La personne que vous appelez sur cette tombe ne répond pas. Téléphone coupé. Et cependant, ils appellent, nous appellons. Il y a l'appel. De la part de qui? Du mort. De la part du mort. On ne peut pas faire autrement. Il faut appeler et sans couper. Ne pas lâcher le fil, de l'appel—du mort—tirer, tirer, c'est pourquoi on doit être deux au moins, relais des souffles à deux, l'appel est continu, à la moindre interruption, c'est évident, le mort se défilerait, fils et fille sont ligués, nous ne laisserons pas le mort filer!

Quelle scène cruelle, insupportable, scène de chasse hallucinée — Oresteélectre poursuivant Agamemnon. Ils cajolent, insultent, exigent,

offense, scratch wounds, grind at amputations, swim in tears and in acids, bait, spit.

Beneath these injuries, Father, will you wake up?

No response.

The door opens. Enter—the Tomb.

In this country, in these times, under these gods here, we repeat it to ourselves, never a resurrection. Here is the cause of the anxious dimension of this persecution. Once blood is spilled it doesn't rise again in the veins. No rewinds. Ever. There is no-one at the end of the line. Not even the ghost of king Hamlet. What a silence!

But on the other hand, in the land of the living, the tomb stampers, what a racket conversely! Here we shout for two. The call of death is just that. We shout for death too. There is strength in death, a heavy energy in the silencer that makes the child scream out two times louder. As if the duo daughterson was playing double, dual role, dual sadness, children giving the order to the father—became no-one—to give the order to his children.

Due to being called, harassed, insulted, this absent one swells, like a tempest, this model gorged with anger that we lend to it, exaggerated by enormous grunts that it doesn't let out. Insidious and frightening phenomenon: because there is no dialogue,—so no noticeable rapport, no communication, so no separation, since death says nothing, doesn't come, doesn't come (since deaths are not made to be brought back from the dead), since then children cause deaths, hollowing out the silent air with sharpened speeches—thus can we no longer separate ourselves from them, nor distinguish them from ourselves, since the children make deaths into a game, and respond for them, it creates a tangle of son, son of son and son of father, a tangle of desires and identities, of deaths and of non-deaths.

Because children preserve the reputation of the dead
Save it like the corks that keep the strings/sons afloat
They save the whole net from the depths.
Listen. These moans are for you,
Honour my words and save yourself by yourself.
(x.505-510)

Weighty powerlessness. But that's not on without an orgy. The Choephori are libation carriers with a taste for death. They come to feed the deaths. Who will feed the survivors? The choir is starving to death.

When we have lost everything, Troy, the paternal city, the house, liberty, we are uprooted, between justice and injustice there is no difference, there is no more love, from whence comes this constant light in the eyes that tears burnt out? It is hate that shines, this beautiful sparkling is hate, the flamboyant lodger in bodies deserted by love. We have never before seen

provoquent, supplient, offensent, grattent les plaies, affûtent les amputations, baignent de larmes et d'acides, appâtent, crachent.

Sous ces injures, Père, te réveilleras-tu?

Pas de réponse.

La porte s'ouvre. Entre:—le Tombeau.

Dans ce pays, en ces temps-là, sous ces dieux là, on nous le répète, jamais de résurrection. Voilà la cause de la dimension angoissante de cette persécution. Le sang une fois versé ne remonte pas dans les veines. Pas de retour en arrière. Jamais. Il n'y a personne au bout du fil. Pas même le fantôme du roi Hamlet. Quel silence!

Mais d'un autre côté, chez les vivants, les trépigneurs de tombeau, quel vacarme inversement! C'est qu'ici l'on crie pour deux. L'appel du mort c'est ça. On crie pour le mort aussi. Il y a une force dans le mort, une lourde énergie dans le silencieux qui fait hurler l'enfant deux fois plus fort. Comme si le duo fillefils jouait double, double rôle, double douleur, enfants donnant l'ordre au père—devenu personne—de donner l'ordre à ses enfants.

A force d'être appelé, harcelé, insulté, comme il grossit cet absent, comme une tempête, ce mannequin gros des colères qu'on lui prête, outré d'énormes grognements qu'il ne pousse pas. Phénomène insidieux et effrayant: puisqu'il n'y a pas de dialogue,—donc pas de rapport appréciable, pas de communication, donc pas de séparation, puisque le mort ne dit rien, ne vient pas, ne vient pas (puisque les morts ne sont pas gardés ressuscitables), puisqu'alors les enfants font les morts, creusant l'air muet à coup de paroles aiguisées—voilà qu'on ne peut plus s'en séparer, ni s'en tenir distingués, puisque les enfants font le jeu des morts, et répondent pour eux, il se produit un emmêlement de fils, fils de fils et fils de père, un emmêlement de désirs et d'identités, de morts et de non morts.

Car les enfants d'un mort qui font sa renommée
Le sauvent comme les lièges qui soutiennent les fils
Sauvent des profondeurs tout le filet.
Ecoute. Ces plaintes sont pour toi,
Honore mes paroles et sauve-toi toi-même.
(v.505-510)

Pesante impuissance. Mais cela ne va pas sans orgie. Les Choéphores sont porteuses de libations au goût de mort. Elles viennent nourrir les morts. Qui nourrira ces survivantes? Le chœur crève de faim.

Quand nous avons tout perdu, Troie, la ville paternelle, la maison, la liberté, nous sommes déracinés, entre le juste et l'injuste aucune différence, il n'y a plus d'amour, d'où vient qu'il y ait encore cette lumière dans les yeux que les larmes ont brûlé? C'est la haine qui brille, ce beau scintillement c'est celui de la haine, la flamboyante locataire des corps désertés par

such shouting, dancing, such a famine. They suffer the worst pain, these deported women, raped: the sadness of having become victims, and for eternity. At least another woman doesn't come to feed their gagged hatred. At least another doesn't bite for them. Electra is the hope of these desperate ones. The delegate of their appetite. From all their enormous slave energies, they insist and inspire. Transfer of electricity. Go on. Go on. Go on.

On the one hand, we are deprived of a father, of flesh, love, family, arms, warmth. On the other, we have never seen such feasting. It is because Aeschylus trains us in the most remote zones of our joys, there at the depths, at the extremity of desperation, where we surprise ourselves to savour the paradoxical pleasures of mourning. Bitter wisdom distils the oldest secrets of the human soul for us, for us always still new.

Lamentation like glory is a sensual delight Orestes reminds us. Yes, there is a joy that vibrates in mourning. A terrible dish is made in the soul. Sadness, regret, lack, when they are expressed, change into syrups, into precious foodstuffs. Given that we are allowed to express in speeches the violent flavour, we make ourselves drunk.

This is why, between Orestes and Electra, it's a banquet of complaints: finally the two thirsty children can feed themselves, the one and the other on their own tears. They are feeders for one another. Eat my hate, my love! Devour my resentment. Swallow my hunger. As if everything given and shared is good, even sadness! It is that which is ripped from us which has a bitter taste. We eat, we drink, we restore the famished soul. It is not by accident that the feeder will arrive, useless character for 'action', essential for inscribing passion. It knows what it means to be a body only fit to be eaten by the other. Whomsoever feeds is fed. It also nourishes its sadness with its tears and the story of its grief—infant and nourishing[1] grief.

The person with whom I can confide my tears, and with whom I can share the bread of mourning, becomes my parents, my fountain. A fabulous regeneration is implemented before our eyes: for Electra we had cut off father, mother, brother, sister. Everything pushes back, thanks to the sharing of lamentations:

> *Radiating face,*
> *For me you will hold four roles.*
> *By the strength of things, I name you my father.*
> *And the love for my mother leans towards you*
> *Because she, I hate her, totally fairly.*
> *You are also she who, born of the same sowing as us,*
> *Was burned without pity.*

1. Cixous plays on the word '*nourrisson*' which means 'infant' or 'nursling' but also sounds like '*nourrisant*' meaning 'nourishing' as well as the double meaning of '*nourricier*' which in its adjectival form means 'nourishing' but as a noun describes a 'foster father'.

l'amour. On n'a jamais vu crier, danser, une telle famine. Elles souffrent du plus grand mal, ces femmes déportées, violées: la douleur d'être devenues victimes, et pour l'éternité. A moins qu'une autre femme ne vienne donner à manger à leur haine baillonnée. A moins qu'une autre ne morde pour elles. Electre est l'espoir de ces désespérées. La déléguée de leur appétit. De toutes leurs énormes énergies d'esclaves, elles insistent et inspirent. Transfert d'électricité. Vas-y. Vas-y. Vas-y.

D'une part, on est privé de père, de chair, d'amour, de famille, de bras, de chaud. De l'autre, on n'a jamais vu de tels festoiements. C'est qu'Eschyle nous entraîne dans les zones les plus reculées de nos jouissances, là-bas au fond, à l'extrémité du désespoir, où nous nous surprenons à savourer les plaisirs paradoxaux du deuil. L'âpre sagesse distille pour nous les plus anciens secrets de l'âme humaine, pour nous toujours encore nouveaux.

La lamentation comme une gloire est une volupté nous rappelle Oreste. Oui, il y a une joie qui vibre dans le deuil. Une terrible cuisine se fait dans l'âme. La douleur, le regret, le manque, lorsqu'ils sont exprimés, se changent en sirops, en aliments précieux. Pourvu qu'il nous soit permis d'en exprimer en paroles la violente saveur, nous nous enivrons.

C'est pourquoi, entre Oreste et Electre, c'est un banquet de plaintes: enfin les deux enfants assoiffés peuvent se nourrir l'un l'autre de leurs propres larmes. L'un pour l'autre est le nourricier ou la nourrice. Mange ma haine, mon amour! Dévore mon ressentiment. Avale ma faim. Comme tout ce qui est donné et partagé est bon, même la douleur! C'est ce qui nous est arraché qui a le goût amer. On mange, on boit, on restaure l'âme affamée. Ce n'est pas par hasard qu'arrivera la nourrice, personnage inutile pour 'l'action', essentiel pour inscrire la passion. Elle sait ce que c'est qu'être le corps bon à manger pour l'autre. Qui nourrit est nourri. Elle aussi nourrit son chagrin avec ses larmes et le récit de son chagrin—chagrin nourisson et nourricier.

La personne à laquelle je peux confier mes larmes, et avec laquelle je peux partager le pain de deuil, devient mes parents, ma source. Une régénerescence fabuleuse est opérée sous nos yeux: à Electre on avait coupé père, mère, frère, sœur. Tout repousse, grâce au partage des lamentations:

Visage rayonnant,
Pour moi tu tiendras quatre rôles.
Par la force des choses, je te nomme mon père.
Et l'amour pour ma mère penche vers toi
Car elle, je la hais, totalement justement.
Tu es aussi celle qui, née du même ensemencement que nous,
Fut immolée sans pitié.
Le frère fidèle, pour moi, tu l'as toujours été,
Par toi je forçais le respect.
(v.238-244)

Faithful brother, for me, you have always been,

Through you I commanded respect.
(v.238-244)

No, it's not a question of roles and functions, it's a question of eating and nourishing. Who doesn't understand that?

We want to live so much! It's not only that we are afraid to die. Clytemnestra isn't afraid. She wants and she is hungry for all provisions. Hungry for youth and hungry for old age too.

But you, I nourished you and with you I want to grow old. (v.908)

No, it's not there, pretext or argument. It's to want to have tasted everything. She, so alive, that even when dead, she will not stop desiring.

And enter a living Orestes and Clytemnestra, hate is not large, uncertain, it vacillates.

Without Pylades for severity and Apollo for stubborn law, Orestes would not succeed in severing love-conquers-all. But all the 'good reasons to kill' accompany him and fortify him. He is such a big, proud, father—in truth, as his mother feels it obscurely:

I lament alive before the stone of a tomb.

He knocks finally. So here is what falls from one side to the other, with lightning speed. A moment ago, he was strong with the rights of the victim. Now here he is, the assassin. Struck by his own blow.

From this non-enviable victory only the stain remains for me. (v.1016)

He no longer loves himself, him who loved himself a moment ago.

He discovers the implacable logic of the passage of the act. In carrying 'the victory', Orestes loses the right, the just, innocence. Here he is already all deformed, twisted like guilty ones are, immediately on the defensive even before being accused, so he himself has brutally become his first accuser. He has lost the past, the present, he is hurled into the foreboding future.

But the great Watcher, the Sun
That one day for my defence it testifies in court
Because it is with justice that I persecuted my mother to the death
(v.986-988)

He needs the Sun: because he can already no longer act as witness for himself. He doesn't believe himself. And so it is only that the flash in him, the greatest hate of the mother, that he killed, because he killed her, and everything is her fault—her, the wildcat. It's you who made an assassin of your son, you killed me! Stupefying trajectory of this Orestes who entered an hour ago with radiant face, and who is slumped now, vanquished, (it's him who says it) first and terrible model of Raskolnikov. To kill kills us, he discovers. And everything is abandonment.

The final scene takes place far away before and above this tragedy,

Non, il ne s'agit pas de rôles et de fonctions, il s'agit de manger et de nourrir. Qui ne le comprend pas?

Comme nous avons envie de vivre! Ce n'est pas seulement que nous avons peur de mourir. Clytemnestre n'a pas peur. Elle a envie et elle a faim de tous les vivres. Faim de jeunesse et faim de vieillesse aussi.

Mais toi je t'ai nourri et avec toi je veux vieillir. (v.908)

Non, ce n'est pas là prétexte ou argument. C'est vouloir avoir tout goûté. Elle, tellement vivante, que même morte elle ne cessera pas de désirer.

Et entre Oreste et Clytemnestre vivante, la haine n'est pas grande, incertaine, elle vacille. Sans Pylade pour dureté et Apollon pour loi entêtée, Oreste n'y arriverait pas, à trancher dans l'amour-malgré-tout. Mais toutes les 'bonnes raisons de tuer' l'accompagnent et le fortifient. Comme il est grand, fier, père—en vérité, comme le sent obscurément sa mère:

Je me lamente vivante devant la pierre d'un tombeau.

Il frappe enfin. Alors le voici qui tombe d'un bord à l'autre, à une vitesse foudroyante. Il y a un instant, il était fort des droits de la victime. A l'instant le voilà assassin. Frappé par son propre coup.

De cette victoire non enviable il ne me reste que la souillure. (v.1016)

Il ne s'aime plus, lui qui s'aimait il y a un instant.

Il découvre la logique implacable du passage à l'acte. En emportant 'la victoire', Oreste perd le droit, le juste, l'innocence. Le voilà déjà tout déformé, tordu comme le sont les coupables, tout de suite sur la défensive avant même d'être accusé, donc devenu lui-même brutalement son premier accusateur. Il a perdu le passé, le présent, il est précipité dans l'avenir menaçant.

Mais le grand Surveillant, le Soleil
Qu'un jour pour ma défense il témoigne en justice.
Car c'est avec justice que j'ai jusqu'à la mort persécuté ma mère.
(v.986-988)

Il lui faut le Soleil: c'est que lui-même ne peut déjà plus témoigner pour lui-même. Il ne se croit pas lui-même. Et c'est alors seulement qu'éclate en lui la plus grande haine pour la mère, qu'il a tuée, parce qu'il l'a tuée, et tout est de sa faute—à elle, le fauve. C'est toi qui de ton fils a fait un assassin, tu m'as tué! Stupéfiante trajectoire de cet Oreste qui est entré, il y a une heure, le visage rayonnant, et qui s'affaisse maintenant, vaincu, (c'est lui qui le dit) premier et terrible modèle de Raskolnikov. Tuer nous tue, découvre-t-il. Et tout est abandon.

La dernière scène s'élève très loin en avant et au-dessus de cette tragédie, le laissant angoissé, petit, livré soudain au vent glacé qui va remplacer à ses côtés tous ceux qui l'accompagnaient hier, et qui ont mystérieusement disparu sans laisser aucune trace. Plus trace de Pylade, plus trace d'Electre. Ils sont laissés si loin derrière Oreste, derrière nous. Oreste reste? Oreste a

leaving him anguished, little, suddenly delivered over to the icy wind that is going to replace from his sides all those who accompanied him yesterday, and who have mysteriously disappeared without leaving any trace. No further trace of Pylades, no further trace of Electra. They were left so far behind Orestes, behind us. Orestes remains?[2] Orestes has lost the possibility of staying, of remaining, of stopping. *I cannot stay!* he shouts, like someone who shouts: I am going to die.

Or maybe, it's that Orestes finds himself thrown into an entirely different time, onto an entirely different land. In an entirely different play. Yes, it's that which produces: solitude blows, chasing Orestes out of the play 'Choephori'.

The play remains gaping, without end.

No-one will ever know, not Orestes, not us, how things will end up in this play. It doesn't finish. It tears itself to pieces. End without end. It bleeds. Still. All of us, we are lost, dumbfounded. Separated. Without goodbye. We don't follow. We are not followed. The Chorus, so decided a short while ago, gives speeches without follow-up.

No-one calls anyone anymore.

What do we hear?

We believe we hear—calls— coming from another time—from another species…

What a way we've come in just a single day!…

Stay—the body. Clytemnestra became an indelible body. All Electra's efforts helped by one hundred Electras will not

succeed in raising this body from the stage of the soul. We don't know just how heavy the body is of the mother who has had her throat slit by the child.

No-one had ever seen them, the Erinyes, neither the gods, nor the humans, nor Aeschylus, nor Ariane Mnouchkine, nor us. The first to have 'seen' them, is Pythia. And she lost balance. Did she 'see' them? This is the stroke of genius by Aesychlus, who continues: you are going to see for the first time what no-one ever saw. Furthermore, it surpasses our abilities, to see, and to describe. Elsewhere, in this play 'The Eumendies', it only happens the first times. It's the first time that we are going to see gods in person, since we are carried away in the legend of the Atreides. Everything is new, unknown, unprecedented, to come. Right up to the world, yes: even the world—with society, cities, customs, religions, and above all else, laws—announce the unknown, full of change. That gives all the characters who shelter the Theatre this uncertainty, this trembling, shaky step, from Pythia right up to the goddess Athena, and all through the public. We are anxious, gristly.

2. Cixous plays on the harmonious assonance of '*Oreste reste*' that is lost in the English translation.

perdu la possibilité de rester, de demeurer, de s'arrêter. *Je ne peux pas rester!* crie-t-il, comme quelqu'un qui crie: je vais mourir.

Ou bien, c'est qu'Oreste se trouve jeté dans un tout autre temps, sur une tout autre terre. Dans une toute autre pièce. Oui, c'est cela qui se produit: la solitude souffle, chassant Oreste hors de la pièce appelée 'Choéphores'.

La pièce reste béante, sans fin.

Personne ne saura jamais, ni Oreste, ni nous, comment cela finira dans cette pièce. Cela ne finit pas. Cela se déchiquète. Fin sans fin. Ça saigne. Encore. Tous, nous sommes perdus, abasourdis. Séparés. Sans adieu. Nous ne suivons pas. Nous ne sommes pas suivis. Le Chœur naguère si décidé, dit des paroles sans suite.

Personne n'appelle plus personne.

Qu'est-ce qu'on entend?

On croit entendre—des appels—venus d'un autre temps —d'une autre espèce...

Quel chemin on a fait en une seule journée!...

Reste—le corps. Clytemnestre devenue corps ineffaçable. Tous les efforts d'Electre aidée de cent Electres ne

parviendront pas à enlever ce corps de la scène de l'âme. C'est que nous ne savons pas comme il est lourd le corps de la mère égorgée par l'enfant.

Personne ne les avait jamais vues, les Erynies, ni les dieux, ni les humains, ni Eschyle, ni Ariane Mnouchkine, ni nous. La première à les avoir 'vues', c'est la Pythie. Et elle en a perdu l'équilibre. Les a-t-elle 'vues'? C'est le coup de génie d'Eschyle, qui continue: vous allez voir pour la première fois ce que personne n'a jamais vu. D'ailleurs, cela dépasse nos aptitudes, à voir, et à décrire. D'ailleurs, dans cette pièce, 'Les Euménides', il ne se passe que des premières fois. C'est la première fois que nous allons voir des dieux en personne, depuis que nous sommes emportés dans la légende des Atrides. Tout est nouveau, inconnu, inouï, à venir. Jusqu'au monde, oui: même le monde,— avec la société, les cités, les mœurs, les religions, et pardessus tout, les lois —s'annonce inconnu, en plein changement. Cela donne à tous les personnages qu'abrite le Théâtre cette incertitude, ce tremblement, le pied chancelant, depuis la Pythie, jusqu'à la déesse Athéna, en passant par le public. Nous sommes inquiets, cartilagineux.

(Mais il y a Apollon. Celui-là, on croirait qu'il est né découpé dans l'aplomb. Rien n'ébranle ce branleur.)

On n'a jamais vu une telle situation: voilà une pièce où des personnages qui se rencontrent pour la première fois vont décider de la figure de l'univers politique pour tous les temps du temps.

Le comble du Théâtre: au Théâtre, d'habitude nous regardons les personnages se débattre dans les situations inextricables que nous réservent le destin. Et nous pensons: nous sommes des jouets pour les dieux. Et voici que les dieux eux-mêmes sont des personnages, les dieux eux-mêmes sont jouets,

(But there is Apollo. Him there, we would believe that he was born jagged with self-assurance. Nothing weakens this wanker.)[3]

We have never seen such a situation: here is a play in which the characters who meet for the first time are going to decide on the shape of the political universe for all time until the end of time.

The height of Theatre: at the Theatre, usually we watch characters fighting one another in inextricable situations that leave us to fate. And we think: we are toys for the gods. And here the gods themselves are characters, the gods themselves are toys, players, played, unknowing…

Theatre (the play) is always surreptitiously a Tribunal, where the characters come to accuse, defend themselves, complain, plead, lay out extenuating circumstances, try to convince the public. The public is the jury. In the end, usually, we are in the grip of the jury's torments who have to arrive at a judgement. This play, 'The Eumenides', is the play of plays. It tells of the origin of the Tribunal, which is to say, the origin of Theatre. Without knowing it, the opposing parties, even before, in front of us, the institution is invented, are in the process of 'playing out' the tribunal. The Erinyes against Apollo and Athena. And vice-versa. We don't know who attacks whom.

What do they look like these old divinities? They look like they have come on foot from the depths of prehistory. Suddenly, the evidence hits us, we recognise them. In truth, the persecutions, the remorse, were not able to be, coming from the rear-soul, anything more than the oldest of the true old women: the forgotten people, injured, humiliated inhabitants of what we call the third age, and others 'the golden age', the most ancient of our mothers, the ones we avoid thinking about, our parents who scare us the most, because they predict death for us, and worse still for mediocre souls: old age. It is necessary and poignant that the punishment of hate crimes is entrusted to grandmothers rather than to a hangman. Every criminal kills the mother. And the worst punishment is to be forced to see the true maternal face of the victim who throws us a look of ghastly astonishment.

But what is a very old woman? The actors know, their thinking body says it all: the grandmothers are childish, these are the former adorable young girls, survivors of themselves. An old woman in a young body; in an old body, youth remains.

Magnificent intuition: the 'genius' of life doesn't grow old, only the envelope fades. What will affect us is to see these women in their old appearance, condemned, trampled, insulted for their old age.

Certainly, until now, solitude was Orestes' characteristic. But, insidiously, in this tragedy, the solitude of the Erinyes rises up. It is the discreet and ruthless work of Aeschylus who slips the tragic portrait of old age for women beneath the central plot of the play. The persecuted ones are not those who

---

3. Cixous plays on the assonance of the words '*ébranle*' meaning 'jagged' and '*branleur*' a slang word meaning 'wanker'.

joueurs, joués, ne savent pas....

Le Théâtre (la pièce de Théâtre) est toujours subrepticement un Tribunal, où les personnages viennent s'accuser, se défendre, se plaindre, plaider, se donner des circonstances atténuantes, tenter de convaincre le public. Le public est le jury. A la fin, d'habitude, nous sommes en proie aux affres du jury qui doit rendre un jugement. Cette pièce, 'Les Euménides', est la pièce des pièces. Elle raconte l'origine du Tribunal, c'est-à-dire, l'origine du Théâtre. Sans le savoir, les parties en présence, avant même que, devant nous, l'institution soit inventée, sont en train de 'jouer' au tribunal. Les Erynies contre Apollon et Athéna. Et vice-versa. On ne sait pas qui attaque qui.

De quoi ont-elles l'air, les vieilles divinités? Elles ont l'air de venir à pied du fin-fond de la préhistoire. Tout d'un coup, l'évidence nous frappe, nous les reconnaissons. En vérité, les persécutions, les remords, ne pouvaient être, venant de l'arrière-âme, que les plus vieilles des vraies vieilles femmes: les personnes oubliées, blessées, habitantes humiliées de ce que nous appelons le troisième âge, et d'autres 'l'âge d'or', les plus antiques de nos mères, celles à qui nous évitons de penser, nos parentes qui nous font le plus peur, parce qu'elles nous prédisent la mort, et pire encore pour les âmes médiocres: la vieillesse. Il est nécessaire et poignant que le châtiment des meurtres haineux soit confié à des aïeules plutôt qu'à un bourreau. C'est que tout criminel tue la mère. Et le pire châtiment c'est d'être forcé de voir le vrai visage maternel de la victime nous jeter un regard d'affreux étonnement.

Mais qu'est-ce qu'une très vieille femme? Les comédiennes le savent, leur corps pensant le dit: les aïeules sont enfantines, ce sont d'anciennes adorables jeunes filles, des survivantes d'elles-mêmes. Une vieille femme dans un jeune corps; dans un vieux corps une jeunesse reste.

Intuition magnifique: le 'génie' de la vie ne vieillit pas, seule l'enveloppe défraichit. Ce qui nous affligera c'est de voir ces femmes dans leur vieille apparence, condamnées, piétinées, insultées pour vieillesse.

Certes, jusqu'ici la solitude était l'attribut d'Oreste. Mais, insidieusement, dans cette tragédie, se lève la solitude des Erynies. C'est le discret et impitoyable travail d'Eschyle qui fait glisser, sous la pièce principale, le portrait tragique de la vieillesse. Les persécutés ne sont pas ceux qu'on croit. 'Personne ne vous aime!' leur répète Apollon, et c'est affreusement vrai. Qui va bercer les vieilles enfants qui appellent leur mère en vain. *O Nuit, mère Nuit, est-ce que tu vois cela?* La Nuit ne répond pas. Comme elles sont seules. On sent gémir l'antique nostalgie de l'amour.

Qui sait—(personne ne sait rien)—si lorsque, tout à l'heure, elles vont céder au chantage charmeur d'Athéna, ce n'est pas dans l'espoir d'être un peu bercées elles aussi? Est-ce que tu m'aimes? Mais cela, elles ne le diront pas. Elles diront: honneur.

Elles arrivent avec leur puissance, leur fatigue, leur formidable résistance, et leurs bêtes, c'est-à-dire, leur férocité, non-intériorisée: les bêtes sont

we believe they are. 'No-one loves you!' Apollo repeats to them, and it is horribly true. Who is going to nurse these old infants who call to their mother in vain. *O Night, mother Night, do you see this?* Night does not respond. They are so alone. We feel the moaning of the ancient nostalgia of love.

Who knows—(no-one knows anything)—if when, soon, they will submit to the charming blackmail of Athena, is it not in the hope of being a little cradled themselves? Do you love me? But that, they will not say it. They will say: honour.

They arrive with their power, their tiredness, their formidable resistance, and their beasts, which is to say, their ferocity, non-interiorised: the beasts are their role, their lot, but not their identity. In the research of the Erinyes, it is thus that the beasts are, little by little, detached from the bodies of the actors to the point of falling over again on the stage, like a sort of exterior wickedness, representative, intimidating, frightened, who already leave their ultimate fate to chance: old loose teeth that are going to fall from themselves. The beasts remain indescribable. Escaping into the public: is it a monkey? A lion? A dog? The beasts are our concern. The announcement or the reminder of our animal part.

As soon as there is a chase between you and me, there is the animal, the taste of blood, our ancestors the cavemen, hate without hate, the terror of the hare, we are game, we are poultry, we are fox, we are crocodile. As soon as we pursue, fangs grow from us.

As soon as we are pursued, we lose father and mother as if they were shoes. Look how Orestes' feet are naked! Not barefoot but without parents.

Enter the pursued. What! This ravaged one, this old one,—it's him? It's Orestes? This great shattered old man? I remember how he was yesterday. You would not have imagined that. Suddenly, the murder scene is rewound several decades. Is this old man the one who killed? This old man is still the young matricidal son. In him the young Orestes speaks. And kills again. Murder has a hard life in this Orestes who is huge and full of time. It's because in that time then, there was no amnesia, no amnesty. But even so, this play is going to finish with 'that time then'. Be careful because now, here, is going to enter:

> Today.
> Today enters: it's Athena.

Another surprise! I believed that Athena was an older woman than herself, mature and hard, more warrior than warrioress, a picture of stability, the sword and the helmet, ally of Ulysses, her spirit strong. But this one is another altogether. It's her from before without doubt: she who doesn't yet know everything, she who is in the process of becoming what she will be, but nothing is certain. She takes, we would say, her first steps towards great divinity. Until now she made weapons with the Greeks.

leur rôle, leur lot, mais pas leur identité. Dans la recherche des Erynies, c'est ainsi que les bêtes se sont peu à peu détachées du corps des comédiennes jusqu'à retomber sur la scène, comme une sorte de méchanceté extérieure, déléguée, apeurante, apeurée, qui laisse deviner déjà leur sort ultime: vieilles dents branlantes qui vont tomber d'elles-mêmes. Les bêtes restent indescriptibles. Echappant au public: est-ce singe? Est-ce lion? Est-ce chien? Les bêtes sont notre inquiétude. L'annonce ou le rappel de notre part animale.

Dès qu'il y a pourchasse entre toi et moi, il y a l'animal, le goût du sang, nos ancêtres les hommes des cavernes, la haine sans haine, la terreur de lièvre, nous sommes gibier, nous sommes volaille, nous sommes renard, nous sommes crocodile. Dès que nous poursuivons, il nous pousse des crocs.

Dès que nous sommes poursuivis, nous perdons père et mère comme s'ils étaient des souliers. Voyez comme les pieds d'Oreste sont nus! Non pas déchaussés mais sans parents.

Entre le poursuivi. Quoi! Ce ravagé, ce vieux,—c'est lui? C'est Oreste? Ce grand vieillard brisé? Je me souviens de lui hier. Je n'aurais pas imaginé cela. Soudain, la scène du meurtre fait en arrière un bond de plusieurs décennies. C'est ce vieux qui a tué? Ce vieux est encore le jeune fils matricide. En lui le jeune Oreste parle. Et tue encore. Le meurtre a la vie dure dans cet Oreste immense et plein de temps. C'est parce qu'en ce temps-là, pas d'amnésie, pas d'amnistie. Mais justement, cette pièce va en finir avec 'ce temps-là'. Attention parce que maintenant, ici, va entrer:

Aujourd'hui.
Aujourd'hui entre: c'est Athéna.

Autre surprise! Je croyais qu'Athéna c'était cette femme plus âgée qu'elle-même, mûre et dure, plus guerrier que guerrière, la stabilité même, la lance et le casque, l'alliée d'Ulysse, l'esprit ferme comme le pied. Mais celle-ci est tout autre. C'est celle d'avant sans doute: celle qui ne sait pas encore tout, celle qui est en train de devenir ce qu'elle sera, mais rien n'est sûr. Elle fait, dirait-on ses premiers pas de grande divinité. Jusqu'ici elle faisait ses armes, avec les Grecs.

La voici, mais sans armes, entrant dans la décisive scène du Droit. Et bien visiblement désarmée mais non sans courage. Mais sans précédent, sans modèle. Tout à faire. Elle en tomberait par terre d'émoi, comme l'enfant qui apprend à marcher. On n'avait jamais vue une telle Athéna. Qui aurait cru que nos tribunaux, et même notre idéologie patriarcale, avaient été l'œuvre d'une fille pareille? Charmante, fraîche, innocemment, redoutablement identifiée au Père, 'en Tout'? Pas encore entièrement saisie dans le moule de l'autorité. Encore pas cuite. Mélange d'assurance future et de tâtonnement enfantin. C'est qu'elle est sur le point d'inventer (elle-même ne le sait pas encore) l'art de la Persuasion. Demain elle persuadera peut-être à tous les coups, aujourd'hui elle essaie. A commencer par elle-même: c'est qu'il faut

Here she is, but without weapons, entering the decisive scene of Right. And even though visibly disarmed, not without courage. But without precedent, without model. Everything to do. She would fall to the ground with emotion, like the child who learns to walk. We have never seen such an Athena. Who would have believed that our tribunals, and even our patrichal ideology, had been the work of such a daughter. Charming, fresh, innocently, undoubtedly identified with the Father, 'in All'? Not yet entirely seized by the mould of authority. Not quite cooked. A mixture of future assurance and childish groping. It is that she is on the verge of inventing (she doesn't know it yet) the art of Persuasion. Tomorrow perhaps she will persuade every time, today she tries. To begin with herself: it is necessary that she persuades herself. And thus what advances, sometimes in a triumphant expansion, sometimes staggering. And all of us, Erinyes, Orestes, public, to follow the events, asking ourselves: where will she end up? Will she win? For this deity, as for all the characters in this extraordinary play, nothing is given in advance. Everyone hopes whilst trembling (except Apollo). Everyone is threatened. Everything hangs by a thread, a son, a voice. Everyone wants to pray. But to whom?

Apollo bears witness to Orestes (which is to say, for male values). The Old Women bear witness to Clytemnestra (which is to say, for the reason of Mothers). But who bears witness for the Old Women?

I call you to witness, they shout, in good faith, calling out to those sworn in judges that Athena has just invented. But the judges don't respond, we don't hear them. We will never see the judges in this house. The Old Women no longer have another interlocutor apart from Athena. Imperceptibly, Athena takes the place of everyone. Who still thinks of Clytemnestra? Athena speaks. The judges are this great silence around her speech.

No witness? Or maybe—the judges were us? The public seated—called to witness, without wanting, without knowing, without power, the public weighed down by silence, we say nothing, at least not out loud. (Because in the room, it whispers. A feminist, sensitive man with a black beard over his sensitivity, calls his wife to witness: 'You hear that, Apollo's argument!' he says indignantly).

So the witnesses—are us? That's right. Thus it is so that the drama of witnessing plays out. The witness testifies millennia later. Yes, we heard today, after millennia, the complaint of the Erinyes. Ourselves, we will have witnesses four millennia after our death.

The tragedies write themselves in this inexplorable interval between the defiant cry of the victim and the response. But there will be a response. It will come. It is always in the future.

At present, we respond, without knowing it, from unknown and ancient assassinated people. The witness is not. The witness is tomorrow.

Who won? Persuasion. (Ah, that one!!) It doesn't lie: it doesn't claim to

qu'elle se persuade elle-même. Et la voilà qui avance, tantôt dans un essor triomphant, tantôt en trébuchant. Et nous tous, Erynies, Oreste, public, de suivre les péripéties, nous demandant: y arrivera-t-elle? Gagnera-t-elle? Pour cette déité, comme pour tous les personnages de cette pièce extraordinaire, rien n'est donné d'avance. Tous espèrent en tremblant (sauf Apollon). Tous sont menacés. Tout tient à un fil, un fils, une voix. Tous ont envie de prier. Mais à qui?

Apollon témoigne pour Oreste (c'est-à-dire, pour les valeurs mâles). Les Vieilles témoignent pour Clytemnestre (c'est-à-dire, pour la raison des Mères). Mais qui témoigne pour les Vieilles?

Je vous prends à témoin, crient-elles, de bonne foi, interpellant ces juges assermentés qu'Athéna vient d'inventer. Mais les juges ne répondent pas, on ne les entend pas. On ne verra jamais les juges dans cette maison. Les Vieilles n'ont plus d'autre interlocuteur qu'Athéna. Imperceptiblement, Athéna prend toute la place du monde. Qui pense encore à Clytemnestre? Athéna parle. Les juges sont ce grand silence autour de sa parole.

Pas de témoin? Ou bien—les juges c'étaient nous? Le public assis—pris à témoin, sans le vouloir, sans le savoir, sans le pouvoir, public sur lequel pèse le silence, nous ne disons rien, du moins pas à haute-voix. (Car dans la salle, ça chuchote. Un féministe, homme sensible portant une barbe noire sur sa sensibilité, prend à témoin sa femme: 'Tu entends ça, cet argument d'Apollon!' s'indigne-t-il).

Alors les témoins—c'est nous? C'est bien cela. C'est bien ainsi que se joue le drame du témoignage. Le témoin témoigne des millénaires plus tard. Oui, nous avons entendu aujourd'hui, après des millénaires, la plainte des Erynies. Nous-mêmes, nous aurons des témoins quatre millénaires après notre mort.

Les tragédies s'écrivent dans cet intervalle inexplorable entre le cri d'appel de la victime et la réponse. Mais il y aura de la réponse. Elle viendra. Elle est toujours future.

Au présent, nous répondons, sans le savoir, d'assassinés inconnus et anciens. Le témoin n'est pas. Le témoin est demain.

Qui a gagné? La Persuasion. (Ah, celle-là!!) Elle ne ment pas: elle ne dit pas qu'elle est la Vérité. Alors tout est devenu incertain, le droit est devenu tortueux. Et personne pour dire que le droit est devenu tortueux.

Le Soleil de la Vérité est devenu tout sec. Les citoyens offrent aux très vieilles divinités des flambeaux artificiels pour éclairer leur demeure dans la cave.

Et personne pour dire que, sous ses dehors souriants, cette fête ressemble à un enterrement.

Là où brillait la lune, l'Oubli lève son visage voilé. Une neige monte et recouvre les traces de ce qui fut un âge.

Comment cela s'appelle, ce matricide sans mère et sans assassinat?

be the Truth. So everything became uncertain, the law became tortuous. And no-one is there to say that the law became tortuous.

The Sun of Truth dried out. The citizens offer artificial flames to the very old female divinities to light their dwelling place in the cellar.

And no-one is there to say that, beneath these exterior smiles, this party resembles a burial. There where the moon was shining, Forgetting raises its vieled face. Snow rises and recovers the tracks of what was an age.

What can we call this, this matricide without mother and without assassin?

Up there, Athena must stop stumbling. Childhoods pass by. Like the old women, we don't know if we are going to get angry or not.

What did I forget? We feel our way along, vaguely distraught. It seems that I left something behind me. It is the spectacle of this hearing that distracted us. Or maybe it's someone that I forgot? It seems that it was a voice. A woman with her throat cut open was making terrible noises, I don't remember, do you remember?

'Pas de Réponse ou l'Appel du Mort' was first published in French in Les Atrides: Les Choéphores, Les Euménides, *Le Théâtre du Soleil, 1992*

Là-haut, Athéna doit cesser de chanceler. Les enfances passent. Comme les vieilles, nous ne savons pas, si nous allons nous fâcher ou pas.

Qu'est-ce que j'ai oublié? nous tâtons-nous, vaguement hagards. Il me semble que j'ai laissé quelque chose derrière moi. C'est le spectacle de ce procès qui nous a distrait. Ou bien, c'est quelqu'un que j'ai oublié? Il me semble que c'était une voix. Une femme égorgée poussait des cris terribles, je ne m'en souviens pas, est-ce que tu te souviens?

'Pas de Réponse ou l'Appel du Mort' in Les Atrides: Les Choéphores, Les Euménides, *Le Théâtre du Soleil, 1992*

The Communion of Misfortunes

They are frightened, they suffer, they hit out, they are hit,
they fall under the blows of the closest beings, Iphigenia,
Agamemnon, Clytemnestra, each one suffers in their place on the
family stage, each one in their own name and in the name of the parent,
Iphigenia since she is the daughter, one part Agamemnon,
the other Clytemnestra, she suffers at least three times, for herself, for him,
for her everyone suffers, kills, is killed, each man and each woman
is in the net of atrocities that weaves the threads of the Atreides family,—
it is not only Agamemnon who is in the net, the whole family
is in the net, the family weaves the net, the family is the net,
each one pulls and kills another by name, by the lines that ill fate poisons,
the Net spreads, next Cassandra, next Orestes, each one takes it,
each one is taken
And not only all these heroes that gather together the lines of blood,
love, hate, and the names that hold them,
But also us, us, that the poet called the Chorus,
we are in the net, and we suffer, and several times, we
suffer differently and in a terrible and otherwise tragic way,
we who are the innumerable Character and Without Name from these stories.
I will speak of the Chorus. Of our role, our action, our destiny.
I will speak of the Hero Without a Name who occupies such an important
place in the plays in which we are told the cruel story
of the Atreides, of its mystery and necessity:
nothing is without him (without them, without those women), nothing is with him. This Character
who does not kill and who is not killed, what is he good for, what
is he doing there?
Later—after the Greeks—, he is going to disappear
this Without Name, have you noticed? We no longer find it in Shakespeare,
nor in Racine, neither in the North or the West, if not in the form of
thin people, reduced to near 'uselessness',

La Communion des Douleurs

Ils craignent, ils souffrent, ils frappent, ils sont frappés,
ils tombent sous les coups des êtres les plus proches, Iphigénie,
Agamemnon, Clytemnestra, ils souffrent chacun à sa place dans la
scène de famille, chacun et chacune en son nom et au nom du parent,
Iphigénie en tant qu'elle est la fille, d'une part, d'Agamemnon,
de l'autre de Clytemnestra, elle souffre au moins trois fois, pour elle
pour lui pour elle, chacun souffre, tue, est tué, chacun, chacune
est dans l'atroce filet que tissent les liens de la famille Atride,—
ce n'est pas seulement Agamemnon qui est dans le filet, toute la famille
est dans le filet, la famille tisse le filet, la famille est le filet,
chacun tire et tue un autre par le nom, par les liens que le destin mauvais
empoisonne,
Le filet s'étend, ensuite Cassandra, ensuite Oreste, chacun y prend,
chacun y est pris
Et pas seulement tous ces héros que rassemblent les liens de sang,
d'amour, de haine, et les noms qui les tiennent,
Mais nous aussi, nous, que le poète a appellé le Chœur,
nous sommes dans le filet, et nous souffrons, et plusieurs fois, nous
souffrons autrement et d'une façon terrible et autrement tragique,
nous qui sommes le Personnage innombrable et Sans Nom de ces récits.
Je parlerai du Chœur. De notre rôle, de notre action, de notre
destin.
Je parlerai du Héros Sans Nom qui occupe une place si importante
dans les pièces où nous est racontée l'histoire cruelle
des Atrides, de son mystère et de sa nécessité:
rien n'est sans lui (sans eux, sans elles), rien n'est avec lui. Ce Personnage
qui ne tue pas et qui n'est pas tué, à quoi sert-il, que
fait-il là?
Plus tard—après les Grecs –, il va disparaître
ce Sans Nom, vous l'avez remarqué? On ne le trouve plus chez Shakespeare,
ni chez Racine, ni au Nord ni à l'Ouest, sinon sous la forme de
personnes ténues, réduit à une presque 'inutilité',

a nanny, a lady in waiting, some deaths. It is all that remains of
this powerful partner.
Look carefully at it; look at these young women who tremble from head to toe, worked over as they are by fateful messages.
Look at these old ones who fight furiously in order to keep standing under the tempest, and that time/the weather brought to the end of the path of life right up to the unsteady state of the last infancy,
look at these beings of which the febrile flesh is shaken up
by foresight and apprehension.
Look closely at them, because they are going to disappear, these mediums. It's
the last time, perhaps, that, with the Chorus, and
as much as it is chorus, we are still admitted to this terrestrial theatre
in convulsion.
– What good does it do, since it doesn't kill, it doesn't revenge, it doesn't cause, and it stops nothing?
– And so, precisely that is the necessity of
the Chorus: it is there to suffer differently, to carry the
sadness of those who, taken in the Net, do nothing, can do
nothing, to live the sadness of disempowerment, the awful sadness without consolation,
without compensation, of those who watch to suffer, our pain.
The Chorus has its own tragedy, that of the Powerless Witness,
the tragedy, always begun again from exile, from the forbidden,
from exclusion, that is the lot of all those who are deprived of
the most precious good: the possibility *to act.*
The Chorus incarnates the passion of passions, that of mothers
who don't save their child. The Chorus is nailed to the spot
by invisible nails and it is doubled over with anguish. Glued to
our places as spectators, there we are, tethered by invisible
lines, we recognise, with the anguish that grips us at the
heart, that we are from the same familial flesh as the Atreides,
the same as the Chorus.
But, the time of fear and complaint that the characters who
carry the familial names don't have, has been passed on to the Chorus.
The Chorus is always there. Without truce. The body of the Chorus
is overrun, trampled on, cut across by the routes of
assassins and victims.
The Chorus always 'knows' too long, too long a time in
advance, and for nothing. It is not divine, it is human: that which it urges on,
it doesn't affirm, it is not a prophet, it is not the spokesman
for a divinity, it is the trembling and furious spokesman of
memory.

une nourrice, une suivante, quelques morts. C'est tout ce qui reste de
ce puissant partenaire.
Regardez-le bien, regardez ces jeunes femmes qui tremblent des pieds à
la tête, traversées qu'elles sont par les messages fatidiques.
Regardez ces vieillards qui luttent furieusement pour tenir debout sous
la tempête, et que le temps a amenés au bout du chemin de
vie jusqu'à l'état chancelant de la dernière enfance,
regardez ces êtres dont la chair fébrile est secouée
de presciences et d'appréhensions.
Regardez-les bien, car ils vont disparaître, ces mediums. C'est
la dernière fois, peut-être, que, avec le Chœur et en
tant que chœur, nous sommes encore admis sur ce terrestre théâtre
en convulsion.
– A quoi sert-il, puisqu'il ne tue pas, il ne venge pas, il ne cause
pas, et il n'empêche rien?
– Eh bien, là justement est la nécessité du
Chœur: il est là pour souffrir autrement, pour porter la
douleur de ceux qui, pris dans le Filet ne font rien, ne peuvent rien
faire, pour vivre la douleur d'impuissance, l'affreuse douleur sans consolation,
sans compensation, de ceux qui regardent souffrir, notre douleur.
Le Chœur a sa propre tragédie, celle du Témoin Impuissant,
la tragédie, toujours recommencée, de l'exil, de l'interdit,
de l'exclusion, qui est le lot de tous ceux qui sont privés du
bien le plus précieux: la possibilité *d'agir.*
Le Chœur incarne la passion des passions, celle des mères
qui ne sauvent pas leur enfant. Le Chœur est cloué sur place
par des clous invisibles, et il se tord d'angoisse. Rivés à
nos places de spectateurs, nous voilà ligotés par les liens
invisibles, nous reconnaissons, à l'angoisse qui nous serre le
cœur, que nous sommes de la même chair familiale que les Atrides,
la même que celle du Chœur.
Mais, au Chœur, est dévolu le temps de craindre et le temps
de se plaindre que n'ont pas les personnages qui portent les noms dans
la famille.
Le Chœur est toujours là. Sans trêve. Le corps du Chœur
est parcouru, piétiné, sillonné par les courses des
assassins et des victimes.
Le Chœur en 'sait' toujours trop long, trop longtemps à
l'avance, et pour rien. Il n'est pas devin, il est humain: ce qu'il presse,
il ne l'affirme pas, il n'est pas prophète, il n'est pas le porte-parole
d'une divinité, il est le porte-parole tremblant et furieux de
la mémoire.
'Pourquoi donc cette Peur

'Why then does this Fear
Standing obstinately before my prophetic heart
Spread through me?
Without being obliged to, without being invited there,
A melody in me reads the future,
And so in the distance we spit all that out again
As we do to dreams that are difficult to understand,
The persuasive trust will not come. Enthroned in the heart of my breast.'
(...)
'I am witness and I have learnt the return with my own eyes
And yet, my heart
Which receives the news,
That came from inside me,
Deserted as it is by trust, companion of Hope,
Beats the funereal rhythm of the Erinyes.
Near the diaphragm that Justice oppresses,
The entrails do not lie
When from my heart the whirlwinds rise.
From my foreboding
Lies fall
That they might be denied!'
The Chorus is the Hero of Foreboding. It is in a state
of Tragic Rage:
'I feel this is going to end badly, this is going to end badly, this is going to end badly'
– Finally , the worst, is that it ends badly
The Chorus suffers the pain of Job: all its fears are realised.
Now, in fear, still beats the feeble hope that fear not be realised.
I am really afraid that she is condemned, she
is going to die, we think, and yet, saying that, we don't believe ourselves,
we flee, head bowed under the storm of thought,
everything we think we don't think it, we lie to ourselves, we deceive ourselves, we don't fool ourselves. We are living, we live in the country of life, and what is over there,
out there, death, we don't have eyes/God[1] to see it, only a chorus
to fear it. We cannot believe in death in advance
– that would be to be its instrument, the living don't
believe that, even if they know death will arrive.
Our mortality, it is this: 'don't-believe-in-death'.
That doesn't stop us from trembling. To die is to lose the immortality that we have throughout the duration of our life. It is this paradox,

1 Cixous plays with the word *'d'yeux'* meaning 'eyes' to and the homophony with *'Dieu'* or 'God'.

Dressée obstinément devant mon cœur prophète
Se répand-elle en moi?
Sans y être obligé, sans y être invité,
Un chant en moi lit l'avenir,
Et bien qu'au loin on recrache tout ça
Comme on le fait des rêves difficiles à comprendre,
La persuasive confiance ne viendra pas
Trôner au cœur de ma poitrine'.
(...)
'Je suis témoin et de mes propres yeux j'ai appris le retour.
Et pourtant, mon cœur
Qui reçoit les nouvelles
Venues de l'intérieur de moi,
Déserté qu'il est par la confiance, compagne de l'Espoir,
Bat le rythme funèbre de l'Erinye.
Près du diaphragme que la Justice oppresse,
Les entrailles ne mentent pas
Quand de mon cœur montent des tourbillons.
De mon pressentiment
Que tombent les mensonges
Et qu'ils soient démentis!'
Le Chœur est le Héros du Pressentiment. Il est dans l'état
de Rage Tragique:
'Je sens que cela va mal finir, cela va mal finir, cela va mal finir'
– finalement, le pire, c'est que ça finit mal.
Le Chœur souffre du mal de Job: toutes ses craintes sont exaucées.
Or, dans la crainte, bat toujours le faible espoir que la crainte ne soit
pas exaucée. J'ai bien peur qu'elle soit condamnée, elle
va mourir, pensons-nous, et cependant, disant cela, nous ne nous croyons
pas, nous fuyons tête baissée sous l'orage de la pensée,
tout ce que nous pensons nous ne le pensons pas, nous nous mentons, nous
nous trompons, nous ne nous trompons pas. C'est que nous sommes vivants,
nous habitons dans le pays de la vie, et ce qui est au-delà, le
dehors, la mort, nous n'avons pas d'yeux pour le voir, seulement un chœur
pour le craindre. La mort nous ne pouvons pas y croire à l'avance
– ce serait être son instrument –, les vivants *n'y
croient pas*, même s'ils savent qu'elle arrivera.
Notre mortalité, c'est cela: 'ne-pas-croire-à-la-mort'.
Cela ne nous empêche pas de trembler. Mourir, c'est perdre l'immortalité
que nous avons pendant la durée de notre vie. C'est ce paradoxe,
cette folie, qui anime le Chœur. Le Chœur résiste, jusqu'au
bout.
Ah! L'horreur que nous éprouvons lorsque ce que nous redoutions

this madness, that animates the Chorus. The Chorus resists until
the end.
Ah! The horror that we experience when that which we dread
is realised: it is what I feared! We exclaim to ourselves,
obstinate humans of hope that we are. Until
the last second we are afraid whilst hoping, hope
whilst fearing. On the one hand we expect the worst, on the other hand
we don't want to wait for it. The anger of the Chorus is immense
when evil triumphs.
We rebel. Century after century.
Massacre after massacre. We don't want to believe that we are
mortal. And yet here is the proof.
The Chorus has an infinite aptitude for hoping against all
hope. The Chorus is made for deception.
But that is not all. The Chorus is not only the public ready
for mourning, plunged into grief though we are. It is also indentified
with each of the characters in the condemned family, separately,
it is one against the other; and it is also the family, this everything that
divides and tears one another to pieces.
– Instead of Agamemnon, I would not kill Iphigenia—
I say to myself.
– Is it true?, I say to myself.
I don't know anymore. I am such a mixture. I no longer know who I
am/follow. I vacillate. Sometimes I want Agamemnon. Sometimes I want
Clytemnestra. I take both sides, the sadness of one
convinces me, the sadness of the other persuades me.
It is because I am one of the family. Under the net, on the stage, around
the bed, the table, the altar, the Chorus is in the same place as
children who are summoned by destiny to choose, in the quarrel,
between father and mother. It is impossible. Every choice leads
to a counter-choice.
As soon as there is Family, the dance of identifications begins. (N.B. Me, personally, H.C., I am pro-Clytemnestra, N.B. N.B.: and I do not agree with Iphigenia. But I only insert H.C. into this parenthesis.) Poor choir, poor old children, orphans of the living, like their parents, voiceless in the matter, and Without Name.
Us, human creatures, when evil strikes us brutally,
all of a sudden we feel alone in the world, persecuted,
find ourselves fleeing without father or mother.
The ancient memory awakens in us from the furthest exiles,
those that struck humans thirty thousand generations ago.
There we are whirling like wisps in the tragic wind,
we don't control events. So we

se réalise: c'est ce que je craignais!, nous exclamons-nous, humains obstinés à espérer que nous sommes. Jusqu'à la dernière seconde nous avons craint en espérant, espéré en craignant. D'un côté on s'attend au pire, de l'autre côté on ne veut pas s'y attendre. La colère du Chœur est immense lorsque le mal triomphe.
Nous nous révoltons. Siècle après siècle.
Massacre après massacre. Nous ne voulons pas croire que nous sommes mortels. Et cependant voici la preuve.
Le Chœur a une aptitude infinie à espérer contre tout espoir. Le Chœur est fait pour la déception.
Mais ce n'est pas tout. Le Chœur n'est pas seulement le public prêt au deuil, endeuillé, que nous sommes. Il est aussi identifié à chacune des personnes de la famille condamnée, séparément, il est l'un contre l'autre; et il est aussi la famille, ce tout qui se divise et s'entredéchire.
– A la place d'Agamemnon, je ne tuerais pas Iphigénie— me dis-je.
– Est-ce vrai?, me dis-je.
Je ne sais plus. Je suis un tel mélange. Je ne sais plus qui je suis. Je vacille. Parfois j'en veux à Agamemnon. Parfois j'en veux à Clytemnestra. Je prends parti diversement, la douleur de l'un me convaint, la douleur de l'autre me persuade.
C'est que je suis de la famille. Sous le filet, sur la scène, autour du lit, de la table, de l'autel, le Chœur est à la place des enfants qui sont sommés par le destin de choisir, dans la querelle, entre père et mère. C'est impossible. Tout choix entraîne un contre-choix.
Dès qu'il y a Famille, commence la danse des identifications. (N.B. Moi, personnellement, H.C., je suis pour Clytemnestra, N.B. N.B.: et je ne suis pas d'accord avec Iphigénie. Mais je n'engage que H.C. dans cette parenthèse.) Pauvre chœur, pauvres vieux enfants, orphelins du vivant même de leurs parents, sans voix au chapitre, et Sans Nom.
Nous, créatures humaines, quand un malheur (nous) frappe brutalement, tout d'un coup nous nous sentons seuls au monde, persécutés, nous voilà fuyant devant nous, sans père ni mère.
En nous s'éveille le souvenir antique des plus lointains exils, ceux qui frappèrent les humains il y a trente mille générations.
Nous voilà tournoyant comme des fétus dans le vent tragique, nous ne maîtrisons pas les événements. Alors nous éprouvons la pénible sensation des Sans-Nom, que connaissent bien ceux qui se trouvent jetés dans les situations d'illégitimité.

experience the painful feeling of those Without-Name, a feeling that is well known
to those who find themselves thrown into positions of illegitimacy.
We are no-one, even if we are the whole city and the whole
world. But we submit personally, in our body without-name
to the desire of the country, of the tribe, of the family, of the race. The Chorus
is there to express the age-old anguish that arises from
a precise threat.
An obscure fear warns us: what we have not lived yet,
our ancestors have lived it in us. Surely, the events
that happen on stage, or that are going to happen, will not take place only
once. They are extraordinary. And yet, feels the Choir, we
(when we were not born), we had already lived that, before our birth.
This is what makes the Choir tremble: the terrors that come
from past lives. And us too, sitting in the room, we sense
that the story that takes place here and that is not ours, had been
ours or will be, one day or another.
The Chorus feels unwell. The 'honours'
(attributions) of the Choir are to experience, in its flesh, in awful translation, all the evils of all the protagonists. And also all the words that are so penetrating.
It has the time, and it is the place, of torments. Those of others and its
own. It has a double ration of desire.
Under the blows of speeches that pronounce Agamemnon, or Clytemnestra, or Iphigenia, or Cassandra
I am wounded by a purple bite
Towards my heart ebbed a stream the colour of saffron,
The mouth of my heart is filled with a bitter taste
My own blood sickens me, it seems that I am going to die,
the malicious speeches act on my organs like daggers
and poisons, yes, I could die of hate, of anger, of
fear.
The Chorus leads us into regions that deal ruthlessly with
the physical worries of the soul, those which come from the heart and
spread in intolerable convulsions from the chest
to the feet, those that make us stagger, the vertigos that turn the world upside-down and spread the earth out above our head.
Look at them, these old, enraged dancers.
What the Chorus expresses, for once, is the seismic calling
of our soul-body. In the pain of the soul, the contracted heart
like a uterus, looks for ways to expel the sadness, and in vain:
because it is the heart itself that the heart looks for ways to

Nous ne sommes personne, même si nous sommes toute la ville et tout
le monde. Mais nous subissons personnellement, dans notre corps sans-nom
la passion du pays, de la tribu, de la famille, de la race. Le Chœur
est là pour exprimer l'angoisse immémoriale qui surgit à
l'occasion d'une menace précise.
Une peur obscure nous avertit: ce que nous n'avons encore jamais vécu,
nos ancêtres en nous l'ont vécu. Certes, les événements
qui se passent sur scène ou qui vont se passer, n'auront lieu qu'une
fois. Ils sont extraordinaires. Et cependant, sent le Chœur, nous
(quand nous n'étions pas nés), nous avons déjà
vécu cela, avant notre naissance.
Voilà ce qui fait frémir le Chœur: des terreurs venues
de vies antérieures. Et nous aussi, assis dans la salle, nous sentons
que l'histoire qui se passe ici et qui n'est pas la nôtre, a été
la nôtre ou le sera, un jour ou l'autre.
Le Chœur a mal. C'est le Chœur qui a pour 'honneurs'
(attributions) d'éprouver dans sa chair, en traduction affreuse,
tous les maux de tous les protagonistes. Et aussi tous les mots si pénétrants.
Il a le temps, et il est le lieu, des tourments. Ceux des autres et les
siens. Il a double ration de passion.
Sous les coups des paroles que prononce Agamemnon, ou Clytemnestra, ou
Iphigénie, ou Cassandra,
Je suis blessé d'une morsure pourpre
Vers mon cœur a reflué un flot couleur safran,
La bouche de mon cœur est remplie d'une saveur amère
Mon propre sang m'écœure, il me semble que je vais mourir,
les paroles méchantes agissent sur mes organes comme des poignards
et des poisons, oui, je pourrais mourir de haine, de colère, de
peur.
Le Chœur nous emmène dans les régions où sévissent
les chagrins physiques de l'âme, ceux qui partent du cœur et
se répandent en convulsions intolérables depuis la poitrine
jusqu'aux pieds, ceux qui nous font tituber, les vertiges qui renversent
le monde et étendent la terre par-dessus notre tête.
Regardez-les, ces vieux danseurs enragés.
Ce que le Chœur exprime, pour une fois, c'est la vocation séismique
de notre âme-corps. Dans la peine de l'âme le cœur contracté
comme un utérus, cherche à expulser la douleur, et en vain:
car c'est le cœur lui-même que le cœur cherche à
vomir. La terre entière est convulsée dans l'effort affolé
d'arracher de sa propre poitrine la source du supplice.
Plié en deux, arqué, crispé, sur le visage la grimace,
le Chœur, en proie à la crise, sanglote les noms des souffrances

vomit up. The whole earth is convulsed in the panicked effort
to rip the source of torture from her own chest.
Folded in two, arched, tensed, on my face the grimace,
the Chorus, plagued by crisis, sobs the names of visceral
sufferings.
– Ah, I have memory-ache, I have tenderness-ache, I have justice-ache, I have mother-ache, I have courage-ache, I am sore in all the subtle and spiritual parts of my being.
I dance the strange wildnesses of the allied heart
Me who cannot break the line that reattaches me to the other.
– Your sadness hurts me, you hurt me, as I hurt you—
we are atoms of a single body.
We take part. Useless to deny it. What happens in Argos happens to us
in Paris. We do everything to forget it, but we don't escape. We are in the circle—we are concerned.
The Chorus in the round draws the human circle. Chanting the rhythm
that reminds us: You too, you too.

'La Communion des douleurs' was first published in French in Les Atrides I: Iphigénie à Aulis et Agamemnon, *Théâtre du Soleil, 1992.*

viscérales.
– Ah, j'ai mal à la mémoire, j'ai mal à la tendresse, j'ai mal à la justice, j'ai mal à ma mère,
j'ai mal au courage, j'ai mal à toutes les parties subtiles, spirituelles, de mon être.
Je danse les étranges sauvageries du cœur allié
Moi qui ne puis rompre les liens qui me rattachent à l'autre.
– Ta douleur me fait mal, tu me fais mal, comme je te fais mal—
nous sommes des atomes d'un seul corps.
Nous faisons partie. Inutile de le nier. Ce qui arrive en Argos nous arrive
à Paris. Nous faisons tout pour l'oublier, mais nous n'échappons
pas. Nous sommes dans le cercle—nous sommes concernés.
Le Chœur dans sa ronde dessine le cercle humain. Scandant le rythme
qui nous rappelle: Toi aussi, toi aussi.

'La Communion des douleurs', in Les Atrides I: Iphigénie à Aulis et Agamemnon, *Théâtre du Soleil, 1992*

The Blow

One day. On a certain day, specific, detailed, stormy, the course of the human Soul completely changed. There had been the day when, in the morning, certain old divinities were still running on the earth, as they did for thirty-five million generations, and in the evening, they came down under the most secret and inner reaches of the earth and they have never again put their foreign foot outside, in the external world.

Our own world, including its religions, prophets, regimes, sciences and ignorance, began the next morning.

In one day–and not in seven–what was above went below to the most buried underworld, what had been named just was declared unjust, what was clear had been declared trouble, truth had been the eyelids of bats–that day, there had been a shaking of thought. Those who believed themselves to be right had been wrong, those who feared being wrong had been justified.

At the end of this day the young rising gods addressed the old descending divinities, their sincere congratulations on the occasion of their sudden triumph. The old day fell.

As it was going down, the old divinities asked, at the juncture of murmur and silence, if the word 'triumph' had the same meaning above and below, but they were already speaking in a voice so tight that, on that day, no-one heard them.

That was a day full of trickery, it all happened so quickly, the biggest trial in the History of trials, the most decisive, the most overturning of spiritual revolutions, so quickly that we didn't even have time to say goodbye to each other, there would never be a Return, only goodbye, adieu, hurriedly. Thereupon the divinities of before and the divinities of after, hastily crossed the planet and our epoch emerged, full of self-assurance, standing up on its virile hamstrings.

That day there was practically no-one from 'our place' on earth, only a character, an ambiguous man, intent on saving his skin and his belongings, a man calling himself the son–son of Agamemnon; all the others were from the immortal race, all of that Greek kind of immortality that doesn't stop them from desiring nor from suffering.

Le Coup

Un jour. Un certain jour, précis, circonstancié, orageux, le cours de l'Ame humaine a entièrement changé. Il y a eu le jour où, le matin, certaines vieilles divinités couraient encore sur la terre, comme elles le faisaient depuis trente-cinq mille générations, et le soir, elles sont descendues sous les replis les plus secrets de la terre et elles n'ont plus jamais mis leur étrange pied dehors, à l'extérieur.

Notre propre monde, y compris ses religions, ses prophètes, ses régimes, ses sciences et ses ignorances, a commencé le lendemain matin.

En un seul jour—et pas en sept –, ce qui était dessus est descendu au plus enfoui du dessous, ce qui était dit juste a été dit non-juste, ce qui était clair a été déclaré trouble, la vérité a eu des paupières de chauve-souris—ce jour-là il y a eu un tremblement de pensée. Ceux qui croyaient avoir raison ont eu tort, ceux qui craignaient d'avoir tort ont été justifiés.

A la fin de ce jour les jeunes divinités montantes adressaient aux vieilles divinités descendantes leurs sincères félicitations à l'occasion de leur triomphe subit. Le vieux jour est tombé.

En descendant, les vieilles divinités se demandaient, à l'angle du murmure et du silence, si le mot 'triomphe' avait toujours le même sens en haut et en bas, mais elles parlaient déjà d'une voix si ténue que personne ne les a entendues, ce jour-là.

Ce fut un jour passe-passe, tout a été si vite, le plus grand procès de l'Histoire des procès, le plus décisif, la plus renversante des révolutions spirituelles, si vite que l'on n'a même pas eu le temps de se dire aurevoir, il n'y aurait jamais de Revoir, seulement adieu, adieu, précipitamment. Là-dessus les divinités d'avant et les divinités d'après se sont croisées en toute hâte sur la planète et notre époque s'est levée, pleine d'assurance, dressée sur ses virils jarrets.

Ce jour-là il n'y avait presque personne de 'chez nous' sur la terre, seulement un personnage, un homme équivoque, acharné à sauver sa peau et ses propriétés, un homme s'appelant fils—fils d'Agamemnon; tous les autres étaient de la race des immortels, tous de cette immortalité grecque qui n'empêche pas de désirer ni de souffrir.

No, that day, there was no-one else except this Orestes, as human–uncertainly, not enough, too much, human.

And if there had been no Aeschylus, a long time after, if Aeschylus the poet was not born to dig up the old buried speeches, and to recreate 'this unprecedented day', total Forgetting would have won out.

That is what Aeschylus did there with that play entitled *The Eumenides,* we have trouble believing it, we have trouble and marvel at the same time. Here is a man who threw, over the abyss that separates two universes, the paltry and transparent poetic footbridge.

He writes the journey. Between two laws, between two loyalties, Law against law, loyalty against loyalty. Between two reigns, two sensibilities. We would call these the first combats, the originary rivalry between man and woman, old and young, gods against gods, father against mother. He writes at sunset. Are we moving towards the day, towards the night? The weather is dreary. We can't see very well, not very clear, neither in oneself nor in front of oneself. This world doesn't know that it is going to end. Although, it's the moment when the epoch-of-Erinyes ends, who would have believed it? Until this day, 'they' were uncontested. Until this morning, all assassins knew that they were there to become her tireless and terrible companions. They were part of the interior landscape of Crime.

The old, very old, the Erinyes don't know that at the end of this working day, they will no longer be called the Erinyes. Not for one moment do they imagine, during their loyal hunt, that they are in the process of becoming 'The Eumenides' ('Benevolents'), their very opposite.

Destiny, which this day, is, on the one hand, the young arrogant profile and baritone of Apollo and, on the other hand, on the lips, the ambiguous smile of Athena, the indecipherable, and already in the process of clipping their tongues, breasts, breaths, but the simple old ladies cannot know it: how would eternity ever be able to imagine its own end?

Suddenly everything stops. It's time. The last. Imagine, the next night, all of a sudden, no more moon, not ever. And no more stars. A strange night surges under the sky. *The Eumenides*, the tale of Aeschylus, is just that. The brutal end of an era of unfathomable antiquity. An extraordinary accident takes place. No, it is not the fall of a meteor. The irreparable break is made in the soul, without axe, without sword, with an inexpressibly muffled violence. Suddenly, to our agitation, the oldest divine women in the world give in.

As if catastrophe was invisibly preparing itself for the last million years. It happens in front of us, during a serious fight. We bitterly debate the crime and the punishment. Naturally, we, as before all trials, we mix ourselves up in the affair. Here we are judges, here we are the accused, councils for the defence, the plaintiffs. We are all born to defend ourselves, to be accused and to accuse. The job of the lawyer is inscribed in the voice of mortals.

Non, ce jour-là, il n'y avait personne d'autre que cet Oreste, comme humain—incertainement, pas assez, trop, humain.

Et s'il n'y avait pas eu Eschyle, longtemps après, si Eschyle le poète n'était pas né pour déterrer les vieilles paroles enfouies, et pour reconstituer 'ce jour inouï', l'Oubli absolu aurait gagné.

Ce qu'Eschyle a fait là, avec cette pièce intitulée '*Euménides*', nous avons peine à y croire, nous avons peine mais émerveillement en même temps. Voilà un homme qui a lancé par-dessus l'abîme qui sépare deux univers la minime et transparente passerelle poétique.

Il écrit le passage. Entre deux lois, entre deux loyautés. Loi contre loi, loyauté contre loyauté. Entre deux règnes, deux sensibilités. On dirait les premiers combats, la rivalité originaire homme contre femme, jeunes contre vieux, dieux contre dieux, père contre mère. Il écrit au crépuscule. Va-t-on vers le jour, vers la nuit? Il fait sombre. On ne voit pas très bien, pas très clair, ni en soi, ni devant soi. Ce monde ne sait pas qu'il va finir. Pourtant, c'est le moment où l'époque-à-Erynies s'achève, qui l'aurait cru? Jusqu'à ce jour 'elles' étaient incontestées. Jusqu'à ce matin, tout assassin savait qu'elles étaient là pour devenir ses inlassables et terribles compagnes. Elles faisaient partie du paysage intérieur du Crime.

Les vieilles, très vieilles, Erynies ne savent pas qu'à la fin de cette journée de travail, elles ne seront plus appelées Erynies. Pas un instant elles n'imaginent, pendant leur chasse loyale, qu'elles sont en train de devenir 'Euménides' ('Bienveillantes'), leur propre contraire.

Le destin, qui a ce jour-là, d'une part le jeune profil arrogant et le baryton d'Apollon et, d'autre part, sur les lèvres, le double sourire d'Athéna, l'indéchiffrable, est déjà en train de leur rogner les langues, les seins, les souffles, mais les simples vieilles ne peuvent pas le savoir: comment l'éternité pourrait-elle jamais penser son propre terme?

Soudain tout s'arrête. C'est l'heure. La dernière. Imaginez, la nuit prochaine, tout d'un coup, plus de lune, plus jamais. Et plus d'étoiles. Une nuit étrangère s'engouffre sous le ciel. Les 'Euménides', le récit d'Eschyle, c'est cela. La fin brutale d'une ère d'insondable antiquité. Il se produit un accident exceptionnel. Non, ce n'est pas la chute d'un météore. La cassure irréparable se fait dans l'âme, sans hache, sans épée, avec une violence inexprimablement feutrée. Soudain, à notre émoi, les plus vieilles femmes divines du monde cèdent.

Comme si depuis un million d'années la catastrophe se préparait invisiblement. Cela se passe devant nous, pendant une querelle grave. On débat âprement de crime et de châtiment. Naturellement, nous, comme devant tout procès, nous nous mêlons de l'affaire. Nous voilà juges, nous voilà accusés, défenseurs, plaignants. Nous tous nous sommes nés pour nous défendre, pour être accusés et pour accuser. La vocation d'avocat est inscrite dans la voix des mortels.

The scene is familiar, serious and ordinary. Everyday, everything provides an occasion for complaint and prosecution, for all of us, our life is made up of angers, apostrophes, attempted assassinations. Here, in the theatre, we are concerned with an affair of rights, we believe. Right, justice, restitution, wrong, account, punishment, crime, purification, we hear only these words. Orestes killed his mother Clytemnestra, and he must pay. It is simple. A storm of arguments is unleashed on us. Our view becomes cloudy. When the storm dissipates, Orestes, in the following hour, returns to reign on his rediscovered throne, Clytemnestra has evaporated, no one yells, a thick consent spreads throughout the room.

'Justice', carried it off thanks to

'Persuasion'.

Justice?

'What is just in all that?', ask the old women, which childhood–with its indignations and secrets–has never left.

– What is just about that? Are we going to acquit a murderer? Is there is going to be a non-event?, worry the spectators still full of childhood, and overrun by their present worries.

– Is that just? According to Apollo, it is fair. According to me, it's not fair.

According to Athena, that's no longer the question. It's not a question of fairness.

– How is that? Explain it to me. Don't we speak of bringing about justice?

Little by little, in an oblique manner, we are pushed into painful (bitter) discoveries. Justice is not an end. Justice is not a right. Justice is the word that keeps bent legs standing, feet spread, it is the tightrope walker. Justice is what makes injustice acceptable. Justice was raised on so many piles of injustice! Justice wasn't made to be fair. *It is made to arrest/stop.* Justice between men, there must be. To cut short the sadnesses that are interminable.

To divide up everything that exceeds, to repress the sobs. The victims are scandalised, they never stop complaining. Justice is there to regulate the cries and cut short the complaints.

Justice is the smooth management of Injustice.

Justice is our necessary tragedy. It inflicts us with its version of our pain. It speaks and we shut up. Justice gives over the secret right to impurity. Without justice we would spend all our lives screaming. Justice doesn't satisfy us. It makes us obliged to change our sadness. Our secret ambition, that of Athena, is to swallow back our fury so that peace can reign.

With great pomp and ceremony it entices, deludes us, captures our desires. It is a legal infamy in the service of a superior cause, peace. Peace justifies Justice. Never has any victim stopped suffering and shedding tears, but at least her sadness will have been declared, set down and handed over in a case file. Justice buries the living with a worry of equalisation.

La scène est familière, grave et quotidienne. Tous les jours, tout est occasion de plainte et de poursuite pour nous tous, notre vie est faite de colères, d'apostrophes, d'attentats. Il s'agit ici, dans le théâtre, d'une affaire de droit, croyons-nous. Droit, justice, rectitude, tort, compte, punition, crime, purification, on n'entend que ces mots. Oreste a tué sa mère Clytemnestra, il faut qu'il paie. C'est simple. Un orage d'arguments se déchaîne sur nous. La vue se trouble. Quand l'orage se dissipe, Oreste, dans l'heure qui suit, retourne régner sur son trône retrouvé, Clytemnestra s'est évaporée, personne ne hurle, un consentement épais s'étend dans la salle.

La 'justice' l'a emporté grâce à la

'Persuasion'.

La justice?

– Qu 'y a-t-il de juste dans tout ça?, demandent les vieilles femmes, que l'enfance avec ses indignations et ses confiances n'a jamais quittées.

– Qu'y a-t-il de juste? On va acquitter un meurtrier? Il va y avoir non-lieu?, s'inquiètent les spectateurs encore pourvus d'enfance, et parcourus d'irritations actuelles.

– Est-ce que c'est juste cela? Selon Apollon, c'est juste. Selon moi, ce n'est pas juste.

Selon Athéna, là n'est plus la question. Il ne s'agit pas d'être juste.

– Comment cela? Expliquez-moi. Ne parle-t-on pas de rendre justice?

Peu à peu, de manière oblique, nous sommes poussés à de pénibles (amères)

découvertes. La Justice n'est pas une fin. La Justice n'est pas droite. La Justice c'est le mot qui se tient debout les jambes fléchies, les pieds écartés, c'est l'équilibriste. La Justice c'est ce qui rend l'injustice convenable. Sur quels tas d'injustice s'élève la Justice! La Justice n'est pas faite pour être juste. *Elle est faite pour arrêter.* La Justice, entre hommes, il la faut. Pour couper court aux douleurs, qui sont interminables.

Trancher tout ce qui dépasse, refouler les sanglots. Les victimes sont scandaleuses, elles ne cessent de se plaindre. La Justice est là pour régler les cris et couper le cours des plaintes.

La Justice est la bonne gestion de l'Injustice.

La Justice est notre tragédie nécessaire. Elle nous inflige sa version de nos peines. Elle parle et nous nous taisons. La Justice se donne le droit secret à l'impureté. Sans la Justice nous passerions nos vies à crier. La Justice ne nous satisfait pas. Elle nous oblige à convertir notre douleur. Son ambition secrète, celle d'Athéna, est de nous faire ravaler nos fureurs, pour que la paix règne.

En grand apparat elle nous appâte, nous leurre, capte nos passions. Elle est une infamie légale au service d'une cause supérieure, la paix. La paix justifie la Justice. Jamais aucune victime ne cessera de souffrir et de verser des larmes, mais du moins sa douleur aura été déclarée, déposée et remisée dans

Was it thus, this awful and inerasable revelation that Aeschylus was counting on us to make?

Is it a question of a tragedy of justice in this story, this perverse subreption?

No. This is the tragedy of *The Eumenides*, these old infantile women, who make, at their expense, the eternal experience and the last human casualties: there is nothing to be done for mortals, nothing, other than to invent this interior dyke that we call suppression.

It is because we mortals have to deal with Blood. It is a question of a Meaning of Blood, blood which, once shed, never returns to the veins. Nothing will make it come back. So blood calling blood, until the end of the world, the entirety of History is nothing but a hemorrhage. We will not satisfy our need for vengeance. Is that livable? Run, pursue, suffer and re-suffer, that is not life either.

What to do? The stroke of genius–the stroke of suppression–it is Athena who brings it. The stakes are enormous.

– And if I changed the world? If I changed the immemorial tradition of desire?, says the famous goddess to herself, product of skillful genetic manipulations. Who else but Athena–this god who has only to act from her woman's body–could make rule the auspicious confusion around the illegalities that want to acquire the full powers of legality. Athena, one would have had to invent her. Closer to the father than any son, and yet a woman by appearance, she is the ferrywoman *par excellence.* The changeling before changing eyes. She knows the difficulties, the tortuous paths one must take, and that often one has to surpass the opposite of that which is desired in order to move forward.

With Athena, humanity wins, but at what price. Too bad, someone has to pay. Peace[1], it can be obtained through war. Such is the pitiless science of she who carries both the sword and the olive branch.

Hard to understand, hard to love, but indispensable to Athena. Still the most modern goddess.

What invents a psychic divinity? Calculation, evaluation, negotiation with one's self: it is in our interest to renounce satisfaction in order to obtain a more tranquil satisfaction and more assured in exchange, she suggests to us.

Is that true? If it is not true, we will never know because Athena drives us with the hand of a master, without hate and with love, without charity, toward the region of submission, to the reality principle. Not resignations but submissions.

We are at our own training, us who yesterday were still savage beasts. What is exultant about all that? Nothing according to me. But to follow Athena, it happens that we experience severe, lusterless joys that we earn by

1. 'Pay' and 'peace', '*paie*' and '*la paix*' are homophones in French.

un dossier. La Justice enterre les vivants dans un souci d'égalisation.

Est-ce donc cette révélation affreuse et ineffaçable qu'Eschyle comptait nous faire?

S'agit-il dans ce récit d'une tragédie de la justice, cette perverse subreptice?

Non. Ceci est la tragédie des 'Euménides', ces vieilles femmes enfantines, qui font, à leur dépens, l'expérience éternelle et dernière des fatalités humaines: il n'y a rien à faire pour les mortels, rien, sinon d'inventer cette digue intérieure que nous appelons le refoulement.

C'est que nous, mortels, avons affaire avec le Sang. Il s'agit du Sens du Sang, le sang qui, une fois versé, ne remonte pas dans les veines. Rien ne le fera remonter. Alors, sang appelant sang, jusqu'à la fin du monde, l'Histoire entière n'est plus qu'une hémorragie. On ne satisfera pas notre besoin de vengeance. Est-ce vivable? Courir, pourchasser, souffrir et re-souffrir, ce n'est pas une vie non plus.

Que faire? Le coup de génie—le coup du refoulement—c'est Athéna qui le porte. L'enjeu est immense.

– Et si je changeais le monde? Si je changeais la tradition immémoriale de la passion?,

se dit la fameuse déesse, produit d'adroites manipulations génétiques. Qui d'autre qu'Athéna—ce dieu qui n'a que faire de son corps de femme—pourrait faire régner la confusion propice aux illégalités qui veulent acquérir les pleins pouvoirs de la légalité? Athéna, il fallait l'inventer. Plus proche du père qu'aucun fils, et cependant femme pour son apparence, elle est la passeuse par excellence. La changeuse aux yeux changeants. Elle sait les difficiles, les tortueux chemins qui font avancer, et qu'il faut bien souvent passer par le contraire de ce que l'on désire pour avancer.

Avec Athéna, l'humanité gagne, mais à quel prix? Tant pis, il faut que quelqu'un paie. La paix, c'est par la guerre qu'on l'obtient. Telle est la science sans pitié de celle qui porte à la fois la lance et le rameau d'olivier.

Difficile à comprendre, difficile à aimer, mais indispensable Athéna. Déesse la plus moderne toujours.

Qu'invente la divinité psychique? Le calcul, l'évaluation, la négociation avec soi-même: on a intérêt à renoncer à une satisfaction pour obtenir une satisfaction plus tranquille et plus assurée en échange, nous suggère-t-elle.

Est-ce vrai? Si ce n'est pas vrai, nous ne le saurons jamais, car Athéna nous conduit de main de maître, sans haine et avec amour, sans charité, vers la région des soumissions au principe de réalité. Non pas démissions, mais soumissions.

C'est à notre propre dressage que nous assistons, nous qui étions hier encore des bêtes sauvages. Quoi d'exaltant dans tout ça? Rien, selon moi. Mais à suivre Athéna, il arrive que l'on éprouve les joies sévères et sans lustres que l'on gagne à se vaincre soi-même. Cette histoire s'est passée avant l'invention

conquering ourselves. This story happened before the invention of a completely different response to our fate, that of the pardon.

The day when we have renounced childhood until grand old age, to rancour, to drunkenness, to the sad joys of not forgetting, there it is, Aeschylus exhumed it with a cruel bravery from beneath centuries of silence.

And for a brief apocalypse, the vision of Erinyes-Eumenides is returned to us. Who? That's the enigma. We have never seen them. There are no stranger creatures.

All, according to them, is strange, strange to think, stranger to our thoughts, to our experience, to our perception. But not to our unconscious. The Powers, the Terrors, the infernal regions that we have never seen, but their presence prowls and makes us shudder, our Dreams see them. But they defy description. Pythia, prophetess of Apollo, is not coming back. These creatures who overthrow her don't even look like the worst known, they are even more, more indescribable, they surpass words, sense. They are as indisputable and loathsome as the great sadnesses.

Even the Divinities have nothing to say of them, and have no relationship with them. The Gods, who speak our language so well, don't have enough words to vomit them up, to stigmatise them, to hate them.

But here is the enigma: irresistibly we understand them, yes, inexplicably we don't vomit them up, and even in secret, a secret between ourselves, without doubt, we love them. Although they are capable of making us frightened. But the Fear (Fears), we will never deny that, no matter how strange it appears to us, it is in us, it is the mask on the flamboyant eyes that looks at us from the farthest corner, the blackest of our interior nights. I say 'the mask' because it is thus that I saw, looking at me from my dream, from the North-West of my night, me lying petrified in the corner of the world without the ability to flee them, even as I heard, from the remotest distance, the ululated warning.

The Erinyes, yes, we (only) see them in dreams.

They are aspects, faces of ourselves that we cannot recognise. We hold them at a distance. Our intolerable aspects, our inseparables. It seems that, in the past, they came to us from outside, from the horizon, and they no longer left us, these Powers dedicated to reproaching us, and to making us feel horror without end.

Their formidable power comes from those parts of them that are us, they are the spawning of our acts, they are our mothers and our children.

Why do they suddenly appear then as old women, these creatures that are consistent with our crimes? I kill, I set on fire, wound, and, straight away, the pack of old women appears. Why not a dragon, or an owl with four heads?

It is these moaning, tenacious old women who make me into a martyr. As if in each crime it was the old woman that I was killing. The crime is

d'une tout autre réponse à nos fatalités, celle du pardon.

Le jour où nous avons renoncé à l'enfance, à la grande vieillesse, à la rancune, à l'ivresse, aux tristes joies de ne pas oublier, le voilà, Eschyle l'a exhumé avec un courage cruel de sous les siècles de silence.

Et pour une brève apocalypse, il nous rend la vision des Erinyes-Euménides. Qui? Voilà l'énigme. On ne les a jamais vues. Pas de créatures plus étranges.

Tout, s'agissant d'elles, est étrange, étrange à penser, étranger à notre pensée, à notre expérience, à notre perception. Mais non pas à notre inconscient. Les Puissances, les Terreurs, les contrées infernales que nous n'avons jamais vues mais dont la présence rôde et nous fait tressaillir, nos Rêves les voient. Mais elles échappent à la description. La Pythie, prophétesse d'Apollon, n'en revient pas. Ces créatures, qui la renversent, ne ressemblent même pas au pire connu, elles sont encore plus, encore plus indescriptibles, elles dépassent les mots, les sens. Elles sont indéniables et innommables comme les grandes douleurs.

Même les Divinités n'ont rien à en dire, et n'ont aucun rapport avec elles. Les Dieux, qui parlent si bien notre langue, n'ont pas assez de mots pour les vomir, les stigmatiser, les haïr.

Mais voici l'énigme: nous, irrésistiblement, nous les comprenons, oui, inexplicablement nous ne les vomissons pas, et même en secret, en secret à nous-même, sans doute, nous les aimons. Pourtant elles sont capables de nous faire peur. Mais la Peur (les Peurs), nous ne pourrons jamais nier que, si étrangère à nous qu'elle paraisse, elle est en nous, elle est le masque aux yeux flamboyants qui nous regarde depuis le coin le plus éloigné, le plus noir de notre nuit intérieure. Je dis 'le masque', parce que c'est ainsi que je les ai vues en rêve me regarder, depuis le Nord-Ouest de ma nuit, moi gisant pétrifiée au coin du monde sans pouvoir les fuir, alors même que j'entendais, au loin du lointain, l'avertissement hululé.

Les Erynies, oui, nous les voyons (seulement) en rêve.

Elles sont les aspects, les figures de nous-mêmes que nous ne pouvons pas reconnaître. Nous les tenons à distance. Nos inadmissibles, nos inséparables. Il paraît donc qu'autrefois, elles venaient à nous du dehors, de l'horizon, et elles ne nous quittaient plus, ces Puissances vouées à nous faire des reproches, et à nous faire sentir l'horreur sans fin.

Leur terrible puissance vient de ce qu'elles sont nous-mêmes, elles sont l'engeance de nos actes, elles sont nos mères et nos enfants.

Pourquoi surgissent-elles donc en tant que vieilles femmes, ces créatures conséquentes à nos crimes? Je tue, je mets à feu, à sang, et aussitôt la meute de vieilles est là. Pourquoi pas un dragon, ou une chouette à quatre têtes?

Ce sont ces vieilles gémissantes, tenaces, qui me martyrisent. Comme si dans chaque crime c'était la vieille femme que je tuais. Le crime c'est ça: c'est ma mère que je tue—la vie, ma mère. L'assassin tue toujours sa mère.

that: it is my mother that I kill–life, my mother. The assassin always kills his mother. (That he calls her 'bad' next, is to declare war. Each killed person is accused of great evil. As soon as Clytemnestra is assassinated, one never stops accusing her.) That is what we cannot face up to: no one can bear to see the mother assassinated, nor to see oneself in the process of killing one's own mother. We want to flee, we want to flee from ourselves and we cannot flee from ourselves by ourselves. The effort it takes to hate ourselves is in vain, no one hates themselves, the more we try to hate ourselves by ourselves, the less we hate ourselves, the more we distill hateful resentment towards 'the assassinated mother', cause of all our torments.

'You need a forgotten in order to separate you from yourself'–here is Athena's great idea. And as soon as we execute it: we persuade the bloodied mother to go and bury herself. From this moment on we will no longer see her coming near us openly.

We declare 'triumph', 'happy end', the descent of the Eumenides under the earth? Will they follow us? We cannot make up our mind. The means by which the old noble women are returned, in a volte-faced lighting, leaves us suffering. Certainly, in this case, they didn't have a choice. But even so. What will become of them?

And us?

Aeschylus comes to bring the subterranean old women to the day of the scene. For a moment, trembling, troubled, we remember everything, all the spectators, among whom certain people are the descendants of Orestes, others the children of Clytemnestra. There is silence. During this silence, the sons and mothers look at one another, perhaps, see one another a little.

Recognise themselves in each other?

What does the male descendant of Orestes think? (Or even the female descendant). What is he going to say?

As the descendant of Clytemnestra, in silence I listen and I don't know.

All of us, who are not divine, we don't renounce vengeance–our unconscious renounces nothing. That which we put on ourselves in the day, the night liberates us from.

In leaving the Theatre at night, we think of them, we lend an ear. Sometimes we despair, and we also we resign ourselves to 'the evidence': never just justice on this earth, matricide will enjoy the use of a throne and paternal riches, and time does its destructive work: it is enough to wait for the Crime to be legitimated. In a generation we will have forgotten that there ever had been murder. It is always thus, thinks our despair.

But sometimes we hope. We cannot yet believe that those who kill their mother will enjoy a prosperous life and have a peaceful death. Surely, we hope, the old women judges are going to return, surely not later than the last day. We ask for neither blood nor punishment, only this: that the criminal be named a criminal, and that the victim be called the victim.

(Qu'il l'appelle 'mauvaise' ensuite, c'est fait de guerre. Toute personne tuée est accusée de grande méchanceté. Dès que Clytemnestra est assassinée, on n'en finit plus de l'accuser.) C'est cela que nous ne pouvons pas voir en face: nul ne peut supporter de voir la mère assassinée, ni de se voir soi-même en train de tuer sa propre mère. Nous voulons fuir, nous voulons nous fuir et nous ne pouvons pas nous fuir nous-mêmes. L'effort pour nous haïr nous-mêmes est vain, nul ne se hait soi-même, plus nous essayons de nous haïr nous-mêmes, moins nous nous haïssons, plus nous distillons le haineux ressentiment à l'égard de 'la mère assassinée', cause de tous nos tourments.

'Il faudrait un oubli qui te sépare de toi-même—voilà l'idée géniale d'Athéna. Et aussitôt de l'exécuter: la mère ensanglantée on la persuade d'aller s'enterrer elle-même. Désormais nous ne la verrons plus venir vers nous ouvertement.

Appellerons-nous 'triomphe', 'happy-end', la descente des Euménides sous la terre? Les suivrons-nous? Nous ne pouvons nous y résoudre. La façon dont les augustes vieilles se sont rendues, en une volte-face foudroyante, nous laisse en souffrance. Certes, en ce cas elles n'ont pas eu le choix. Mais quand même. Que vont-elles devenir?

Et nous?

Eschyle vient de ramener les souterraines vieilles au jour de la scène. Pendant un instant, tremblants, troublés, tous nous nous souvenons, tous les spectateurs, parmi lesquels certains sont des descendants d'Oreste, d'autres les enfants de Clytemnestra. Il y a un silence. Pendant ce silence, les fils et les mères se regardent, peut-être, un peu, se voient.

Se reconnaissent?

Que pense le descendant d'Oreste? (Ou bien la descendante). Que va-t-il dire?

En tant que descendante de Clytemnestra, en silence, j'écoute et je ne sais pas.

Nous tous, qui ne sommes pas divins, nous ne renonçons pas à la vengeance—notre inconscient ne renonce à rien. Ce que nous nous imposons le jour, la nuit le libère.

En sortant du Théâtre, la nuit, nous pensons à elles, nous tendons l'oreille. Parfois nous désespérons, et nous aussi nous nous rendons 'à l'évidence': jamais de juste justice sur cette terre, le matricide jouira d'un trône et des richesses paternelles, et le temps fait son œuvre fossoyeuse: il suffit d'attendre pour que le Crime trouve sa légitimité. Dans une génération on aura oublié qu'il y a eu meurtre. C'est toujours ainsi, pense notre désespoir.

Mais parfois nous espérons. Nous ne pouvons encore pas croire que ceux qui tuent leur mère jouiront d'une vie prospère et d'une mort paisible. Sûrement, espérons-nous, les vieilles justicières vont revenir, sûrement pas plus tard que le dernier jour. Nous ne demandons ni sang ni châtiment, seulement ceci: que le criminel soit appelé criminel, et que la victime soit

What? Even this is too much?

'Le Coup' was first published in French in Hélène Cixous's translation of Aeschylus– Les Euménides d'Eschyle, *Théâtre du Soleil, 1992, pp. 5-13*

appelée victime.

Quoi? C'est encore trop?

'Le Coup', in Les Euménides d'Eschyle, *traduction d'Hélène Cixous, Théâtre du Soleil, 1992, pp. 5-13*

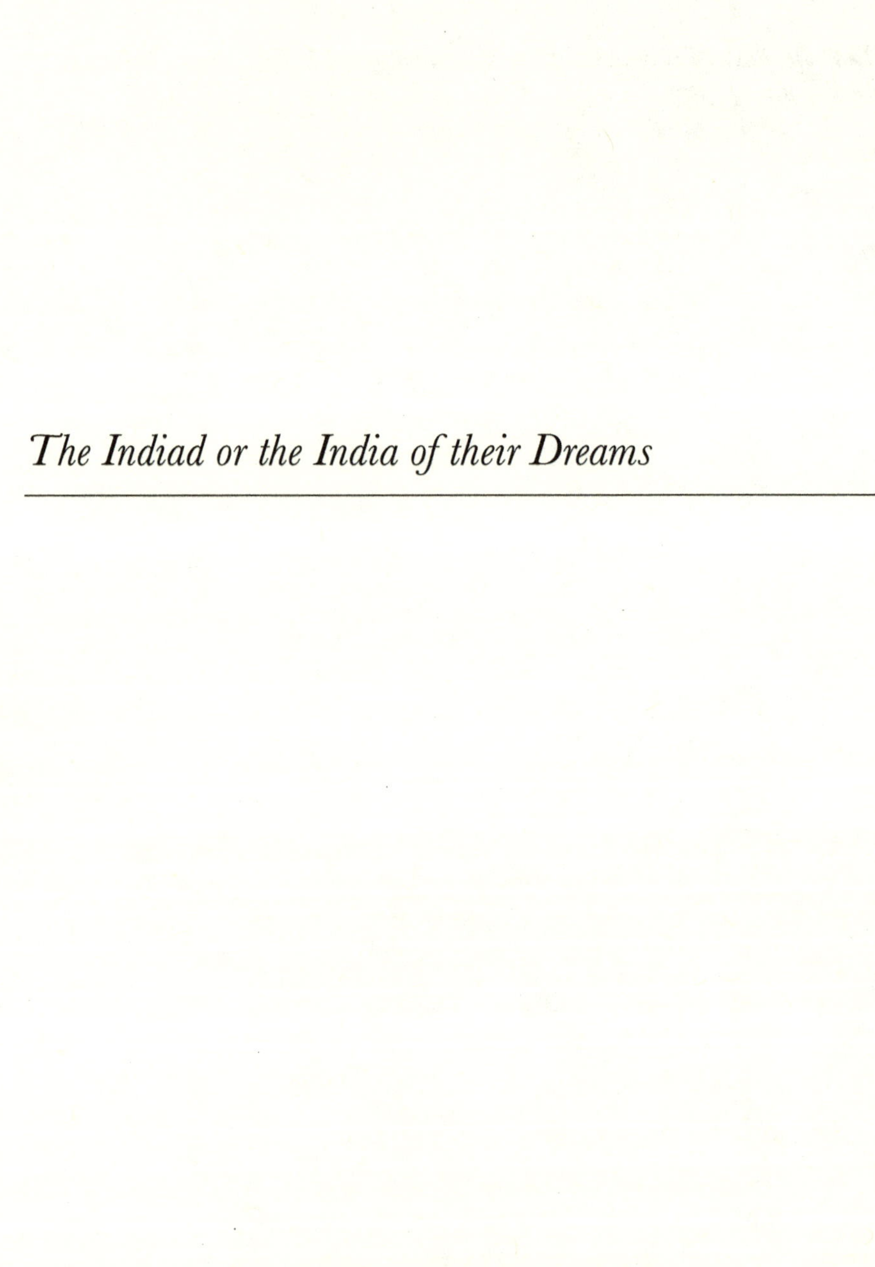

The Indiad or the India of their Dreams

The play: *The Indiad or the India of their Dreams*
Creators: The Théâtre du Soleil
First performed: 30 September 1987 at the Cartoucherie of Vincennes, Paris
Director: Ariane Mnouchkine
Text: Hélène Cixous
Music: Jean-Jacques Lemêtre
Set: Guy-Claude François
Costumes: Jean-Claude Barriera and Nathalie Thomas
Masks: Erhard Stiefel

Synopsis: *The Indiad or the India of their Dreams* is an epic recounting of a tumultuous period of change in the history of India. The play focuses on India's independence from British colonial rule in 1947. The central characters of the play are fictional re-imaginings of the real historical figures of Jawaharlal Nehru, the first Prime Minister of India, Mohandas Karamchand Gandhi, leader of the non-violent Indian independence movement and Muhammad Ali Jinnah, the founder of Pakistan. The production used the stylised techniques of Oriental acting and design principles as well as Indian musical instruments and the melodic structures and motifs of Indian music.

Résumé de la pièce: *L'Indiade ou l'Inde de leurs rêves* est une pièce-épopée qui ré-imagine la période de changements tumultueux de l'histoire de l'Inde. La pièce se focalise sur la domination coloniale britannique, l'indépendance de l'Inde et sa partition en 1947. Les personnages principaux sont des re-créations fictives des vrais leaders historiques comme Jawaharlal Nehru, le Premier ministre; Mohandas Karamchand Gandhi, le dirigeant du mouvement non-violent pour l'indépendance; et Muhammad Ali Jinnah, le fondateur du Pakistan. Le spectacle a fait appel aux modes orientaux et stylisés, pour les comédiens tout comme pour les éléments du décor, ainsi que pour les instruments fabriqués par Jean-jacques Lemêtre, qui donne au spectacle mélodies, rythmes et motifs de la musique indienne.

If you allow me, I am going to speak to you about love…

Triumph and Mourning

On 15 August 1947, India is born. For thirty years the Indian people fought to bring about that day so desired. Thirty years of servitudes, prisons, great waves of non-violence. A long desire. Thirty years of anger and dreaming. 'When we will be free, old India will give birth to a young India that…'

This blessed day finally arrives, freedom arrives, the saffron, white and green flag goes up. But the sky is black and thus this joyful day is a day of mourning. Such it is that smiles have dried on lips and bitterness inflames eyelids. Because destiny has dealt India one of its tragic turns. The day of birth is also a day of goodbye and of ripping/heartbreak.

On 14 August 1947, Pakistan is born. Carved in the large Indian body, pulled from the stomach of the continent by an implacable operation, this new country surges from India in a flood of blood. Everything is separated, populations, villages, rivers, communities. Punjab to the west and Bengal to the east are sliced alive down the middle.

The Indian soul twists with sadness and rage. For a long time, knives flew. History has never lived through such a mass exodus. In one day, ten million beings are uprooted. Death is vast.

So was this the party you were preparing for? This Partition? And yet, amongst the tears, there is, even still, a sad joy, since we are independent.

Why, how, by what fault, madness, or necessity, has this division come about?

Everything had begun in one single hope that united and carried 400 million Indians from all religions, from all casts, towards the same goal.

Then, little by little, the ark cracks, the division puts the massive body to the test, fractures the joints. An opposite dream rises up and opposes the union. And the dreamer of this dream of division is a haunted man, powerful, inflexible. A man built of willpower, Mohamed Ali Jinnah. And thus he assembles sections of the Muslim Indian community around him, thus does

Si vous permettez, je vais vous parler d'amour…

Triomphe et Deuil

Le 15 août 1947, l'Inde est née. Trente années le peuple Indien a lutté pour qu'advienne ce jour tant désiré. Trente années à travers servitudes, prisons, grandes vagues de non-violence. Une longue passion. Trente ans de colère et de rêve. « Quand nous serons libres, de la vieille Inde renaîtra une jeune Inde qui… »

Vient enfin ce jour béni, vient la liberté, monte le drapeau safran blanc et vert. Mais le ciel est noir et voici que ce jour de joie est un jour de deuil. Voici que les sourires ont séché sur les lèvres et l'amertume enflamme les paupières. Car le destin a joué à l'Inde un de ses tours tragiques. Le jour de la naissance est aussi un jour d'adieu et de déchirement.

Le 14 août 1947 est né le Pakistan. Découpé dans le grand corps indien, tiré de la poitrine du continent par une opération implacable, ce nouveau pays surgit de l'Inde dans un flot de sang. Tout est séparé, populations, villages, fleuves, communautés. Le Punjab à l'ouest et le Bengale à l'est sont tranchés vifs par le milieu.

Et l'âme indienne se tord de douleur et de rage. Longtemps les couteaux ont volé. L'Histoire n'a jamais vécu un si grand exode. En un jour dix millions d'êtres sont déracinés. La mort est innombrable.

Alors, c'était cela la fête que vous prépariez? Cette Partition? Et cependant, parmi les larmes, quand même une triste joie, puisque nous sommes indépendants.

Pourquoi, comment, par quelle faute, folie, ou nécessité, cette division?

Tout avait commencé par une seule espérance qui unissait et portait 400 millions d'Indiens de toutes les religions, de toutes les castes, vers le même but.

Puis peu à peu l'arche se fendille, la division travaille l'immense corps, fait craquer les jointures. Un rêve contraire se lève et s'oppose à l'union. Et le rêveur de ce rêve de division est un homme hanté, puissant, inflexible. Un

Jinnah the atheist call Indian Islam towards a Promised Land, he who does not believe

in Allah. Fate juggles with sincere hearts.

A second story is now coming to cross over with the fight for Independence. The combatants move forward stumbling. Their own brothers attack them. And it is a fray that carries itself, panting towards the goal.

If at first the dream did not entirely believe in itself, it soon gains self-confidence. In 1940 it enters into History and calls itself: Pakistan. Now that it has a name, it only lacks land. And despite the desperate efforts of the great Indian leaders (Hindus, Muslims, Sikhs, Christians, Atheists...), everything helps to make it happen: the second world war, the political uncertainties, the English, only too happy to weaken the Freedom-fighters of the Indian Congress by backing up Jinnah's Muslim League. In the night of war, Jinnah strides out. So when the global conflict is finally over, the hour of 'the meeting with destiny' approaches, as Nehru spoke of.

Yes, India finally belongs to Indians, but in what state: divided against herself, damaged, gangrened, distraught from hatred. And to save it, one can only believe in amputation.

Only one opposes the vivisection: Gandhi.

Him, the mother, shouts to King Solomon: 'don't divide up the child, give it alive to she who asks for it at any price'. But there is no Solomon. The sword falls.

The Epoch of Blood, but the Epoch of the Heart

The story that carries the fatal name of Partition is, in truth, an immense story of love. Love, that was a matter beyond politics and religion.

Can we speak of love today, publically, loudly, in public spheres, political spheres? Can we speak of love with love and without derision in the television-era?

No, today love is regulated to restricted depths, forbidden in high places.

Do we love one another? What head of State can permit himself to say that?

Even so, the Indians never stopped talking about love throughout the thirty years, right up to the head of State. The glorious entry of love into public affairs, right in the middle of the twentieth century, such is the gift that India gave to the universe, thanks to Gandhi. And since love had, thanks to the Mahatma, the right of speech and of residence, he gave it away with a free heart. On the same stage of love unfolded—whether certain people liked it or not—all the political battles. We loved one another, fell out, searched for, found, separated, lost, in the grips of love. The great rippings had the convulsing faces of hating lovers.

The separations, the rejected regions of India, the party alliances, the

homme taillé dans la volonté, Mohamed Ali Jinnah. Et voici qu'il rassemble autour de lui une partie de la communauté musulmane indienne, voici que Jinnah l'athée appelle l'Islam indien vers une Terre Promise, lui qui ne croit pas

en Allah. Le destin jongle avec les cœurs sincères.

Une deuxième histoire vient maintenant traverser la lutte pour l'Indépendance. Les combattants avancent en trébuchant. Leurs propres frères les attaquent. Et c'est une mêlée qui se porte en haletant vers le but.

Si d'abord le rêve ne s'est pas tout à fait cru lui-même, il prend bientôt de l'assurance. En 1940 il entre dans l'Histoire et s'appelle: Pakistan. Il a maintenant un nom, il ne lui manque plus qu'une terre. Et malgré les efforts désespérés des grands leaders indiens (indous, musulmans, sikhs, chrétiens, athées...), tout l'aide à se réaliser: la deuxième guerre mondiale, les aléas politiques, les Anglais trop contents d'affaiblir les Freedom-fighters du Congrès Indien en s'appuyant sur la Ligue Musulmane de Jinnah. Dans la nuit de la guerre, Jinnah va à grandes enjambées. Alors, quand enfin s'achève le conflit mondial, approche l'heure du « Rendez-vous avec la Destinée » dont a parlé Nehru.

Oui, l'Inde vient enfin aux Indiens, mais dans quel état: divisée contre elle-même, blessée, gangrenée, affolée de haine. Et pour la sauver on ne croit plus qu'à l'amputation.

Un seul s'oppose à la vivisection: Gandhi.

Lui, la mère, crie au roi Salomon: ne tranchez pas l'enfant, donnez-le vivant à qui le réclame à tout prix. Mais il n'y a pas de Salomon. L'épée tombe.

Epoque de sang, mais époque de coeur

L'histoire qui porte le nom fatal de Partition est en vérité une immense histoire d'amour. L'amour, voilà ce dont il s'agissait au-delà de la politique et de la religion.

Peut-on parler d'amour aujourd'hui, publiquement, haut, dans les sphères publiques, politiques? Peut-on parler d'amour avec amour et sans dérision à l'époque-télévision?

Non, aujourd'hui l'amour est relégué dans les étroites intimités, interdit en hauts lieux.

Aimons-nous les uns les autres, quel chef d'Etat peut-il se permettre de dire cela?

Eh bien les Indiens n'ont pas cessé de parler d'amour pendant trente ans et jusqu'au sommet de l'Etat. L'entrée glorieuse de l'amour dans la chose publique en plein XXe siècle, tel est le cadeau qu'à travers Gandhi l'Inde fit à l'univers. Et puisque l'amour avait, grâce au Mahatma, droit de parole et de cité, il s'en donnait à cœur libre. Sur la scène même de l'amour se sont déroulées—bon gré mal gré pour certains—toutes les batailles politiques.

torments of populations, the promises made, kept, worn-out, the events appear in the poignant and familiar figures of our desires. The tempests of the heart, the recognitions, deceptions, rancours, repudiations, reunions, everything is there, but lived through the magnificent ladder of India.

Yes, in that time then, hardly yesterday, when the Occident was tattooed by Hitler, we burned with love in Asia, and one part of humanity was living through a sublime epoch on this same earth.

The Knights of the Absolute

The unexpected feature of this story is that, right in the middle of the XXth century, beings lived near us who belonged to spiritual eras that had evolved over centuries and millennia.

Biblical and comparable to Abraham are men such as Gandhi and Abdul Ghaffar Khan, who have men, as well as their Gods, as interlocutors. And as if they conform in their terrestrial life to celestial law, they are sometimes as incomprehensible as stars. And Jawaharlal Nehru, Abul Kalam Azad, Sarojini Naidu, Vallabhbhai Patel live in a region of high honour. To follow their adventures is to find one's self before an Indian Round Table. No one among them is smaller or bigger than the other. Oh Golden Age of loyalty and respect!

But when these characters, with their souls cut from the cloth of myth, meet reality, what does that achieve?

The sainthood of Gandhi growing with political expediency? The idealism of Nehru with historical contradictions, what does that signify?

This play is born of India. It is not India, it is only an Indian molecule, a footprint.

It is a play about the human being, about heroes and dust, about the combat of angel and beast in every one of us.

There are all sorts of human creatures there—angels, saints, women, men, small, big. And souls alter in size according to the test.

But all that this play was not able to carry on its human back, I will never cease saying it.

There are not

The camels that pass by as in dreams

The sleeping cow in the middle of the road

The little kids from Durgapur who cavort at the very heart of hell on the road

The vultures on the dome of the tomb of Lodi Garden

Those innumerable bodies sleeping like death on the pavements in front of Calcutta station, and some among them are dead

The three-hundred famished people jostling each other like birds around the pot of soup at Nizamuddin and who show us just what human hunger is.

On s'est aimé, désaimé, cherché, trouvé, séparé, perdu, agrippé d'amour. Les grands déchirements avaient les visages convulsés des amants haineux.

Les séparations, les régions rejetées de l'Inde, les alliances de partis, les tourmentes des populations, les promesses faites, tenues, rompues, les événements apparaissent avec les figures poignantes et familières de nos passions. Les tempêtes du coeur, les reconnaissances, les déceptions, les rancœurs, les répudiations, les retrouvailles, tout est là, mais vécu à l'échelle magnifique de l'Inde.

Oui, en ce temps-là, hier à peine, quand l'Occident était tatoué par Hitler, on brûlait d'amour en Asie, et une partie de l'humanité vivait sur cette terre même une époque sublime.

Les Chevaliers de l'Absolu

Le trait inouï de cette histoire, c'est qu'en plein XXe siècle ont vécu près de nous des êtres qui appartenaient à des époques spirituelles révolues pour nous depuis siècles et millénaires.

Bibliques et comparables à Abraham sont des hommes comme Gandhi et Abdul Ghaffar Khan, qui ont pour interlocuteurs également les hommes et leurs Dieux. Et comme ils se conforment dans leur vie terrestre à la loi céleste, ils sont parfois aussi incompréhensibles que les étoiles. Et Jawaharlal Nehru, Abul Kalam Azad, Sarojini Naïdu, Vallabhbahaï Patel vivent dans une haute région d'honneur. Suivre leurs aventures, c'est se retrouver devant une Table Ronde indienne. Nul n'est plus petit ni plus grand que l'autre. O âge d'or de la loyauté et du respect!

Mais quand ces personnages, aux âmes taillées dans l'étoffe du mythe, rencontrent la réalité, qu'est-ce que cela donne?

La sainteté de Gandhi croisant avec le calcul politique? L'idéalisme de Nehru avec les contradictions historiques, qu'est-ce que cela donne?

Cette pièce est née de l'Inde. Ce n'est pas l'Inde, elle est seulement une molécule indienne, une empreinte de pas.

C'est une pièce sur l'être humain, sur le héros et la poussière, sur le combat de l'ange et de la bête en chacun de nous.

Il y a là toutes sortes de créatures humaines, des anges, des saints, des femmes, des hommes, des petits, des grands. Et les âmes changent de taille selon l'épreuve.

Mais tout ce que cette pièce n'a pu porter sur son dos humain, je n'en finirai pas de le dire.

Il n'y a pas

Les chameaux qui passent comme des rêves

La vache endormie au milieu de la route

Les petits chevreaux de Durgapur qui cabriolent en plein cœur de l'enfer routier

The rats that pass by the exultant rhythms of Kawali

The child without legs who runs like the wind on his crutches on the esplanade of the Red Fort

The wretched royal women who wear pyramids of bricks on their little heads to such a height that they shake like bamboo scaffolding

The mysteriously beautiful children who are like tears fallen from the wretched eyes of the gods above

The crows that are as numerous as the Indians

The passenger in the train compartment from Bolpur who asks: 'And you, tell me, where do you believe God lives?'

The Baul guru in the ashram planted among the Bengali rice fields who really understood Gandhi's philosophy

The very old man sitting in the corner of a street in Calcutta, so small that we don't see him in front of a single box of shoe shine, so little that we don't see it, and who waits for a god to send him a shoe to shine, that will manifest itself or not manifest itself, and the old man does not beg because he works, while waiting, he works by waiting for no-one or someone.

But all that is not said here, is here however, silently, I hope. Nothing is forgotten. 'That which really exists cannot cease to exist'

Everything that doesn't figure here has become the murmuring and multitudinous earth in which this play took root and breath, to rise up, inch by inch, onto the stage.

Program Extract

'Si vous permettez, je vais vous parler d'amour...' was first published in French in the introduction to L'Indiade ou l'Inde de leurs rêves, *Théâtre du Soleil, 1987, pp. 11-17 and in* Acteurs, *No. 53, October 1987, pp. 8-9.*

Les vautours sur la coupole du tombeau de Lhodi Garden

Les dormeurs comme des morts innombrables sur le trottoir devant la gare de Calcutta et certains sont morts

Les trois cents affamés se bousculant comme des oiseaux autour de la marmite de soupe à Nizamuddin et qui nous montrent ce qu'est la faim humaine

Les rats qui passent à travers les cadences exultantes du Kawali

L'enfant sans jambes qui court comme le vent sur ses béquilles sur l'esplanade du Fort Rouge

Les misérables femmes royales qui portent sur leurs petites têtes des pyramides de briques là-haut à la pointe tremblante de l'échafaudage de bambous

Les enfants mystérieusement beaux qui sont comme des larmes tombées des yeux de dieux misérables là-haut

Les corbeaux aussi nombreux que les Indiens

Le passager dans le wagon du train de Bholpur qui demande: et vous, dites-moi, où croyez-vous que Dieu réside?

Le guru des Bauls dans l'ashram planté parmi les rizières bengalies qui a vraiment compris la pensée de Gandhi

Le très vieil homme assis dans le coin d'une ruelle de Calcutta si petite qu'on ne la voit pas devant une unique boîte de cirage si petite qu'on ne la voit pas, et qui attend qu'un dieu lui envoie un soulier à cirer, cela se produira ou ne se produira pas, et le vieil homme ne mendie pas car il travaille, en attendant, il travaille en attendant personne ou quelqu'un.

Mais tout ce qui n'est pas dit ici, est cependant silencieusement ici, je l'espère. Rien n'est oublié. « Ce qui réellement existe ne peut cesser d'exister »

Tout ce qui ne figure pas ici est devenu la terre murmurante et multitudineuse dans laquelle cette pièce a pris racine et souffle pour s'élever ensuite, pouce par pouce, sur le plateau.

Extrait du programme du spectacle

Texte intégral en introduction de L'Indiade ou l'Inde de leurs rêves, *Théâtre du Soleil, 1987, pp. 11-17 et dans* Acteurs, *n°53, octobre 1987, pp. 8-9.*

The Crime Scene, the Place of Forgiveness

How can the poet open his universe to the fate of the people? He who is firstly an explorer of the Me, how, in which foreign language to his me, by what means would he be able to write of much more and everything other than Me?

And another question: how does me, who is of the species 'woman of letters', could I ever give speech to an illiterate peasant without taking it back from her, with one strike of my verb, without burying it in one of my beautiful sentences? So there will only ever be people who know how to read and write in my texts, and juggle with signs? And yet, I love him, this Khmer peasant, I love her, this royal mother from a village in Rajasthan who knows so many things and doesn't know that she lives in a country that me, I call India. For a long time I believed that my texts would only live in those rare and deserted places where only poems grow.

Until I arrive at the Theatre. There was the stage, the earth, where the me remains imperceptible, the land of others. There their speech is made to be heard, their silences, their shouts, their song, each one according to its own world and in its foreign language.

Once arrived, everything begins to be illuminated, and firstly, the nature of my need for theatre.

I need *a certain* Theatre, of which the first name was Shakespeare or Verdi, or Schoenberg or Sophocles or Rossini. I need this theatre to tell me stories, and for it to tell me them as only the theatre can tell them—legendarily, and yet, straight in the eyes.

If this Theatre is necessary it is because it allows us to live that which no 'genre' allows us: the difficulty we have in being human. The Evil. What happens at the theatre, it is Passion, but passion according to Oedipus, according to Hamlet, according to you, according to Woyzeck, according to me, according to Othello, according to Cleopatra, according to Marie, according to that enigmatic human being, tortured, criminal, innocent as I am, I who am you or all of you.

Le lieu du crime,
le lieu du pardon

Comment le poète peut-il ouvrir son univers aux destins des peuples? Celui qui est d'abord un explorateur du Moi, comment, dans quelle langue étrangère à son moi, par quels moyens pourrait-il écrire du beaucoup plus et tout autre que Moi?

Et une autre question: comment moi, qui suis de l'espèce des lettrés, pourrais-je jamais donner la parole à une paysanne illettrée sans la lui reprendre, d'un coup de mon verbe, sans l'enterrer d'une de mes belles phrases? Alors il n'y aurait jamais dans mes textes que des gens qui savent lire et écrire, jongler avec les signes? Et cependant je l'aime ce paysan khmer, je l'aime cette royale mère d'un village du Rajasthan qui sait tant de choses et ne sait pas qu'elle vit dans un pays que moi j'appelle Inde. Longtemps j'ai cru que mes textes n'habiteraient que dans ces lieux rares et désertiques où ne poussent que des poèmes.

Jusqu'à ce que j'arrive au Théâtre. Là était la scène, la terre, où le moi reste imperceptible, le pays des autres. Là se font entendre leurs paroles, leurs silences, leurs cris, leur chant, chacun selon son propre monde et dans sa langue étrangère.

Une fois arrivée, tout commence à s'éclairer, et d'abord la nature de mon besoin du théâtre.

J'ai besoin d'*un certain* Théâtre, dont le prénom était Shakespeare ou Verdi, ou Schönberg ou Sophocle ou Rossini. J'ai besoin que ce théâtre me raconte des histoires, et qu'il me les raconte comme lui seul peut les raconter légendairement et cependant droit dans les yeux.

Car si ce Théâtre est nécessaire c'est parce qu'il nous permet de vivre ce qu'aucun 'genre' ne nous permet: le mal que nous avons à être humains. Le Mal. Ce qui se passe au théâtre, c'est la Passion, mais la passion selon Oedipe, selon Hamlet, selon vous, selon Woyzzeck, selon moi, selon Othello, selon Cléopâtre, selon Marie, selon cet être humain énigmatique, torturé, criminel, innocent que je suis, je qui est toi ou vous.

Je crois que nous avons besoin aujourd'hui plus que jamais de notre

I think that today we need our own theatre more than ever, theatre where our heart is the stage upon which our destiny and our mystery play out, and of which we very rarely see the curtain lifted.

To tell the truth, we go less to the theatre than to our heart, and it is when we go to the heart, ours and the heart of things, that we feel the lack. We live outside ourselves, in a world in which the walls are replaced by television screens that lost their substance, their depths, their treasures, and we take the newspaper columns as our thoughts. We are imprinted daily. Even the wall, the real wall upon which the divine messages are written, we lack. We lack earth and flesh.

We live in front of the paper curtain, and even often as a curtain. But what is important to us, that which hurts us, that which makes us feel that we are characters in a great adventure, is what happens behind the curtain. And behind the curtain there is the naked stage.

We need this nudity. We need to see the hidden faces behind the faces, these faces that Theatre unveils.

And under the charm of costumes and makeup, under the mask, that which rises to the light is truth, which is to say, only the best or the worst. And behind the curtain of words, the naked voice. What a relief when in entering this place, the lie—which is our everyday politeness—stops and we begin to listen to the dialogue between hearts! We would shout about it. And we rejoice that it is not forbidden in this marvelous country to yell, to throw punches, to translate into breath, into sweat, into song, the suffering that comes with being a human inhabitant in our time.

We are characters of an epic that is forbidden to us by the laws of mediocrity and the prudence of living. And yet it is an epic. And what is frightening and beautiful is that, even though the epic of nation states appears so majestic, its motives—those which cause wars, peace, massacres, heroisms—all there is to see close up when parting the curtain, are lowly and powerful humans. The world is a theatre. Each character that enters believes themselves to be the centre of the world. And, in a certain sense, because they believe it, they are. Each one of us is the Centre. And each Centre is besieged by the other Centres.

Theatre kept the secret of History that Homer had sung: History is made up of stories of husbands and wives, of lovers, of fathers, of daughters, of mothers, of sons, of jealousy, of pride, of desire. And there are faces that launch fleets of a thousand ships and destroy cities.

The human being needs to become human. Human? I mean to say that he is the stage of the war between good and evil. That there is war is a chance for good: a chance to distinguish oneself and to conquer.

And he needs destiny: he needs to tell himself a story with a beginning and an end, to get from one day to the next. Our fate, what is it today? Since Shakespeare, it has changed a little. I am an island. Am I still only an island?

propre théâtre, le théâtre dont notre cœur est la scène, sur laquelle se jouent notre destin et notre mystère, et dont nous voyons très rarement se lever le rideau.

A vrai dire nous allons aussi peu au théâtre qu'à notre cœur, et c'est d'aller au cœur, le nôtre et celui des choses, que nous sentons le manque. Nous vivons à l'extérieur de nous-mêmes, dans un monde dont les murs sont remplacés par des écrans de télévision, qui a perdu son épaisseur, ses profondeurs, ses trésors, et nous prenons les colonnes de journaux pour nos pensées. Nous sommes imprimés quotidiennement. Même de mur, de vrai mur sur lequel s'écrivent les messages divins, nous manquons. Nous manquons de terre et de chair.

Nous vivons devant le rideau de papier, et même souvent en tant que rideau. Mais ce qui nous importe, ce qui nous blesse, ce qui nous fait sentir que nous sommes les personnages d'une aventure immense, c'est ce qui se passe derrière le rideau. Et derrière le rideau il y a la scène *nue.*

Nous avons besoin de cette nudité. Nous avons besoin de voir les visages cachés derrière les visages, ces visages que le Théâtre dévoile.

Et sous le charme des costumes et des maquillages, sous le masque, ce qui monte à la lumière c'est la vérité, c'est-à-dire seulement le meilleur ou le pire. Et derrière le rideau des mots, la voix nue. Quel soulagement, lorsqu'en entrant dans ce lieu, le mensonge, qui est notre politesse quotidienne, s'arrête et l'on commence à entendre le dialogue des cœurs! On en crierait. Et on se réjouit qu'il ne soit pas interdit, dans ce pays merveilleux, de pousser des cris, de porter des coups, de traduire en souffle, en sueur, en chant, la souffrance d'être un habitant humain de notre époque.

Nous sommes les personnages d'une épopée qu'il nous est interdit, par les lois de la médiocrité et de la prudence, de vivre. Et pourtant c'est une épopée. Et ce qu'il y a d'effrayant et de beau c'est que, si majestueuse que paraisse être l'épopée des nations, ses mobiles—ce qui cause les guerres, les paix, les massacres, les héroïsmes—à y regarder de près, en écartant le rideau, sont les infimes et puissants humains. Le monde est un théâtre. Chaque personnage qui entre se croit le centre du monde. Et d'une certaine manière, parce qu'il le croit, il l'est. Chacun de nous est le Centre. Et chaque Centre est assiégé par les autres Centres.

Le Théâtre a gardé le secret de l'Histoire que Homère avait chanté: l'Histoire est faite d'histoires de maris, d'amants, de pères, de filles, de mères, de fils, de jalousie, d'orgueil, de désir. Et il y a des visages qui lancent des flottes de mille voiles et détruisent des villes.

L'être humain a besoin de devenir humain. Humain? Je veux dire qu'il est la scène de la guerre entre le bien et le mal. Qu'il y ait guerre est une chance pour le bien: une chance de se distinguer et de vaincre.

Et il a besoin de destin: il a besoin de se raconter une histoire avec un commencement et une fin, pour avancer d'un jour à l'autre. Notre destin,

My island, even England, is raised on explosions, I can hear the bombs exploding, the canons firing, I am surrounded by wars, I am haunted by the sadness of hostages. The last bomb didn't kill me, we live under a sky of injustice in which we are victims or miracles. Is it not in our home that madness passes with its scythe? But if it is in our home, Paris, New Delhi, Beirut, Stockholm, we walk under the same blood sun. Sometimes death approaches and beats at a street in me, sometimes I don't hear it, once it knocks… and that will be me. It's already me.

Yes, from time to time we have this thought that I name here but most often we chase it away because it stops us from living. But in chasing it away we lose a big part of life. It's this part that Theatre gives back to us: the living part of the dead, or perhaps the mortal part of life.

I go to the theatre because I need to understand or, at least, to contemplate the act of death, or at least to admit it, to meditate on it. And also because I need to cry.

Also to laugh: but laughter is only the sigh of relief that bursts in the path of the scythe: it missed us by a hair!

I confess that Theatre is a form of religion: I want to say that we experience together there, in the religious space, the re-lieging,[1] the re-binding, the gathering together of emotions. I say 'confess' because it is one of the reasons that I can resist the call of Theatre: by anti-religion. By the need for individualism.

But I declare that we need these temples without dogma and without doctrine (but not without a great number of gods) where our torments and, above all, our blindness play out.

We are blind. We don't see what we do. We don't hear ourselves saying what we say. We don't understand ourselves. And we lie to ourselves. Because we are afraid of ourselves. We are afraid of our wickedness. We have guessed, thought, suspected or seen that we are bad. A little or a lot. But we don't really like being bad. And yet? Or we are bad without wickedness?

The enigma of wickedness, of human cruelty, that of others and my own, it is that which we come to ask the Theatre to show us.

Because Theatre is the place of the Crime. Yes, the place of the Crime, the place of horror, but also the place of Forgiveness. What do we gain from seeing? The primitive passions: adoration, assassination. All the excess that I leave at the door of my apartment: suicide, murder, the part of mourning that is in all passionate human relations: thirst and hunger. Sacrifice, cannibalism.

Because we don't only kill what we hate. We also kill what we love. We always kill a little of the being that we love.

And by twisted love, because love is twisted, we end up killing

1. '*Re-ligere*' is a neologism that combines '*religieux*' and '*lige*', meaning 'religious' and 'liege', hence theatre as a sovereign and a religion.

quel est-il aujourd'hui? Depuis Shakespeare il a un peu changé. Je suis une île. Suis-je encore seulement une île? Mon île, même l'Angleterre, est soulevée par les explosions, j'entends des bombes éclater, des canons tirer, je suis entourée de guerres, je suis hantée par la douleur des otages. La dernière bombe ne m'a pas tuée, nous vivons sous un ciel d'injustice, dont nous sommes les victimes ou les miraculés. Ce n'est pas chez nous que la folie passe avec sa faux? Mais si, c'est chez nous, Paris, New Delhi, Beyrouth, Stockholm, nous marchons sous le même soleil de sang. Parfois la mort s'approche et frappe à une rue de moi, parfois je ne l'entends pas, une fois elle frappe... et ce sera moi. C'est déjà moi.

Oui, par instants nous avons cette pensée que je nomme ici mais le plus souvent nous la chassons parce qu'elle nous empêcherait de vivre. Mais en la chassant nous perdons une grande part de vie. C'est cette part que le Théâtre nous rend: la part vivante de la mort, ou bien la part mortelle de la vie.

Je vais au théâtre parce que j'ai besoin de comprendre ou au moins de contempler l'acte de la mort, ou au moins de l'admettre, de le méditer. Et aussi parce que j'ai besoin de pleurer.

De rire aussi: mais le rire n'est que le soupir de soulagement qui éclate au passage de la faux: elle nous a manqués d'un cheveu!

J'avoue que le Théâtre est une forme de religion: je veux dire que l'on y éprouve ensemble, dans le re-ligere, le re-liement, le recueillement des émotions. Je dis 'j'avoue' parce que c'est une des raisons pour lesquelles il m'arrive de résister à l'appel du Théâtre: par anti-religion. Par besoin d'individualisme.

Mais je déclare que nous avons besoin de ces temples sans dogme et sans doctrine (mais non sans un grand nombre de dieux) où se jouent nos affres et surtout nos aveuglements.

Nous sommes des aveugles. Nous ne voyons pas ce que nous faisons. Nous ne nous entendons pas dire ce que nous disons. Nous ne nous comprenons pas nous-mêmes. Et nous nous mentons. Parce que nous avons peur de nous-mêmes. Nous avons peur de notre méchanceté. C'est que nous l'avons deviné, pensé, soupçonné, ou vu, que nous sommes méchants. Un peu ou très. Mais nous n'aimons pas vraiment être méchants. Et pourtant? Ou bien nous sommes méchants sans méchanceté?

L'énigme de la méchanceté, de la cruauté humaine, celle des autres et la mienne, c'est cela que nous venons demander au Théâtre de nous révéler.

Car le Théâtre c'est le lieu du Crime. Oui le lieu du Crime, le lieu de l'horreur, aussi le lieu du Pardon. Que nous donne-t-il à voir? Les passions primitives: adoration, assassinat. Tous les excès que je mets à la porte de mon appartement: le suicide, le meurtre, la part de deuil qu'il y a dans toute relation passionnément humaine: soif et faim. Le sacrifice, le cannibalisme.

Desdemona, Marie, our people or another people, or Indira Gandhi or Olof Palme.

Why do we love so immediately, so eternally, certain works of theatre or opera? Because by showing us our crimes at the Theatre, before witnesses, they accuse us and, at the same time, they pardon us.

We are all victims, but we are also hangmen. The Beast and the Knife. What does Theatre say to us? Death exists. What does Theatre give us? Death. We love Carmen and Don Jose equally. And, by the magic of music, we become one and other, we can stand being the killer or the killed, killed and killer.

The stage gives it to us, returns it to us, this death that we are ashamed of, that we fear, that we repel. It gives us life, in an instant or slowly, this source of so much sense, death, the dead part of all life, and right up to the drunk desire to kill Marie, the young woman or the old, the mother, the father, the child, a whole people.

And thus it is that, in this moment where, no longer fleeing, we accept looking at the victim or the murderer in the eyes—like Myshkin looks at Rogojine—that we remind ourselves that we are human, that it's a misfortune, but that it's a trying joy. Humans equally: humanity passes by you and by me, and by Macbeth and by the king and by the beggar, and we understand ourselves.

There are essential things that make us equal: that we arrive by such different paths to the same door, death.

And there are moments when the monster (the evil one, the '*villain*', the bandit, the assassin) discovers his humanity. There is always the moment of hesitation and temptation: and if I killed? And if I was wrong? And if I was a monster? And if I was blind? This moment is given to us by Theatre, it is the tragic moment when everything could be changed. No longer comes. This moment also occurs in our lives. And we must, Theatre reminds us, be highly vigilant in order not to miss it. Because between the bad and the good, the step is as fine as a blade.

Theatre doesn't give us a brutal death like a kick in the back. No, it does not assassinate us. Because, at its core, Theatre has pity. It gives us one of the rarest moments in the grind of our daily existence, the time of pity. We have become capable of no longer crying in front of the severed legs of a small Asian beggar, isn't it true? Fortunately, Theatre stops us and strikes us in the heart and brings us to tears. Suddenly I hear the complaint and I discover my deafness. And in recompense for our rediscovered suffering, the performance gives us tears, and the beauty of song reminds us that sadness can be beautiful when there is compassion. By beautiful I mean: human, shared.

Yes pity, terror, remain the most precious emotions in the world. They are love. And they

need so much to be reanimated in the hearts of our time.

Parce que l'on ne tue pas seulement ce que l'on hait. On tue aussi ce que l'on aime. Nous tuons toujours un peu l'être que nous aimons.

Et par amour tordu, parce que l'amour est tordu, nous en arrivons à tuer Desdémone, Marie, notre peuple ou un autre peuple ou Indira Gandhi ou Olof Palme.

Pourquoi aimons-nous si immédiatement, si éternellement certaines oeuvres de théâtre ou d'opéra? Parce qu'en nous montrant nos crimes au Théâtre, devant témoins, elles nous accusent et en même temps elles nous pardonnent.

Nous sommes tous victimes, mais nous sommes aussi bourreaux. La Bête et le Couteau. Que nous dit le Théâtre? Il y a de la mort. Que nous donne le Théâtre? La mort. Nous aimons Carmen et Don José également. Et par la magie de la musique nous devenons l'un et l'autre, nous supportons d'être tueur et tuée, tué et tueuse.

La scène nous la donne, nous la rend, cette mort dont nous avons honte, dont nous avons crainte, que nous repoussons. Elle nous donne à vivre, en un instant ou lentement cette source de tant de sens, la mort, la part de mort de toute vie, et jusqu'au désir ivre de tuer Marie, la jeune femme ou la vieille, la mère, le père, l'enfant, le peuple.

Et c'est alors, dans ce moment où ne fuyant plus nous acceptons de regarder la victime ou le meurtrier dans les yeux—comme Mychkine regarde Rogojine—que nous nous rappelons que nous sommes humains, que c'est un malheur, mais que c'est une joie éprouvante. Humains *également*: l'humanité passe par vous et par moi, et par Macbeth et par le roi et par le mendiant, et nous nous comprenons.

Il y a des choses essentielles qui nous rendent égaux: c'est d'arriver par des chemins si différents à la même porte, la mort.

Et il y a des moments où le monstre (le méchant, le "*villain*", le bandit, l'assassin) découvre son humanité. Il y a toujours le moment d'hésitation, et de tentation: et si je tuais? Et si je me trompais? Et si j'étais un monstre? Et si j'étais aveugle? Ce moment nous est donné au Théâtre, c'est l'instant tragique où tout pourrait être changé. Ne plus arriver. Cet instant arrive aussi dans nos vies. Et il nous faut, le Théâtre nous le rappelle, être d'une vigilance extrême pour ne pas le rater. Car entre le mal et le bien, le pas est mince comme une lame.

Le Théâtre ne nous donne pas la mort brutalement comme un coup dans le dos. Non, il ne nous assassine pas. Car essentiellement le Théâtre a pitié. Il nous donne un des temps les plus raréfiés dans le marché de nos existences quotidiennes, le temps de la pitié. Nous sommes devenus capables de ne plus pleurer devant les jambes coupées d'un petit mendiant asiatique, n'est-ce pas vrai? Heureusement le Théâtre nous arrête et nous frappe au cœur et nous ramène aux larmes. Soudain j'entends la plainte et je découvre ma surdité. Et en récompense de notre souffrance retrouvée, le spectacle nous donne les

If we have pity…

To begin with, let's take theatre seriously. I mean: it's good to go there seriously, like children. Because we can pretend to go to listen to an opera. And so nothing happens. But if we participate in *Woyzeck* or *King Lear*, with a simplified heart, discovered, and if by chance we shed tears, so perhaps a woman will be saved on earth, a prisoner will be set free—and perhaps an innocent person will be vindicated, and a forgotten one will be remembered.

'Le lieu du Crime, le lieu du Pardon', in was first published in French in L'Indiade ou l'Inde de leurs rêves, et quelques écrits sur le théâtre, *Théâtre du Soleil, 1987, pp. 253-259.*

This text was first written and published in a slightly different version for the reopening of the theatre 'La Monnaie De Munt' in Brussels in November 1986 under the title 'The Country of Others'.

larmes, et la beauté du chant nous rappelle que la douleur peut être belle lorsqu'il y a compassion. Belle je veux dire: humaine, partagée.

Oui la pitié, la terreur, restent les émotions les plus précieuses du monde. Ce sont elles l'amour. Et elles

ont tant besoin d'être ranimées dans les cœurs de notre époque.

Si nous avions pitié…

Pour commencer, prenons le Théâtre au sérieux. Je veux dire: il est bon d'y aller sérieusement, comme des enfants. Parce qu'on peut faire semblant d'aller écouter un opéra. Et alors rien ne se passe. Mais si l'on participe à *Woyzzeck* ou au *Roi Lear,* avec le cœur simplifié, découvert, et si par chance on verse des larmes, alors peut-être sur la terre une femme sera sauvée, un prisonnier sera libéré,—et peut-être un innocent justifié, et un oublié sera rappelé.

'Le lieu du Crime, le lieu du Pardon', in L'Indiade ou l'Inde de leurs rêves, et quelques écrits sur le théâtre, *Théâtre du Soleil, 1987, pp. 253-259.*

Ce texte, dans une version légèrement différente, a d'abord été écrit et publié à l'occasion de la réouverture du Théâtre de la Monnaie de Bruxelles en novembre 1986 sous le titre a 'Le Pays des Autres'.

The Terrible and Still Unfinished Story of Norodom Sihanouk, King of Cambodia

The play: *The Terrible and still Unfinished story of Norodom Sihanouk, King of Cambodia*
Creators: The Théâtre du Soleil
First performed: 11 September 1985 at the Cartoucherie of Vincennes, Paris
Director: Ariane Mnouchkine
Text: Hélène Cixous
Music: Jean-Jacques Lemêtre
Set: Guy-Claude François
Costumes: Jean-Claude Barriera and Nathalie Thomas
Puppets and mask: Erhard Stiefel

Synopsis: *The Dreadful but Unfinished History of Norodom Sihanouk, King of Cambodia* recounts Cambodia's history from the country's independence in 1955 until the collapse of the Khmer Rouge regime in 1979 through the creation of a fictionalised character based on the real historical Cambodian King, Norodom Sihanouk. The play stages the tensions between the old and new worlds of East and West, North and South, religion and politics. In 2011 the play was translated and adapted by Georges Bigot and Delphine Cotty into the Khmer language and performed at the Cartoucherie and in the festival Sens Interdit by 30 Cambodian actors from Phare Ponleu Selpak.

Résumé de la pièce: *L'Histoire terrible mais inachevée de Norodom Sihanouk, roi du Cambodge* retrace l'histoire du Cambodge de 1955 jusqu'à la chute du régime Khmer rouge en 1979. Découpée en 2 époques et 50 tableaux, la pièce montre les tensions entre le nouveau et le vieux monde, l'Est et l'Ouest, le Nord et le Sud, la religion et la politique. En 2011, 30 jeunes Cambodgiens issus de l'école d'art Phare Ponleu Selpak de Battambang, se réapproprient leur histoire: la pièce est traduite et adaptée en langue khmère par Georges Bigot and Delphine Cottu. Le spectacle est présenté à la Cartoucherie, puis au festival Sens Interdit à Lyon, avant de partir en tournée en France et à l'étranger.

An Inextinguishable Spark

Cambodia, country of the Khmers, the fate of this ancient peasant kingdom is that it is geographically situated right next to Vietnam.

The Indochinese wars come. After France, America attacks Communist Vietnam. Neutral Cambodia is carried into the tempest. In order to reach it, America doesn't hesitate to walk on its body and trample it. This tragedy brings with it an even more bitter tragedy. Fleeing America, the Khmer people find themselves in the murderous arms of the Khmer Rouge, frightening nannies of Communist ideology. From 1975 to 1979, the Khmer people descend the rungs into the hell of Pol Pot.

Our play finishes on 6 January 1979, at the beginning of our current era. That day, Vietnam, armed by the USSR, separates from Pol Pot's Democratic Kampuchea, rejects the underground Khmer Rouge, saves the rest of the dying people. And then absorbs the country. Because since 1979, there is no more Khmer Cambodia. Cambodia is the slave of its Vietnamese neighbour who, in days gone by, under the name of Annam, dreamed of swallowing it up. Five million Khmers against 50 million Vietnamese—such is fate's number.

In 1979 the third tragedy of contemporary Cambodia began. We still don't know the ending.

Political Man, Theatrical Hero

When we saw Prince Sihanouk crop up in the beautiful book by William Shawcross, *Sideshow* ('An Unimportant Tragedy'), which played the role of 'chronicle' for us, he seemed destined to become a theatre hero. Because Sihanouk is 'theatrical'. Which means worthy of Theatre. The man who appears on stage has to unveil his heart and his ulterior motives. He says what in ordinary life would be kept hidden, and even more rigorously because he is a political figure. The character doesn't trick the public. Prince Sihanouk lives on earth as much as on a theatrical stage. He takes the entire world apart. He shows it as it is. And he shows others as they are. He adopts the Shakespearean mischievousness: 'All the world's a stage'.

Prince Sihanouk is not unaware that he made, around his fate, a work of

Une étincelle inextinguible

Le Cambodge, pays des Khmers, antique royaume paysan, a pour fatalité sa situation géographique tout contre le Vietnam.

Viennent les guerres Indochinoises. Après la France, les Etats-Unis s'attaquent au Vietnam communiste. Le Cambodge neutre est emporté dans la tempête. Pour l'atteindre, l'Amérique n'hésite pas à lui passer sur le corps et à le piétiner. Cette tragédie engendre une tragédie plus amère encore. Fuyant l'Amérique, le peuple khmer se retrouve dans les bras meurtriers des Khmers Rouges, effrayants nourrissons de l'idéologie communiste. De 1975 à 1979, le peuple khmer descend les degrés de l'enfer Pol Pot.

Notre pièce s'achève le 6 janvier 1979, à l'orée de l'époque actuelle. Ce jour-là, le Vietnam, armé par l'URSS, s'empare du Kampuchea Démocratique de Pol Pot, rejette les Khmers Rouges dans les maquis, sauve un reste de peuple à l'agonie. Et puis absorbe le pays. Car depuis 1979, il n'y a plus de Cambodge khmer. Le Cambodge est l'esclave du voisin vietnamien qui jadis, sous le nom d'Annam, rêvait de l'avaler. Cinq millions de Khmers contre 50 millions de Vietnamiens—tel est le chiffre du destin.

En 1979 a commencé la troisième tragédie du Cambodge contemporain. Nous en ignorons la fin.

Homme Politique, Heros de Théâtre

Lorsque nous avons vu surgir le Prince Sihanouk dans le beau livre de William Shawcross, *Sideshow* ('Une Tragédie sans Importance'), qui a joué pour nous le rôle de 'chronique', il nous a semblé fait pour devenir un héros de théâtre. Car Sihanouk est 'théâtral'. C'est-à-dire digne de Théâtre. L'homme qui paraît sur la scène doit dévoiler son cœœur et ses arrière-pensées. Il dit ce qui dans la vie ordinaire serait tenu caché, et plus rigoureusement encore lorsqu'il s'agit d'une personne politique. Le personnage ne trompe pas le public. Le Prince Sihanouk vit sur la terre comme sur une scène de théâtre. Il prend le monde entier à part. Il se montre tel qu'il est. Et il montre les autres tels qu'ils sont. Il a fait sienne la malice shakespearienne: 'All the world's a stage'.

Le Prince Sihanouk n'ignore pas qu'il s'est fait, autour de son destin, une

theatre. We informed him about it as a matter of courtesy. The Prince had the true elegance to never forget his absolute discretion.

A Sampeah

In December 1984, at Tatum, at Ampil, in the camps of the nationalist resistance, situated on a remainder of Khmer soil on the border of Thailand, tiny little children welcomed foreigners by joining their hands together for the sampeah, the gracious salute of royal times. Thus the sampeah, which led to death during the terror of Pol Pot, had returned. This time around, the mother teaches the baby who doesn't yet know how to walk, to join fingers in front of their little nose. And the older children were softly shouting the magic password: 'OKbyebye!', to the foreigner. So the passing Frenchman bowed his head, his heart tense with shame and love. And he echoed, with an untrained mouth: 'OKbyebye!'

In the clear blue sky, claps of dry thunder. 'Where is the storm?', exclaimed the foreigner. The storm was the Vietnamese army, it came, with its canons and its tanks, to reduce the Khmer people after the Annamese people. The hours in camps were counted by explosions from canons. On 25 December 1984, the assault comes on all sides. The free Cambodian earth is now embedded in hearts. We cannot chase the Khmers out of the land that beat in our breasts. Our play is a sampeah. A tender and respectful salute to a people who, at this moment, for land, only have the future.

And the Khmers Rouges?

There are still some. Some of them are easily visible in the Vietnamised Cambodia. Yes, we are too often unaware of it—Heng Samrin and his governing team are former Khmer Rouge, who, in 1978, were stained by the red blood of the Pol Potites, Moscow's façade. Others make up the tripartite coalition of resistance to the Vietnamese invader. Disgusted, the foreigner has no desire to approach them. But that is part of his privilege as a foreigner, to be able to protect himself from such associations. The Khmers themselves, the victims, today consent to rub shoulders with their hangmen: unfortunate alliance but without hesitation against the archenemy, Vietnam. What that must cost their mourning hearts defies our imagination. Must one cross hatred in order to regain one's fatherland? Tears in eyes, the Khmers cross it. And Prince Sihanouk, who presides over this resistance coalition since June 1982, is greeted obsequiously by those who deposed him in 1970, and by those who, in 1975, killed his five children, his 14 grandchildren and half of his people.

œuvre de théâtre. Nous l'en avons informé par courtoisie. Le Prince a eu la juste élégance de ne jamais sortir d'une absolue discrétion.

Un Sampeâh

En décembre 1984, à Tatum, à Ampil, dans les camps de la résistance nationaliste situés sur un reste de sol khmer au bord de la Thaïlande, les tout petits enfants accueillaient les étrangers en joignant les mains pour le sampeâh, le gracieux salut du temps royal. Ainsi le sampeâh, qui entraînait la mort sous la terreur Pol Pot était revenu. A nouveau, la mère apprend au bébé qui ne sait pas encore marcher, à joindre les doigts devant le petit nez. Et les enfants plus grands criaient doucement à l'étranger le mot de passe magique: 'OKbyebye!'. Alors le passant français baissait la tête, le cœœur crispé de honte et d'amour. Et il faisait écho d'une bouche malhabile: 'OKbyebye!'

Dans le ciel nettement bleu, des éclats de tonnerre sec. 'Où est l'orage?' s'étonnait l'étranger. L'orage, c'était l'armée vietnamienne, venue, avec ses canons et ses tanks, réduire le pleuple khmer après le peuple annamite. Les heures des camps étaient comptées à coups de canons. Le 25 décembre 1984, l'assaut est donné de tous côtés. La terre du Cambodge libre est maintenant plantée dans les cœurs. On ne peut pas chasser les Khmers de la terre qui bat dans nos poitrines. Notre pièce est un sampeâh. Un salut tendre et respectueux à un peuple qui n'a en ce moment pour terre que l'avenir.

Et Les Khmers Rouges?

Il y en a toujours. Certains sont bien en vue au Cambodge vietnamisé. Oui, nous l'ignorons trop souvent, Heng Samrin et son équipe gouvernante sont d'anciens Khmers Rouges, qui, en 1978, ont passé par dessus le rouge sang des Polpots dont ils sont maculés, le masque de Moscou. D'autres font partie de la coalition tripartite de la Résistance à l'envahisseur vietnamien. Ecœœuré, l'étranger n'a aucune envie de les approcher. Mais cela fait partie de ses privilèges d'étranger que de pouvoir se garder de telles fréquentations. Les Khmers eux, les victimes, consentent aujourd'hui à côtoyer leurs bourreaux: alliance douloureuse mais sans hésitation contre l'archi-ennemi, le Vietnam. Ce que cela doit coûter aux cœurs endeuillés dépasse notre imagination. Il faut traverser la haine pour regagner sa patrie? Les larmes aux yeux, les Khmers la traversent. Et le Prince Sihanouk, qui préside depuis juin 1982 cette coalition de résistance, est salué bien bas par ceux qui en 1970 l'ont déposé, et par ceux qui, en 1975, lui ont tué 5 enfants, 14 petits-enfants et la moitié de son peuple.

To Work

Such it is that history must become Theatre. In passing from one genre to another, the truth (historical here) doesn't change. What changes is the rhythm.

To create something for theatre is firstly to submit one's self to urgency. The book can wait to be read: it has eternity. But theatre only has the time of the performance. The present, only the present. So one must write in the immediate. We see the book flowing like a river, the theatrical play rises up and hurries like a succession of battles. We must win… time. For a historical play, the work of theatre is similar to the work of the dream: our epic dreams last for five minutes thanks to condensation and movement. We only have time to play 'life or death'. At the theatre, fate beats very quickly to the rhythm of the heart. In each beat (a scene), life risks being lost. 1955-1979: our play spans 24 years in a few hours. Sometimes three years speed up into a single scene. Sometimes a fateful day for the whole world plays out in four scenes, in four capitals. Sometimes three years pass in between two scenes, like nothing, like death. There are fifty tableaus. All are fictional. Everything would have been able to occur in reality.

The Characters Arrive

The first to be presented to the author's imagination, was the highly visible ghost of the Father of Prince Sihanouk, the deceased King Suramarit. This deceased, so alive, so charitable, isn't he the very symbol of the obstinacy of Cambodia to not disappear? Moreover, isn't he the very sign of the Art of Theatre: the art of incarnation, of reincarnation, of reanimation? Before any writing, in him the second era of performance was already shaping up: 1970-1979. In these years, Cambodia becomes a country peopled by as many dead as there are living. Now, the dead must help the living to resist total erasure, thought the author…

In reality, King Sumarit was not dead in 1955, when the play starts. Seceding to his son Sihanouk, he reigned from 1955 to his actual death in 1960. But during this reign, it is Prince Sihanouk who was governing and making History.

Theatre chose to give Suramarit the immense power of those who we think about and who haunt us for our own good. In his magical way he 'incarnates' all loyalties.

What happens to the author when the text seems finished: some cutting remarks from the theatre

The actors enter. So in passing through the huge living sieve of the game and the staging, the play takes its own measure, refines itself. Some scenes

Au Travail

Voici que l'Histoire doit devenir Théâtre. Dans le passage d'un genre à l'autre la vérité (historique ici) ne change pas. Ce qui change c'est le rythme.

Créer pour le théâtre c'est d'abord se soumettre à l'urgence. Le livre peut attendre la lectur: il a l'éternité. Mais le théâtre n'a que le temps du spectacle. Le présent, seulement le présent. Alors il faut écrire à l'immédiat. On voit le livre s'écouler comme un fleuve, la pièce de théâtre se dresser et se presser comme une succession de batailles. Il faut gagner... du temps. Pour une pièce historique, le travail du théâtre est semblable au travail du rêve: nos épopées de rêve durent 5 minutes, grâce à la condensation et au déplacement. On a seulement le temps de jouer à 'la vie ou la mort'. Au théâtre, le destin bat très vite, au rythme du cœur. A chaque battement (une scène), la vie risque d'être perdue. 1955-1979: notre pièce dure 24 ans en quelques heures. Parfois trois ans se précipitent en une seule scène. Parfois un jour mondialement fatidique se joue en 4 scènes, en 4 capitales. Parfois trois ans passent entre deux scènes, comme rien, comme la mort. Il y a 50 tableaux. Tous sont fictifs. Tous auraient pu se passer en réalité.

Arrivent les Personnages

Le premier qui se soit présenté à l'imagination de l'auteur, ce fut le spectre bien visible du Père du Prince Sihanouk, le défunt Roi Suramarit. Ce défunt si vivant, si charitable, n'est-il pas le symbole même de l'obstination du Cambodge à ne pas disparaître? Et n'est-il pas en outre le signe même de l'Art du Théâtre: l'art d'incarner, de réincarner, de ranimer? En lui, s'annonçait déjà, avant toute écriture, la deuxième époque du spectacle: 1970-1979. En ces années, le Cambodge devint un pays peuplé d'autant de morts que de vivants. Maintenant, il faut vraiment que les morts aident les vivants à résister à l'effacement total, pensait l'auteur...

En réalité, le Roi Suramarit n'était pas mort en 1955, lorsque la pièce commence. Succédant a son fils Sihanouk, il a régné de 1955 jusqu'à sa mort réelle en 1960. Mais pendant ce règne, c'est le Prince Sihanouk qui gouvernait et faisait l'Histoire.

Le Théâtre a choisi de donner à Suramarit le pouvoir immense de ceux auxquels nous pensons et qui nous hantent pour notre bien. A sa manière magique il 'incarne' toutes les fidélités.

Ce qui arrive à l'auteur lorsque le texte à l'air fini: Quelques coups de patte de la part du Théâtre

Entrent les comédiens. Alors en passant par l'immense tamis vivant du jeu et de la mise en scène, la pièce se mesure, s'épure. Des scènes s'évaporent. D'autres accourent. Une scène que l'auteur aimait beaucoup entre un matin.

evaporate. Others rush. One scene that the author really liked arrives one morning. And leaves again that same evening: it was wrong for the play, the style. Sorry. An intimidating scene presents itself. It is exactly this one that we were waiting for! The space suddenly expands by a look thrown from far away: the author sees a river flowing there where a wall was lifted! As quickly, the river streams into the text. Theatre reveals its marvelous mathematics to us; on the stage a crowd shrivels up, but three actors place themselves such that the author sees a whole people. So the masses of Khmer Rouge? To the trap door! There remains the individual, each one as immense as ten thousand. I rediscover that it is by the singular that the universal manifests. If one makes a thousand, two alike make less than one. Nixon plus Kissinger was too much, one of them was sent away because of a dual role. The same for Hou Youn and Hu Nim. Of the three US ambassadors, no more than one remained. One American general contains half a dozen of his equals. Zhou Enlai, he alone and without Mao became the embodiment of China.

But here appeared one extra character! A gift from Theatre to the author. He entered on the stage under the name 'servant'. This becomes useful, then captivating, then indispensable. Thus it is in haste that we allot him his place in the story/history. In the end, all together we have baptized him Dith Boun Suo. From now on, he is part of this work in which he entered forever with his oblique step, just as a whole people that we hadn't thought about for a long time entered our lives. And the author asks herself again: What is an author? What is this world that creates and that we call Theatre?

Program Extract

Et re-sort le soir même: elle s'était trompée de pièce, de style. Pardon. Une scène intimidée se présente. C'est justement elle que l'on attendait! Par un regard lancé très loin un comédien agrandit soudain l'espace: l'auteur voit couler un fleuve là où s'élevait un mur! Aussitôt le fleuve se jette dans le texte. Le Théâtre nous révèle sa mathématique merveilleuse; sur la scène une foule se ratatine, mais trois comédiens se placent et l'auteur voit tout un peuple. Alors les masses des Khmers Rouges? A la trappe! Reste l'individu, chacun aussi immense que dix mille. Je redécouvre que c'est par le singulier que se manifeste l'universel. Si un fait mille, deux semblables font moins qu'un. Nixon plus Kissinger c'était trop, l'un d'eux fut renvoyé pour cause de double emploi. De même pour Hou Youn plus Hu Nim. De trois ambassadeurs US il n'en restait déjà plus qu'un. Un général américain contient une demi-douzaine de ses pareils. Chou En-Laï à lui seul et sans Mao est devenu la Chine en personne.

Mais voici qu'apparaît un personnage en plus! Un cadeau du Théâtre à l'auteur. Il est entré sur la scène sous le sans-nom de 'serviteur'. Le voilà qui devient utile, puis attachant, puis indispensable. Alors c'est en hâte qu'on lui fait place dans l'histoire. A la fin, tous ensemble, nous l'avons baptisé Dith Boun Suo. Désormais il fait partie de cette œœuvre dans laquelle il est entré de son pas oblique et pour toujours, comme est entré dans nos vies tout un peuple, auquel, pendant longtemps, nous n'avions pas pensé. Et l'auteur se demande encore: qu'est-ce qu'un auteur? Qu'est-ce que ce monde qui crée et que nous appelons Théâtre?

Extrait du programme de L'Histoire terrible mais inachevée de Norodom Sihanouk, roi du Cambodge

www.ingramcontent.com/pod-product-compliance
Lightning Source LLC
LaVergne TN
LVHW091129080826
845145LV00008B/2093

* 9 7 8 0 9 8 7 2 6 8 2 1 1 *